A SOUL HOUSED UP

A SOUL HOUSED UP

A Selection of the Writing

of

ETHEL NEAL YEAGER

Edited by

Bruce W. Coggin

with a Foreword by

Jane Yeager Coggin

Copyright © 2000 by Bruce W. Coggin
All rights reserved.
No part of this book may be reproduced, restored in a retrieval system, or transmitted by means, electronic, mechanical, photocopying, recording, or otherwise, without written consent from the author.

ISBN: 1-58820-237-2

1stBooks - rev. 09/21/00

Foreword

by Jane Yeager Coggin

A native of Rochelle, McCulloch County, Texas, my mother, Ethel Neal, was a vivacious girl who was so proud of being a Neal, as she said in later life, that she would never embarrass herself or her family by making a low grade in school. She developed a love for learning that was an important motivating force in all of her life. She never ceased to learn, graduating from Howard Payne College in Brownwood, Texas, in 1925, and earning a Master of Education degree from North Texas University in Denton in 1954. The latter adventure in learning was a highlight of her later life which she enjoyed with all the eagerness of one whose interest in all aspects of life never flagged.

A person whose greatest joy in life was sharing, Ethel was a natural—some would say supernatural—teacher. Marrying Aaron Vaughan Yeager in 1917, Ethel soon found herself living in Brownwood. When their only child was old enough to go to school, Ethel entered the teaching profession, at the same time working to complete her Bachelor of Arts degree at Howard Payne, where she had gone to school before marrying. She began teaching at Mt. View, near Brownwood, in 1923; moved to McCulloch County in 1926, where she taught at the Claxton community school—serving also as principal—until 1930; and then went from Claxton to Lohn High School, where she taught until 1935.

At this point Ethel's health dictated that she leave the classroom for an interim. In retrospect, it is apparent that this turn of events was fortunate. While she rested herself and tried unsuccessfully to put on some weight, she found time to release a great flow of delightful and earthy and deeply philosophical ideas that welled up in her endlessly. Her writing was a way of sharing her unique and always evocative interpretation of life. Not only did she write two columns for the Brady papers over a period of several years, but she also frequently entered and won contests, gaining statewide recognition. Her column "Country Commonplaces" was written as a series of feature stories, while her "Yeagitorial" was an editorial.

Selections from those articles have been chosen with the purpose of setting forth a sampling of the essence of Ethel. These excerpts from her writing reveal the soul of Ethel and shed much light on the social, political, and economic conditions that prevailed during those years. A loving, nurturing person, Ethel could use a unique turn of phrase to strike home when constructive criticism was needed. Her unfailing sense of humor tempered her use of irony so that, while it does bite, it seldom draws blood. Her essays feed the soul, nurture the intellect, and delight the aesthetic hunger for the well-turned phrase.

One of the most distinctive characteristics of Ethel was her very practical, workable—yet spiritually complex and constantly expanding—Christian faith. A lifelong Baptist, Ethel was truly the universal Christian, constantly studying to know more about and to understand better her God and her Savior, the Bible, and her fellow man. A good friend and co-worker of Ethel's once told me, "Your mother ought to live forever!" Privileged to live in the aura of her presence for much of my life, I say that she does still live in the lives of those folks whom she touched during her almost eighty-four years on earth. And she will live for any who read this collection of samples from her essays on life as she distilled it during the years between 1936 and 1944.

Enjoy Ethel, and she can also live in you!

Table of Contents

Foreword v

Introduction ix

Out of the Depths 1

Country Commonplaces 11

People 79

Granny Cates 107

Two Essays 115

Yeagitorial 121

The Coke Stevenson Story 161

The War 175

Introduction

by Bruce W. Coggin

In the breathless heat of early September in McCulloch County, Texas, a kerosene lamp sends its gentle light into the night through the window of a tiny frame farmhouse. On the screened sleeping porch, a man in his fifties tosses on his bed. Across the porch his sister lies awake, listening to the silence and praying for a break in the weather. By the lamp, before an Underwood typewriter is a thin woman in her forties, braided hair piled atop her head, eyes closed. She sits a long while, then opens her eyes, straightens her narrow back, addresses the typewriter, and begins to write: "I wish it would rain. As I write, the earth lies baked and dry. Waterholes have been licked up by the arid winds, leaving their cracked surfaces turned to the hot sky." It is 1936 and Ethel Yeager is beginning a mini-career as a journalist.

God knows why it is some people *will* write. More than sixty years after Ethel Yeager began to write publicly, United States educators with almost one voice will tell you that, for a plethora of reasons, *nobody* writes any more, which means really that most of their students cannot write. Certainly a person who likes to write letters is often hard put to find a correspondent when telephone companies compete ferociously to convince us simply to save the trouble and call. Probably not since writing was invented and replaced the oral tradition (causing, no doubt, endless head-wagging among grumpy Sayers, lamenting the forgetful younger generation's penchant for the new craze) has the business of setting words to paper suffered such a beating as it has in our culture in the last half of this century. People *don't* write as much or as well as they used to.

Yet now as in 1936 and as always since writing has been, there are people who write, who craft words and record them, people who enjoy what Auden called "the farming of a verse," indeed cannot let it alone. Stendahl said he could not help it, described himself as a *gratte-papier*, a paper-scratcher who could not resist the urge to say it in ink. Or as Grendel, in Barth's retelling of the story, observes about the mountain goat he is about to brain because it has, despite his warning, climbed too close to him, "Goats climb." Fish gotta swim, birds gotta fly. Writers write. At least in part, Ethel Yeager was one of those.

But in September 1936, she was writing for money and to maintain her sanity. The house in which she sat was on a little hard-scrabble farm north of Rochelle to which she had moved with her husband and daughter just before the onset of the Depression. From a family well-known and connected in the county, she found work teaching in the tiny, unaccredited school at Lohn and taught there for five years. Her husband farmed, though he would have preferred ranching or railroading. Farming gave him migraines. Their daughter finished high school and went away to college, for which the schoolteaching helped pay. All in all, it was a life, until in 1935 her body rebelled: not only did her doctor believe he detected advanced tuberculosis, but also gum disease which would cost all her teeth. As it turned out, she did not have tuberculosis, but rather histoplasmosis, carried in bird droppings with which she, intrepid henhouse cleaner, had long acquaintance. For six months she lay in a ward in a TB sanatorium in Carlsbad, Texas, healing her lungs and shedding teeth. Then it was time to come home, home to enforced bed rest and reduced activity, to fear of what her husband would feel, what people would think, to real anxiety about how to pay for college. She got in touch with the editor of the local paper in Brady, the county seat, and asked for work as a columnist. For each column she got a dollar—and just the outlet she needed to help make sense of a world in which she had always been an actor and would for a time have to become an observer. Quite literally, she was writing for her life.

It turned out well. Her two columns — "Country Commonplaces" and "Yeagitorial" — proved to be winners. She won the only Texas award in a "crossroads" contest conducted in 1936-1937 by *Country Home Magazine*, and in 1938 the same magazine named her the champion country newspaper correspondent in Texas. In the *Dallas News* First All Southwestern Newspaper Contest celebrating the golden jubilee of the State Fair of Texas in 1938, she won third prize in the local column competition and won first place for her editorial "What the State Fair Means to Texas and the Southwest." She won an admirer in the *Fort Worth Star-Telegram's* Otto Bordenkircher who regularly featured her in his *Vignettes*, a recueil of "comment and jottings from the Texas press." He called her "a Diogenes in petticoats." In 1940 the Democrat power brokers in her area implored her to become a candidate for Congress, but that was not her *métier*. She stayed on the farm and wrote until 1944, when her octogenarian mother came to live with her. By then she was strong enough and sane enough to take up the protracted battle to the death with nature, with everything parent and child had known of each other, with the sheer inertia of roles long played and well learned. Now there was no time to meet newspaper deadlines, even weekly ones. She gave up the columns, but with no regrets.

Writing released from Ethel Yeager a powerful flow of epiphanies, almost always delightful, at times profound. The tentative, pitiful beginnings—"I wish it would rain"—formed the *De profundis* of her darkest moments. When she found that people enjoyed her, she turned increasingly outward to embrace them with her writing. By the end of her career as a journalist, she had increased her range to include the wide world and its leaders. Some of her readers thought *she* should have a share of the leading. When the time came to take up one of her life's biggest tasks, she was ready for it. She had written her way back to health.

o o o o o o o o o o o o o o o o

Journalists have seldom been satisfied to report the news and let it go at that. From Addison and Steele's uplifting bent, through Mark Twain's deflating barbs and Mencken's managed invective, to officious television commentators, journalists like to put in a word or two of their own. "Everybody likes to make concise and pointed comments on the news of the day" (Flint, p. 5). This urge is the sire of newspaper columns as they have developed in this country. By 1800 the editorial essay was firmly established in any newspaper worth the name, though usually it was pretty earnest stuff, especially in the politically fermenting United States. Less weighty, sometimes humorous comment was offered by "paragraphers," who provided pointed commentary in short form, work which could be done by virtually anyone in the newspaper office. Paragraphers did not get by-lines.

As newspapers became more common and appeared more frequently, however, publishers needed more fill material, and in the later nineteenth century there grew up to meet the demand a breed of satirical essayists—often disguised as clownish, semi-illiterate, at times outrageously hypocritical boobs—whose writings were distributed and reproduced widely, the forerunners of the later columnists. By 1900 popular columnists were known across the country, and by 1925 newspapers would compete by pitting syndicated writers against one another, sharpening reader interest and boosting circulation. When the Depression arrived in America, personal columns with by-lines were common in all the big dailies and copied in many of the smaller weeklies. After the reader scanned the news, he turned over a couple of pages to see what Westbrook Pegler or Walter Winchell had to say about it.

As do many things, column writing came more slowly to the countryside. Often conservative and working short-handed, country editors found outlet for their need to have a say in their own editorial columns. Most of their limited space went to news from the wire services, advertising, and local happenings. Certainly they avoided controversy. A New York columnist could be polemical with relative impunity. Distance and the city protected him. But a small town journalist who popped off in print could end up dead, like Brann of the *Iconoclast*, shot in the back—right where the suspenders cross—on a sidewalk in Waco. More often those small weeklies followed an editorial policy geared to meet business considerations.

In the 1930s and 1940s Americans kept their rendezvous with destiny. The Depression and World War II meant that just about all the news was bad, so bad in fact that many thought the Apocalypse was upon them. People needed a break. Hollywood and radio broadcasting provided part of that break with glitzy musical reviews and zany comedy shows. In the non-urban press too a more entertaining kind of writing began to appear in the form of personal columns, written by local people—possibly the editor under a pen name or some other person who was in touch and qualified to comment on the news. Not precisely editorials, they were nevertheless connected to local goings-on and contained more or less pointed observations as a matter of course. Their principal impetus, however, was not reporting, but rather to provide a kind of intimate chat with the readers, not unlike FDR at the hearth with his radio audience. They offered some emotional release from the brutal facts of the news, and—most importantly—they pulsed with the life of the community. By 1940, about 2,000 small-town newspapers already featured such columns; in the 1940s, some 6,000 more began using them (Hinkle and Henry, p. 15). In 1936, when Ethel Yeager began to write for *The Brady Standard* and *The Heart O' Texas News*, she was one among many who offered a kind of writing much livelier than—and, in her case at least, far superior to—the general run of news reporting.

The fact that she was a woman in some degree separates Yeager from the crowd. In 1936, journalism was still a place where women might not be welcome, not an entirely "civilized" profession. As late as 1926, Columbia University's school of journalism conducted an experiment which pitted "the girls" against "men." The women set up an independent newspaper project and demonstrated that, compared to the men, they were "equally competent" (Ross, p. 476). Up to then, women had had to fight for a place in U.S. newspapers, and when they found one, it was usually "special." The murder trial of Harry K. Thaw in 1906 was a case in point. New York editors assigned four women to cover the trial and produce a highly colored version of events, pitched to appeal to the emotions of women readers. These four "sob sisters" ushered in one kind of "specialized" journalism for women. Others, like Elsie Robinson of the Oakland *Tribune*, wrote and illustrated serialized children's stories, filled with eupeptic philosophy. If women formed part of the newspaper's team, they knew their place, and it was usually marginal.

Some, however, managed to move up the ladder and, like Helen Rowland, joined the ranks of the syndicated columnists. She wrote for King Features, and her advice to any woman hoping to pull away from the crowd was, "Get a typewriter. Get a copy of Roget's *Thesaurus*. Get a specialty" (Ross, p. 381). Indeed enough women were working in journalism by the 1920s to form a national sorority—Theta Sigma Pi—publishing its own magazine, *The Matrix*. In Texas in 1936, women with a by-line included Mary Caroline Holmes of the Dallas *Journal*, Allena Duff James of the Dallas *Times-Herald*, Bess Stephenson of the *Fort Worth Star-Telegram*, and Clara Ogden of the *Houston Chronicle*.

In the small town Texas papers, however, women were not so exalted. An examination of the extensive microfilm newspaper collections in the Barker Texas History Center at the University of Texas at Austin reveals that most of the space filled by women writers was of two kinds which persist in any county-seat newspaper today. The "woman's" column dealt with news of weddings and parties, fashion, cooking, or household help. The rest were "crossroads correspondents," usually from the tiny unincorporated communities in the county, who reported comings and goings in the country. The latter, particularly, did not often display distinguished writing skills. A local woman with a by-line writing beautifully and intelligently about things in no special way feminine was hard to find. Ethel Yeager was an exception, and her long string of prizes and the fondness of some Texas editors for quoting her testify to her singular talent.

o o o o o o o o o o o o o o o o

Very much a woman of her time, Ethel Yeager would have found contemporary feminist issues a conundrum. She would have identified quickly enough the business of stereotypes and roles, as well as the negative economics of being a woman in America. Her portrait of Fay Stevenson, wife of Texas Governor

Coke Stevenson, patently shows its age and identifies its author as someone who accepted the idea that women and men *should* move in different spheres and behave differently. That acceptance would have included, perhaps grudgingly, the notion that, though she was desperate to work and earn money, the only serious profession open to her, even in a community in which her family had been influential for over a generation, was school teaching. As often as not, she was paid in script, not money. Just as quickly she would have recognized the curious ambivalence of being idolized and oppressed at the same time. Her husband was in many ways in awe of her and adored her until the day he died. His letters to her while she was in the sanatorium are quite simply lovestruck—and this after two decades of marriage. Yet he was also overbearing in many ways, including the ubiquitous male need always to be right. To all this her writing alludes, though never with rancor.

She would have found far less recognizable the need for fierce competition with men in order to extort from them some kind of recognition of her human worth. One commentator on these vexed issues notes that, aside from the aristocracy, women in earliest colonial society in America were of necessity equal to their men. When there was a forest to be cleared, house to be built, garden to be planted, livestock to be tended, women cleared, built, planted, and tended right along with their men. If need be, they fought and killed beside them. When in the nineteenth century the circumstances of living permitted it in great parts of the country, women were put on the pedestal of domesticity, a kind of idealized captivity in uselessness, from which they have been sedulously descending in the last part of the twentieth (Chafe, p. 259). Yeager's comments after reading Marjorie Hillis' *Live Alone and Like It* shed light on her thinking about idealized femininity.

Yet in the truly frontier society in which Ethel Yeager was raised, that elevation beyond reality was perhaps an "ideal" aimed for, but seldom realized. Women worked, and they worked hard. Life, especially in the Texas countryside, was a daily round of familiar contentions with the elements from which men *and* women wrested their very existence. It may be difficult for some today to recall that as recently as half a century ago, in some places there was water to be drawn and carried, wood to be chopped, animals to be fed and corralled and doctored and slaughtered and butchered. If you ate, it was because you and your animals dealt intimately with the soil. If you stayed clean, it was because you built a fire and heated water and washed your clothes and yourself in a tub. These conditions were not uncommon in rural Central Texas as late as the 1940s. It was democratic: women worked just as hard and just as long as men, and they needed no man to remind them of their value.

Yeager would have sympathized with the economic agenda of feminists. Anyone who could see through Roosevelt's reasoning for the 1937 veto of low-interest rates for farmers could also piece it out that women in this country have been historically relegated to "their" professions and there have been underpaid. But the economic would not have translated to the personal. Living with men all her life (she had two sisters and *eight* brothers) might have been a chore, but it did not drive her sense of herself underground. Her writing shows a fully realized humanity, glad of itself and not infrequently luxuriating in a sense of being somewhat brighter than the "countryman" with whom she shared the house. Beside, there was external corroboration: the same voters who begged her to run for Congress in 1940 rejected her husband for County Commissioner in 1942. Ethel Yeager knew she was relatively worthless when it came to earning a dollar, but she knew just as surely that in her corner of the world nobody was loved and valued any more than she was.

o o o o o o o o o o o o o o o o

Though Ethel Yeager's household was small, it was busy. Soon after she started writing, she found she had to leave the house to think. She picked a favorite shaded place in a pasture and, the weather cooperating, wrote there, her hair lifting with the breeze and her feet on caliche, surrounded by the smells—of which she writes so often—of earth and (rarely) water and wild flowers and farm animals. Above and beyond stretched the wide, noisy Texas sky, whose commotion was the subject of daily discourse. Above all, her writing shows a spirit completely connected to the universe it inhabits, fascinated by the ways of garden weeds and awe-struck by thoughts of eternity. That spirit found no venue alien to its genial nose-poking, and Yeager's columns provide a window onto those explorations of the world she beheld from her pasture and found wonderful. They reward the reader in at least four ways.

First, the columns provide a precisely accurate picture of life on a poor-farm in Central Texas during the last years of the Depression and World War II. Though the Yeagers lacked for little they needed, they had little beyond those needs. They did not have to hit the road with the Joads, but right across the road from their house Verge and Zora Mooring lived without a water well. They joshingly called it a poor-farm—"Belly Acres"—but there is a saying in Texas that "poor folks got poor ways," and Ethel Yeager found her existence challenging but by no means poor. How she brings that world to life! The reader at once plunges into the feel, the smell, the taste, the sounds, the sights of that world—especially the tastes and smells. The daily round of early rising, cow milking, fire building, vermin fighting, house mending, meal fixing, weather watching is on almost every page, and from the details of that round Yeager compounds structures of commentary. Also she peoples the pages with those who shared her life, and the portraits—some a single line, others whole essays—are the equals of any. The prose elegy on the death of Granny Cates is a transcendent masterpiece. Her people move in their spheres—Rochelle, Brady, Austin—and show the reader a difficult but very lively world rather removed from the gelled popular impression of that time. Yeager shows us a society whose economy was depressed. Its people were not.

Second, Yeager's political and social comments, limited usually though not always to the "Yeagitorial," interest us in at least two ways. They remind us, in the first place, that the common-sense opinions of ordinary people should count. Long before Tip O'Neill said it, Yeager intuited that politics is indeed local: she suggests the best education on farm problems for FDR would be a February visit to Rochelle. Unacquainted with advanced economic theory, Yeager was convinced that common sense was in short supply in Washington. As the Beltway closes tighter around the nation's leaders, a two-headed calf can see she was right. In the second place, we are reminded that the Depression and the run-up to WWII found a lively house of dissent in the United States, not only at the noisy public levels of the America Firsters, but also in places like McCulloch County. Meg Greenfield has valuably pointed out the fallacy that those days were, in the popular jargon, "a simpler time" when large decisions came only in black and white (*Newsweek*, June 6, 1994). Simple-minded historians reduce; but reading Yeager's comments shows that there was no *lumpen intelligentsia* granting imprimatur to every word issuing from the seats of power. She had a good many ideas to the contrary. So did lots of people.

Third, there is the joy of meeting Ethel. A decade after her death, many people remember her vividly. Most recall with gratitude the effect she had on their lives. The reader of her columns encounters her *nel mezzo del cammin* of her life. She is bright, but not sassy; mature, but not set; experienced, but not jaded; kind, but not ingenuous. Her mood is almost always genial, the more surprising when one considers the circumstances which impelled her to write. The synthesizing and penetrating qualities of her mind are astonishing. Four-o'clocks blooming in the doorway call up memories of tent revivals and intimations of immortality. A visit to a pilot training school produces a sonnet which makes the reader wish she had written much, much more poetry. Her agrarian philosophy is often archaic and, to modern ears, a little stilted. Paeans to supposedly American virtues sound somehow naïve to ears accustomed to the sounds emanating from Vietnam-Watergate-era television sets. Yet we forgive that, because through everything gleams the woman's sweetness and her unabashed joy in loving life. She was and she remains an antidote for self-absorption and inaction.

Finally and most important, there is the writing. The list of prizes and awards begun in the early part of this introduction could be extended considerably, indicating that people highly placed in journalism thought she was better than good. When Bordenkircher learned she was being "spoken of" for Congress, he regretted it in print. He was afraid she would be elected and then stop writing. But the reader will not depend on outside judgment to form his own. The writing—vigorous, original, unpretentious, supple, evocative, joyful—validates itself. Ethel Yeager farmed words the way she farmed plants—study the sunshine, devise protection, fool with the dirt, contemplate the alternatives, choose just the right seed, and put it just so into the ground. She said she lacked her mother's green-thumbed natural way with plants, but she had the itch for it. A winter garden usually came, but grudgingly, not naturally. Her itch for words, however, stemmed from as natural a knack for them as you could want, and the product was consistently good, at times breathtaking. For better for worse, she was a writer. For all their possible usefulness as history, as social commentary, as recollection of people or places known, the real value in Ethel Yeager's columns is their excellence as literature. The reader takes an almost effortless trip through time and space into the spirit of a truly remarkable woman whose view of life was both acute and generous. From that journey, he will not return unchanged.

SOURCES

Belford, Barbara. 1986. *Brilliant Bylines: A Biographical Anthology of Notable Newspaperwomen in America.* New York City: Columbia University Press.

Chafe, William H. 1987. "Women and American Society," in *Making America*, Luther S. Luedtke, Ed. (See below)

Flint, L.N. 1920. *The Paragrapher's Sprightly Art.* Lawrence: University of Kansas Journalism Press.

Greenfield, Meg. June 6, 1994, "Misusing World War II," *Newsweek.*

Hinkle, Olin and Henry, John. 1952. *How to Write Columns.* Ames: The Iowa State College Press.

Luedtke, Luther, Ed. 1987. *Making America: The Society and Culture of the United States.* Washington, D.C.: United States Information Agency.

McEnteer, James. 1992. *Fighting Words: Independent Journalists in Texas.* Austin: The University of Texas Press.

Ross, Ishbel. 1936. *Ladies of the Press: The Story of Women in Journalism by an Insider.* Harper & Brothers.

Out of the Depths

At home I was needed. Who'd have dinner on time and plan the day? Jane getting ready to go to school without me. Who'd . . . but they didn't need me there sick. Rest . . . . Have you ever tried resting on a windswept porch day after day with eighteen others in narrow white beds in a long row?

In her fortieth year, Ethel Yeager got some bad news. She was a sick woman. For over ten years she had worked both as a homemaker and schoolteacher, and the double load eventually brought her down. She developed serious gum disease, and in 1935 she saw a dentist who told her the condition was more than serious, that she would lose all her teeth—but also that his examinations showed she might be infected with tuberculosis. In fact, she learned later, she had contracted histoplasmosis, a cousin of tuberculosis, but the effect was the same: she would have to have extended, supervised bed rest, and in her little community she would be marked as a carrier and therefore no fit person to teach school. She spent the next months of her life in a sanatorium in Carlsbad, Texas.

The following account of her stay in the sanatorium reveals the kernel of fear which eventually goaded her into writing for the public. She was afraid that when she got home she would be useless—and that was a condition she could not tolerate. Here also she shows early signs of the incisive observation of people and events which so enlivens all her subsequent writing.

o o o o o o o o o o o o o o o o o

So What?

"Tuberculosis." That's what the doctor said to me. He said it to *me*, who'd been born in pioneer simplicity without benefit of medical science and had lived forty years without the same benefit because of an almost indecent lack of illness.

The doctor was a kindish sort of fellow, but the hospital was very big and he was in a hurry. A knock on the door, and he left me wrapped up in a sheet, shut into four bleak, white walls with that word while he talked to a starched apron in the hall.

"Tuberculosis!" There was a dry, sickish taste in my mouth like ashes that hadn't been there before the kind-faced doctor had told me, and my stomach had rolled into a tight knot the way it does when someone hands you an unexpected telegram. Surely he must be mistaken. Not tuberculosis! Not me. I had no pain, no cough—only a weariness. Lots of folks are weary. I'd come to the clinic to see about whether or not my teeth could be saved. I hadn't come to be told that I had tuberculosis. I didn't have time. The doctor was back.

"A sanatorium. More than rahls—a cavity. You've been sicker than you are now. And you kept working? Ambitious folks are funny. Yes, get the teeth out—under the supervision of a specialist—if your health can stand the extractions."

Tuberculosis. I'd have to tell my husband . . . and Jane, in her second year of college. How could college be managed now? I'd have to leave my position. *Everybody would know.*

Outside, the hall was wide and high and long, and I was very small as my legs carried me down the length of it to them to gulp, "Tuberculosis!" and see their white faces, blank like china dinner plates.

I said the word, but still I didn't believe it. Six weeks later I sat in the consultation room of the State Tuberculosis Sanatorium and doubted out loud to the specialist. He listened resignedly, as if he'd heard doubters before. Then he said, "One doesn't have to hurt to have tuberculosis. All one needs is an abrasion in the lung tissue and an exposure to TB germs. You get the abrasion, and in this civilized world, the chances are a million to one that exposure will follow. If you should tell me that you had a common cold with a cough that lasted two weeks, and that your sputum was stained with blood, ever so little blood, or that you had coughed two weeks without noticing 'streaking,' I'd diagnose you tuberculosis over the telephone—and I'd not be mistaken."

"Very well," I countered. "You are telling me that practically everybody has tuberculosis at one time or another. Everybody has had colds that lasted two weeks, and they have coughed. I've done it, and I have tuberculosis. You've done it, and you have tuberculosis. Everybody's done it, and everybody's got tuberculosis. So what?"

"Now," said he, "we're getting somewhere! You are luckier than those who don't know they have tuberculosis. And there's an answer to your question. The answer is, 'So rest!' Rest that ever-moving lung so it can heal up that abrasion. It will seal up the embryo of the germ, and if you keep it sealed up for five years, the embryo will die and you'll be free of tuberculosis. However, if you break open the scar at any time during the five years, you sentence yourself to another five years."

There was a tap at the door. Another doctor with a stethoscope dangling about his neck entered. He had an adhesive patch above a swelled eye, a controlled cough, and a rueful tone. "Last night I met another fellow," he explained to my doctor's raised eyebrow, "that was a better man than I am. The town seems to be having a Gunga Din convention."

An exchange of technical palaver followed, and the patched-up one left.

"There," said my doctor grimly as the door clanged. "There goes a fellow who says, 'So what?' instead of 'So rest.' A spot of cognac last night, a street brawl, and he's too nervous to do an operation this morning. He is the best tuberculosis surgeon west of the Mississippi, but he keeps a blow-torch going on both ends of his candle for fear it won't burn fast enough. Soon he'll be gone, and this sanatorium will lose the best brain and surest fingers it has ever known. Yes, he's tubercular—active! He's lived the last two years on one-fifth of one lung—and he says 'So what?'"

That settled it for me. I'd rest!

It wasn't easy.

At home, I was needed. Who'd have dinner on time and plan the day? Jane getting ready to go to school without me.

Who'd . . . but they didn't need me there sick. Rest . . . . Have you tried resting on a windswept porch day after day with eighteen others in narrow white beds in a long row—eighteen others who have tuberculosis? It isn't easy, but it can be done.

Funny people, folks that have tuberculosis. The diagnosing doctor had dropped the hint, and as I lay eighteen hours out of twenty-four between sheets, I began to think they were mighty funny people. There's my little roommate—that is, we share dressing and storing privileges in a cubbyhole adjoining our beds on the long porch. She's sixteen, vivacious, funloving, and utterly homesick for Mumsie and Dad and Ginger and Bobby and Ned, who are four hundred miles away and too poor to come for a visit. She collects verse, mostly by Eddie Guest, about home and families.

The next-bed patient is in love with somebody else's husband and cries a lot. She snores, too. Beyond her is Dora. Dora's husband has just finished his six-months' period in the san and is "chasing" in a little shack in the mountains. Just across the road from our porch, Dora can see the Healthatorium, where her three children are taking the rest cure. Sometimes she can see them at play. Dora smokes when the nurse is off duty. But lots of the patients do that. The nurses know, but what can they do?

Dora's roommate is a harmless little moron who has left her baby with her mother-in-law and is having the time of her life in the san. Here she has real food, the first she has ever tasted. And clean sheets. She prattles endlessly. Like me, like most of us, she is here at the entire expense of the state. Whether we are pay patients or not, the treatment is identical. No one would know a pay patient unless the pay patient told—and sometimes she does and sometimes she doesn't.

Beyond the moron is a woman to whom the san is a refuge from an overbearing husband. She is a bundle of nerves, wholly without courage. Her roommate is an MA in bacteriology from the state university. She quotes Dorothy Parker and Ogden Nash, but reads "Thanatopsis," which she will not discuss.

Next is a woman whose husband smuggles in to her a very vile brand of hootch, and then she goes on a jag for days, while we bring her meals from the dining hall. Sometimes she will be found out and sent home. There is in the next bed a mother whose little girl started across the street, but there was a big car and the driver didn't see the baby . . . . In the stillness of the rest hours her sobbing sigh comes all the way down the long porch and sits for a while on every heart. A nervous, high-voiced girl is her roommate. Common, coarse, sex-perverted—she's like the things that crawl out from under rocks. One would despise her, but in long hours one learns that hate is expensive; so one is only mildly interested in the nude kodak pictures of herself she exchanges somehow or else with the boys in the men's dormitories.

Another has a needle. Queer people! Suddenly I am aware that most of these are maladjusted folk emotionally, eager to talk about themselves in the false security of chance acquaintances. Not all, but most. *Am I like them?* I've had no "affairs," being a bit more than content with a budget of one husband-and-lover combined. No tragedy has come my way. I'm not like these people, I tell myself desperately. I'm normal—normal!

Am I? Ambition is a cancerous thing, eating into hours—a merciless thing that drives like Jehu. I find myself scrambling lines of Kipling:

> If you can force your nerve and mind and sinew
> To serve your turn long after they are gone,
> And so hold on when there is nothing in you
> Except the will that says to them "Hold on!"—
> If you can fill the unforgiving minute
> With sixty seconds worth of distance run—
> YOURS IS THE EARTH—SIX FEET OF IT, OLD TIMER
> AND WHAT'S MORE YOUR DEATH CERTIFICATE WILL READ
> "TUBERCULOSIS," MY SON!

So I rest.

Routine! Breakfast, bed; lunch, bed; supper, more bed. Then back to breakfast again. I am an up-patient. Finally my homesick heart rebels. "There's nothing here for me but bed and food. I can get that at home!" Surreptitiously, I pack my bag. Lots of them leave. My teeth are out, and I have a new set. I don't hurt, and how homesick I am! There's nothing but . . . And I stop and think. What am I taking home? A sick body—one emotionally unstable if it can not REST. Then I admit the truth: there's more than bed and food in the san for me. Twice each week in the precious up-hours there are lectures. The san is also a College of Rest, where two kinds of education are aimed at—informal and emotional. I unpack.

I sit with the moron and the M.A. and Dora and others and listen to the doctor with one-fifth of one lung lecture in a voice he can scarcely raise above a conversational tone. I learn that everybody in this civilized world is exposed to tuberculosis germs every day from the cradle to the grave: dad's hands that lift the infant from the cradle when he comes home from contact with humanity, his feet when he walks in the street; mother's hands on the grocery counter; anybody's hands trailing the stair railing of a public building—school, church, office, the post office—in grandma's chin chucking, in a friendly hand clasp, in the very air we breathe. The possibility of infection is everywhere. The best protection one can give oneself is keeping well, so that germs can find no place to cling. But once one knows himself to be the host of tuberculosis bacilli, his duty to himself, his family, and humanity is to seal up the abrasion and evermore be conscious of the fact that he carries within himself the seed of his own destruction.

I am given these emotional problems to solve:

Can you take it easy?

Are you willing to let somebody else run the world till you are an arrested case?

Can you throw over from your life unnecessary cargo?

Can you rest on schedule at home, which means denying yourself to well-meaning but uninformed friends—and to your family—and not let them own you?

Can you forget the strenuous life, contenting yourself with simple things, providing your own amusements, schooling your soul to growth?

Then, when the specialist finally says the abrasion is healed, the germs are sealed in, that you are an arrested case, that you are non-infectious, can you forgive friends who fear you, the home doctor who ignorantly raises a barrier between you and your old position, and the public that calls you unclean?

Can you?

It isn't very easy. For the very love of life, I try to say, "I can." Otherwise . . . Well, there are things that can be done, but science nor surgeons nor skill can avail UNLESS the attitude of mind of the patient is tuned to Rest.

So I am one of eighteen, waiting on my porch for another day—one of seven hundred in this state supported sanatorium, one of millions who have been told; "You carry within you the seed of your own destruction." Today's business is to rest. It is night again. I fluff up my pillow, hush my homesick heart a little, wait for the moron to begin the Lord's Prayer (tonight is her turn to start it) and I mumble it to the end. Then we say good night to each other. The night nurse rustles past the foot of the beds to see that all are in. Goodnight, nurse. Goodnight, little roomie. Goodnight, Dora. Stillness. Little roomie stirs restlessly in her bed. I hear her murmur, "Goodnight, Mumsie . . . Mumsie . . ." She lingers on the word as if it were a heart's ease just to mouth it. "Goodnight, Ginger. Goodnight, Dad and Bobby and Ned." There's a sigh, such a sigh as can come only from a young heart learning to school itself.

"Dear God," says the sigh, "I wish I didn't have the bugs!"

o o o o o o o o o o o o o o o o

Though the preceding account was written a while after she was well, Ethel also wrote letters during her convalescence. They too have the spoor of loneliness and fear, but they also ring with the steel of determination to get well and go forward. Here are excerpts.

o o o o o o o o o o o o o o o o

To be prepared for a no-letter day, then to get the two loveliest letters ever written—well, that's worth waiting a long, long time for—and my box of good old *home* things. It was a gala day . . . .

I'm dreading tomorrow. Now I have not worried and am not worrying about having my teeth out. I did five years of that, so now I'm letting the dentist worry. (He doesn't seem to be losing weight over it.) But I do reluctantly part with my front ones. I'm afraid I've formed a sentimental attachment for them. Too, they have rendered me valiant service during hamburger season. This is my swan song to them. I still can't think of having "fresh teeth" myself. I do hope . . . well, a lot of things . . . .

Dearest family in the world, your letters do me a lot of good, for I enjoy your being *at home*. I liked what Jane said about loving the old place. Aunt Carrie always said it looked "different." Don't you suppose it's because it's loved? Now take me: I won't be really ugly with all my teeth out, 'cause *I'm loved*. Conceit?

I think perhaps I shall feel like going out for dinner. I had a good night's sleep and am resting hard for Monday's trip. These uppers hurt less but longer, for they were so crowded with pus . . . . These last six won't be so bad, for my three "good" (according to the X-ray) ones are in the bunch . . . . I don't look like anything so much as Dr. Hornburg when he pauses in the middle of his sermon with his mouth open like a perch. I still know I don't want you to come on Sunday, although my heart does a double-quick every time I see a husbandish pair of khakis on the campus . . . .

My sweets, that *compound* letter at dinner time—well, I just don't how the others take it, not getting to share in it. I thought I loved you both before, but I hadn't had time to think it over. Now I think I shall never be able to love you enough, but I am putting in time at it . . . .

I went to lecture this A.M. A long-legged lunger built after the type of Dr. Anderson made a dry lecture—very much like

Dr. Anderson. Then he read a few jokes. Here's the naughty one: the church was taking up a collection to buy a new carpet. A good old sister, not having her change in her pocket book, wished to write a pledge. Said she, "Bring me a piece of paper. I want to do something on the rug." It near laughed the lungs out of the gents . . . . I enjoyed my new pajamas when I was sick. I couldn't keep still, and it was a favor not to worry about exposure!

I, too, little Jane, had a "complexity of emotions" when I tried a while ago to bite a thread. It was an *all gone* feeling—and funny, too! . . .

I'm so proud of the new sheep. I told myself this P.M. during rest hour, "Mrs. Yeager, you are the only sheep woman on the whole porch!" I'd like to meet each mutton individually—and soon! Honest, they don't seem ugly and stupid like the ones that ate the moss, do they?

My face is quite swollen still. The dentist stopped me at noon and asked how it was. I told him not so hot. He said, "Yes, I know. It looks like something the cats had had." That was very apt, I think. But there is little pain. I have a snuffy articulation . . . .

You make me very happy when you say how well you are feeling. I think you have been a *brick* about staying well under this strain. I promise to get well and nurse you and Aunt Carrie and Jane for everything or for nothing at all as long as you want to be petted. And I'll love the job.

o o o o o o o o o o o o o o o o

When Ethel went home, her fears of losing her job permanently were confirmed. The local school board didn't think children should be exposed to her. So she went to the Brady newspaper and offered to write for a dollar a column. The money would be sent to Jane at college. Her husband built her a place to write in a secluded woods in a back pasture, and there she sought her muse.

Country Commonplaces

I like Four-o'clocks. Somehow that flower is mixed up for me with revival meetings, starched dresses, new shoes, and thoughts of God, my soul, and eternity.

The bulk of Yeager's writing portrays throughout the scene on the small farms of Central Texas in various seasons and changing times. Her focus is always on home, farm, and family, but she also alludes frequently enough to events both political and historical which were significant both to her and to her readers.

o o o o o o o o o o o o o o o

September 11, 1936
I wish it would rain. As I write, the earth lies baked and dry, the grasses gone to seed or grazed to the nub. Young cotton shimmers in the dry, hot air. Waterholes have been licked up by the arid winds, leaving their cracked surfaces turned to the hot sky. The family feels the strain of the drought. Pa's as jumpy as a short-tailed bull in fly time. Ma soft pedals as best she can. Even small children watch tantalizing piles of clouds in the sky and the impertinent flash of lightning at night, barren signs—not promises—of moisture. Anxiety is the keynote while the Heart of Texas waits for rain.

October 6, 1936
The first bright blue weather—October's specialty—flaunts line full after line full of clean washed clothes in my neighbors' yards. Judging by the output, one might suppose that Congress had passed a law compelling everybody to observe washday. What a new lease on life the emptying of the clothes hamper after a week of rough weather brings on! Washday is, of course, universal, but to me it seems particularly American. History

records that the first day spent by Pilgrim women on the American continent was spent washing clothes—after some weeks of bad weather, sickness, death, and children. I doubt that even a Maytag could produce the equivalent in satisfaction of the empty clothes hamper feeling of that first American washday.

The rains descended with the customary results. A weather-watcher who rarely trusts God to tend to the weather alone remarked wryly that it takes only two hours to break up a ten-year drought.

++++++++++++++++++++++

War and drought and floods and tax muddles and sudden death are relieved by country commonplaces: the quack-quack-quack and gabble-gabble-gabble of Mother Engdahl's turkeys in the early morning, unseen but challengingly talking turkey; the swoop of a blue-darter over a frantic mother hen; Vernon Brown, striding in ten-league swinging measure half a mile away across the valley, whistling in the fog, a vibrant rolling tune with a note of melancholy; neighborly smoke drifting up from Ida Stewart's chimney; hot biscuits and new honey for supper; the warmth of the first open wood fire in the fall; a good book and somebody to share it with.

++++++++++++++++++++++

Last year there was a poor market for small pelts, and as Fall comes on, farmer matches farmer with multiplied reports of poultry devastation by possums, polecats, and even the sly fox. Added to this, there is an increase in the number of hawks and owls. Eggs bid fair to be scarce. Then, too, consider what must be the day and night life of Mrs. Hen. Ben Allen in this community has been the most successful shooter-atter of hawks, but we need some skillful trappers.

++++++++++++++++++++++

Some small grain is responding to the moisture and growing warmth. From the top of the hill, McCulloch County's farming country is remindful of quilts in frames at a neighborhood quilting—splotches of green and even-furrowed plowed stretches separated here and there by fields of picked and unpicked cotton and maize still in shocks, with patches of pasture lands between. There is not a prettier spread of countryside in the South than that of the Lohn Valley from the adjoining mountain tops—say the Fullagar ones. But find your favorite spot and then enjoy it in "October's bright blue weather"—just before Indian Summer sets in in earnest.

And don't miss Indian Summer. Its bright beauty lasts only three or four days, generally, before the sumac begins to dull and the woodsy odor loses its freshness. Ride horseback; better still, walk in the woods. It will do something wonderful to your soul.

February 5, 1937
February. It is the month the earth yawns and begins to wake up. "Hope," sang the poet, "springs eternal in the human breast." Often I have conned the line using farmer instead of human—a farmer at his early spring plowing. Last year's drought? flood? worms? market? freeze? blight? hail? Oh, that was LAST year. So with head down and heart ahead, he plows his furrow straight—again! And the world eats what is left from the plowman's table.
++++++++++++++++++++

During the last freeze-in, I read America's best selling non-fiction book, *Live Alone and Like It*, by Marjorie Hillis. Never have I felt more inelegant. With the hydrants all frozen, the last pair of once-clean sheets an icy lamination, the next fresh house dress something to conjecture about, swaddled in an outing night gown, I read about "glamour in the bedroom; four bed jackets—a sheer, a lacy, a Shetland wool, and a quilted silk; breakfast in bed; bath salts; fingernails soaked in olive oil." We had spare ribs and sausage, corn pone and turnips with liver and onions while I read of "twiglets, Newbergs, mousse of halibut, chutney, Bombay duck, Greek (not green) olives, Russian borscht, and ham cooked in cider." I don't know about the other things, but that is an inhuman thing to do to a ham. Then think of the cider wasted.

There was a chapter devoted to Old Fashioneds, Martinis, highballs and Manhattans. One bit of wisdom that Miss Hillis wishes to impress upon a waiting world is, "Remember, never, never to mix Scotch with anything but plain or charged water."

All in all, the book is not good enough to be really bad nor bad enough to be really good.

A better non-fiction American book is one written eighty-three years ago by an American who lived alone and liked it, and it offers more valuable wisdom than the "remember-never-never." The book is Thoreau's *Walden* in which a real countryman says, "A man is rich in proportion to the number of things he can afford to let alone." Then in support of his theory, this young Harvard graduate, living in his self-made hut, planted a garden and supported himself for two years on a yearly grocery bill of eight dollars, while he fronted the essential facts of life to see, as he said, what it had to teach lest when he came to die he should discover that he had not lived.

I think Thoreau would not have cared much for Miss Hillis' book, for he said, "A sentence should read as if its author, had he held a plow instead of a pen, could have drawn a furrow deep and straight to the end." I failed to find anything deep and very little straight about Miss Hillis' book. Yet it is America's best non-fiction seller this winter, which gives one cause to ponder.

++++++++++++++++++++++

A census taken by the Rochelle Baptist Church reveals the fact that the large-size family exists, with its blessings and its woes. Its blessings have been told in song and story, but chief among its woes, as I remember it, is the problem of The Towel. Unless you were reared in a family approximating a dozen, you wouldn't believe how vexing the whereabouts of that elusive common drying piece can be. If you have never been all drippy with soap suds and groped blindly in the great empty space where the preceding dryer should have left The Towel, you'll not know what this is all about. Who knows how many new homes have been established by towel-gropers with the secret purpose of stabilizing the abiding place of the face mopper-upper! Statistics will probably show that roller-towel families produce more old maids and bachelors than the loose towel families.

March 9, 1937

March. This is the month nobody loves. I imagine it must be mighty discouraging to be a month like that. March doesn't have nice ancestry, either. It was named for the God of War, and Sherman said that about war, even before the dustbowl sandstorms. The head of the house is not enthusiastic about it because he has been knowing since last September that March is the month for the other Federal Farm Payment. And also there is that little matter of new tags for the family motor-omnibus before that month is up. Women dread it because the clothes twist round and round and round the line on washday, and all month they fret to launder the curtains but know it will be a waste of time—and housecleaning is casting pearls before swine. Caesar got into trouble on the Ides of it.

However, the month does have some talking points. Like a lot of other famous, infamous, and inconsequential folks, I was born in it, and regardless of what that may mean to outsiders, it does give us a sort of friendly feeling for the old month. The lamb market begins to gambol, and this is fast becoming of interest to farmers of this section. Everybody anticipates a rain. Tulips bloom in March if you have them, and some days when white clouds romp across, the blue March sky is prettier than any other. Algeritas bloom in it, and no woodsy odor is sweeter.

August 3, 1937

August with its dry, hot winds for maturing and curing. Seed time and harvest. August's little sounds: the busy whirr of the cicada from his hiding place among the leaves, the shrill call of the ground squirrel sitting straight and high on his haunches, dirt daubers plastering in forbidden places, the ceaseless year-round chirp of English sparrows.

A fall sound that is particularly full of goodness to me is the rattle and bump of wagon wheels and the creak and rumble of an empty market wagon returning from town after nightfall behind the measured clump of the tired horses' hooves and the busy jangle of harness. There is more here than pleasant sounds. One knows that there is supper waiting in the oven—a supper of victuals for a hungry man; little ones waiting up to see what daddy brought; a recounting of the details of marketing to be shared with mother; then sleep.

The return of the producer from the market to his home is the completion of a great cycle which makes and has always made great nations. When anything goes wrong with any part of that cycle, something goes wrong—even as far away as Capitol Hill.

November 16, 1937

Wild ducks and geese are flying over in wedges, honking and barking at us earth-bound creatures getting ready for winter. In the woods there is the raucous call of blue jays. Stinging scorpions are bunching up under rocks. Leaves are yellowing on the limbs. Without twenty trunks or flurry in diplomatic circles, without official greetings from governmental dignitaries, without anything more disturbing than a blast of winter wind, the yellow and red and brown leaves are about to set off on a journey more important to mankind than any visit of royalty or dignitary.

November means Thanksgiving dinner all over our land. If I wanted oysters in the dressing on that day, I'd drop in on Ma Lohn. If I felt a yen for caramel pie, I'd dine with Bill Bryson at his hill-top ranch house. For angel food cake, I'd have dinner with Ma Gainer. There'll be smearcase at the Rudolphs' and cornbread with "vittles" at Granny Cates'. And superb coffee at the James Boyds'.

March 11, 1938

Early spring mornings free from chores are akin to heaven in boydom. A group of Lohn youngsters brings in the prize story of a day well spent: half a dozen boys about the bumpkin age started adventuring under the leadership of Myers Johnson with the Johnson fox hounds for a day in the woods. Boys and dogs exceeded expectations when they hit a fox trail. After a yipping, breathless foot race, the bewildered fox found safety on a high limb—helpless till Myers' hand sought the environs of his pocket. There, mixed up with top, topstring, two agates, a button hook, four goobers, and a soda-pop bottle top, he found his sling shot.

With Little David precision, he let the quarry have it, and down tumbled the fox into a mad snarling and biting of expert fox hounds. The boys then waded in and beat off the dogs, killed the stunned fox, and brought him back to town. The last account of the adventure reported one pelt for sale for which the joint owners hoped to realize a ten or twenty-and-a-half cent payoff. Myers, true son of a careful business man, was holding out for the big end of the take, since his were the hounds and his was the sling shot.

++++++++++++++++++++

Is the wharf rat tendency common to farmers or peculiar to a few of them? A block of medicated stock salt, a half-barrel of seed corn, new wire stretchers, or some other he-some possession too precious to be cached in the barn finds its way to the house, gets tucked hopefully behind the "outside door" or secreted in the "back room." Once I remember the smell of new leather pervading the house for weeks while a squeaky new saddle hung pendant-like from the center of the "side room." After a week to himself, my countryman, I found on my return, had dragged to his lair a new lariat, a block of sheep salt, a sack of something, and a box I couldn't open.

April 12, 1938

Mamie Snodgrass, mother of six, paid tribute to April by having the children help her "red up" the house bright and early so she could come to school and bring the teacher a bouquet of early Crimson Ramblers and Sweet Locust. Something of a poet and philosopher is this dainty little lady. "Flowers are like people," she said. "There is something good in the most homely ones." Then she told of a late summer party she gave once when the drought had left not a flower in bloom over the countryside—except oceans of broomweeds, with which she made the house gala. "Did you ever notice," she asked with a twinkle, "that the drier and hotter it gets, the harder the broomwood tries to be beautiful?"

June 23, 1938

June is alliteratively the month of romance and roses, brides and building. Big doin's in the Roosevelt family with John and Ann putting the finishing furbelows on their honeymoon house by the sea. Big doin's too in the romance and building business as observed from my sleeping porch. A pair of orchard orioles that have been that way about each other for some time started building in the tickle-tongue bush yesterday. That is, the bride started building.

A hundred trips she has made, winging her way back with a bit of straw, a length of horse hair, a wisp of wool, a pliable stick, which she deftly weaves into a strong, snug nest. Her consort seems tremendously interested in the project, making each trip with her, sitting excitedly on the window flap as she builds, but carrying nary a load nor weaving nary a strand. At first, I was no end provoked with the fellow, but as I watched, I think I learned a thing or two. The bride is a pretty little trick, energetic and vivacious. Too, she has a coquettish turn of the head that promises interesting complications. Other fine gentlemen of the oriole family are alert to her every move. Her selected suitor seems to know he will have little time for prosaic home puttering until he's sure of keeping his bride.

Another couple, this time doves, have secured an HOLC loan and are remodeling a mocker's nest in the mulberry. They didn't bother a great deal about details. Mrs. Dove simply started bringing in rather stiffish twigs about eight o'clock and had a white egg in the worked-over job by eleven. Rather a shiftless couple, or perhaps they are philosophers and are little concerned with mere housing.

But a bull-bat gives society cause for some alarm. Without a stick, a wisp of anything, or any preparation whatever, Mrs. Bull-bat unconcernedly deposited two eggs on the very bare ground out in the sunshine in the midst of rolling pebbles. There she sat day after day until two ugly but hardy bull-bats were hatched. These she offers more or less protection whenever she happens to find them upon her return from fly catching. No thought of a rainy day, of prowling enemies, apparently no thought of family obligations as she brings her fledglings into a world already too full of bull-bats. Queer, thoughtless one she is.

Since the rains, the country bathing season is open. It is wise to let yourself be known before approaching any gravel bottom tank or spring-fed creek in this neighborhood. During the next few months, a senatorial investigation would reveal a higher percentage of washed bodies among the poorly housed rural population of the South about which we have been hearing so much of late than a winter investigation would reveal.

There are those, however, that doubt the felt need of bathing facilities in some rural homes. A town-dwelling Austin farm owner once told of providing his farm house with a bath tub and hot and cold running water. At Christmas time when he repaired to the farm for an escape from town living, he found the water system frozen, his tenant carrying water from the spring, and the winter's pork salted down in the tub.

Another neighbor who felt that efforts for comfort had gone unappreciated told a tale of a tenant who set hens in the bathtub.

Nevertheless, everybody gets a washup at the old swimmin' hole, so this can't be an all bad world.

++++++++++++++++++++++

Out at Sam Cloud's farm where I went for early fryers, I found a country uncommonplace. Although it was the middle of the week and no cyclone was in evidence, Mrs. Sam and her mother were sitting on the pleasant front porch reading the Bible aloud to each other. A white oleander nodded from its tub. Sam estimated that he had toted the flower pot a hundred miles, carrying it inside from the cold and outside again for the sun and rain. But he didn't seem to mind a bit.

July 28, 1938

In the pastures and along the roadsides, tall lady slippers are in bloom as in early spring. No old timer has been able to recall a parallel to this siege of July rains. Jack Crew, who has lived always and looks as if he intends to keep it up, says it never happened in McCulloch County before.

The threshers barely got clear of the fields before the rains set in. This year closes a half-century of threshing in the section for T.W. Mooring. He recalls a wide range of grain prices and yields, as well as a scale of threshing charges from a one-tenth toll to war time high. Personally he declares himself in favor of oats as against wheat and barley as the most profitable grain crop for this part of the country. "I know what to do with oats," he says, "even cheap oats."

Tall bloodweeds are beginning to show up on the farms and in the draws of this neighbornood. They threaten to become an East Texas nuisance for us if we don't watch out. As it is, we have enough to keep us out of mischief fighting the hoarhound, Johnson grass, and potato weeds. Several fields have become fouled, too, with yellow daisies while lying idle under cut acreage compensation.

The sun, a sort of mildewed edition, holds out a half-hearted promise that we can take up the pans and buckets from under the leaks, open the windows and let out the musty odors while we let in clean, washed outside air.

++++++++++++++++++++++++

When flooded Brady Creek ripped the town in two, crowds stood for hours on both sides in the spitting drizzle, as the flood passed in review fragments from a community's living: chicken coops, telephone cross arms, packing crates, loose lumber, household furniture, bundles of shingles, trailer houses, shacks, small houses, a frantic horse swimming bravely.

Disaster draws its gallery. On the north side, Bridge Street milled with awed spectators cut off from the main part of town— residents, country people, and folks from next towns. Idle curiosity had scant representation. Across and under the rolling water lay devastation for many of them. Others remembered friends or relatives who were paying the cost of the rampage. Imagination supplemented reports of the extent of mischief on the town side of the creek.

Homeowner Dodson, with the waters licking at the eaves of his house, showed the kind of fight that is America. He was a spectator till his home was threatened. Against the flood he made no war until it assaulted his door. Then he became militant. With a sea of water about him, he stayed on the roof of his home and, with a scantling, pushed away the drift to keep his home secure. He won.

As the wet crowd elbowed each other, unmindful of the stealthy advance of the waters and the danger of unanchored live wires, Bud Westbrook rose like the genie of the stream and was everywhere at once. He moved parked cars, pushed back the spectators from water's edge, and herded them away from the live wires.

A little black and white dog paced an island made of an overturned trailer house in midstream. As night came down, his apprehensive helplessness gave the crowd an object upon which to bestow an accumulation of sympathy. On Sunday morning, the water was gone, and the little dog frisked about the scene of his late terror, the memory of the night how far removed?

On Saturday night the water was back in its bed after one grand spree. It was clean-up time.

Something there is about a high bridge and a stream slithering under it that makes me want to drop things and see the current carry them on. Since the bridge was built over Bridge Street, I have passed over it from my home to Brady and back. For all these years, I have had a strong urge to drop in my banana peels as I leave town—long, yellow banana peels—and have them carried on by the waters. But having been reared on a belief that it is some sort of a crime for a citizen to pollute the streams of his country; and being myself a blood brother of Mr. Milquetoast, I have restrained myself dutifully and tucked my peels back into the sack. Imagine then my surprise to see truck after truck back up to the abutment of the washed-out bridge and dump loads of filth into the same creek. I worried about the thing for a long time. By Monday it had begun to stink. I worried some more, but was reassured by citizens that "everything is in hand," and "there is a division of the State Health Department in charge." Eventually my last worry was dispelled when one patiently explained to me that the serum dumped into people would make them air-tight to the filth dumped into the creek; and besides, it was pointed out, the fall from the dump cart into the stream broke the necks of the germs and that was where the stink came from.

Now I don't have anything to worry about but those who live down the stream and failed to get full of serum.

Losses? A hundred dollars? A thousand? Many thousand? What's the difference? With broom and mop and scoop, from one end of the flood-swept town to the other, Brady started over again Saturday night. Outsiders inquired among themselves, "How can they try it again?" But Brady was too busy to answer. Among them one heard the words "new channels," "engineers," "impounding," "raised wall."

August 25, 1938

Country people know the summer sky a little better than we do the winter sky because the weather is kind and this allows us to see more of it. We go outdoors to see it. We sit on the porch and visit by starlight. We sleep on beds in the yard. We go hunting. And some of us walk through the magic of coming night to the tabernacle where there is a revival, or we visit neighbors. We are thus exposed to the mystery and beauty of the summer night, yet too few of us are familiar with the lore of stars and constellations, even the summer ones. The loss is ours, for sky acquaintance broadens the horizon of the soul. Poor little cooped up souls! We've hemmed them in so tightly with things, things, things that they have not had much room for expansion.

September 2, 1938

When fall weather calls for another blanket before morning and sends housewives inspecting the supply of longies and a hint of frost is in the air, the while romantic souls write songs about the harvest moon, it is comforting to take a tally of man-won victories over nature, who says, "I've got what you want, but you'll have to come and get it." In the face of cold days, there is comfort in marching fences, tight of stay, hemming in domestic brutes; deep, mysterious wells, bringing water to an arid land; windmills that harness a fraction of nature's great force wasting above us; stacks of hay; acres of ground upturned and seeded for the winter rains; dams across draws; cords of fire wood; and roofs that shut out the cold and rain and shut in peace and love.

November 3, 1938

The melancholy days are come to our house—those sad, long days between the last milking of Old Pide and the first milking of Old Jersey with her new calf, when and if it ever arrives. We never miss the water till the creek runs dry nor realize the full poetry of the cream in our coffee until the cow goes dry. So far, friendly neighbors have supplied the poetry for the morning cup—some quarts from Mama Mackie's; a gorgeous, ropy separated offering that had to be spooned from the pitcher from Ida Stewart's; and a big, fat half gallon I found in the ice box from neighbor Densman's. The milk and cream are even better than ours from Old Pide, for they are flavored with neighborliness.

There is something indecent feeling about dish-washing when there are no milk things to be done. Two cups, two saucers, two scarcely mussed plates, a brace of knives, forks, and spoons—and the job's done. Of course, I appreciate the vacation from prolonged sudsings—but the whole ritual seems so sort of temporary, so rootless.

I am dismayed at the collection of town-sacks from the grocery store that has been accumulating since the melancholy days are come.

November 17, 1938

Washday. At our house the occasion has always required a washboard and tubs, a fire around a pot, and much lifting of water. For a number of years the system worked well enough. However, of late I have suspected that my countryman has taken a tip from the aborigines of this land. I think he's smoke signalling. Anyway, I have observed that pretty soon after the first blue pencilling of smoke spirals heavenward on washday, there are callers at our house, always neighboring menfolks. Uncle Walter appears from nowhere, or Papa Brown hobbles up on his yucca walking stick, or Pete Stewart or Jewel Densman or even Papa Engdahl stops the mules long enough to join my countryman and lifter of suds in some manful project far removed from the old wash place. And I am left holding the rubboard and my temper.

So by way of counter revolution, the other day I suggested the Help-Yourself Wash and was introduced to a whole new way of life. No lift, no rub, no wait (once you are started), and the toll is considerably less than buying a machine.

Life goes on at the Help-Yourself Wash. The proprietor said that she had men, women, and children customers. Some she had to teach how to wash; others she did the wash for at a small increase in price. I found that I had time for a pleasant visit with the owner and other customers and time to read a short short in the Collier's which was lying on a table, like the magazines in a doctor's office. This experience will likely put an end to the smoke signal finagling at our house.

+++++++++++++++++++++++

An early morning fog is duck soup to the blue darter that has been fattening himself on my broilers. Hordes of chattering sparrows, crammed fear-crazed into an algerita bush, say that he is somewhere about and on the stalk, but he always finds me before I find him. On a clear morning, he hid in the big oak by the windmill and allowed me to go indoors and get the shotgun. But no hawk could I find in the thick leaves till he was on the wing. I think he was amused at my lack of marksmanship as I fired him a farewell, just in case he thought I didn't mean business.

December 1, 1938

Winter living in the country makes one rub elbows with reality. Cold days emphasize the dependence of living things on man, and the day's chores have a point to them that leaves the husbandman feeling a bit important at the end of the day. Indoors, most farm houses lack much for comfortable living. This is an open secret, now that the government has told it to the world about life as she is lived in the South and Southwest.

Yet indoors and out there is definite satisfaction for having lived twenty-four hours out of twenty-four. There are sunrises and sunsets, for instance. Now, modern poets look askance at a poem made on a sunrise or a sunset. They feel the subject is more than slightly frayed around the cuffs, but yesterday I saw a sunset that was so new that it crinkled. And after the rain this morning the earth was young.

Geese flew over in wedges and tantalized my imagination. I questioned where they were heading for, what freedom, what escape they would find. I thought of the things that held me home. Yet I knew I wouldn't go with them, even if they asked me, because I need to make my beds and sweep my floors. Besides, I think I shall plant some poppy seeds for next spring this afternoon. Do you suppose the wind is warm and the water runs in little teasing washes along the sandy beach where they are today?

An awareness of the ground, the dirt under our feet, comes with winter in the country. Soon it begins threateningly to show through the grassy covering of the growing season. It clings clammily to the shoes after a wet spell; its warm smell in the noon sun promises. In the snow and frost, it threatens and warns of waste. Altogether it is different from the feel of the swelling earth in the springtime. A favorite story has been that of the giant who, when knocked to the ground, got up stronger than before because he got his strength from contact with the ground. So do we all.

Another story of the ground: from the slums of New York, a waif, a victim of diabetes, was picked up and sent for treatment to the country estate of a philanthropist. In the city the boy had lived month following month with the streets and sidewalks under him, hidden in the backwash of humanity where there were no trees nor yards nor gardens nor grass—only dry, hot pavement. When his nurse rolled his wheelchair out upon the lawn under the trees, she expected some expressions about the beauty of the growing things. But the patient wobbled from his chair, went down on hands and knees, dug with his hands through the grass, and brought up a trickle of dirt through his fingers. With eyes glowing, he whispered, "Doit! Real doit!"

A country kid has "doit." Does he have appreciation for it? If not, why not?

++++++++++++++++++++

"Sleeping sickness" took the saddle horse. But as saddle horses go, it didn't take a lot. He was the sort of animal that one never gets around to naming—largely because no polite name seems to cover adequately all the varieties of cussedness bound up in his hide. In appearance he was as alluring as sin. Sleek, high-headed, he had the grace of a deer—and the heart of a demon.

With every ounce of him he hated the gates and fences. It was a mean, nasty job to pen him, and he had fiendish delight in tantalizing us on such occasions. He told us what he thought of us! Head held high, tail outstretched, nostrils wide, he snorted his disdain of a guy that would put a rope about his neck, a bridle in his mouth, and a saddle on his back. He seemed to have an understanding with himself, while being penned, that it wasn't cricket to have much more than one hoof on the ground at a time. I think I wouldn't have been surprised to see him swoop into the air after one of his long, earth-spurning dashes. He was the kind of brute profanity was invented for.

Even when he was dead, he didn't seem really still. It was only when they dragged him away and left a wide swath in the dust that I realized that we wouldn't be corralling him again, ever. It made me sort of lonesome, somehow, and I was surprised that it did. That swath in the dust—how he would have hated so much of him at once to be on the ground! The life of rebel is a hard one, but surely it is highly flavored.

December 15, 1938

The last of November is a part of the year especially set apart in this Yeager family, for it was on the 29th of that month twenty-one years ago that my countryman, then a young city slicker from Brownwood, stood with me before the Rev. A.E. Baten in front of the fireplace at the old Neal home, and the both of us said, "I do." There was a roomful of neighbors present, but to this day I can remember seeing only my daddy, sitting in the chimney corner crying—the way a bride's mother is supposed to do.

I couldn't say whether Mackie Ma cried or not. I don't remember seeing her. But I'll bet she didn't. She was never one for tears. Rather, Mackie Ma belongs to the lip-straightening, chin-lifting school.

By and large, we have found in the twenty-one years that the royal road to material wealth for us lies in schooling ourselves to be content with what we have—and in cutting off behind impossible, impractical desires that spoil contentment. In other words, we have found what the philosophers knew all the time and we wouldn't believe—that is, that we are rich in proportion to the things we can do without and not wish for after the light is out.

We have found, too, that many of the things we value have no taxable worth: an open fire, flapjacks for supper, getting ready for comp'ny, a silly kitten chasing its tail, odds and ends of small nephews and nieces, a four- or five-sided conversation.

On this November anniversary, we clipped a coupon from our most valued possession: we closed up, lock, stock, and barrel, and went to visit the children—we were impressed with the plural—at Alvin, Texas, below Houston.

Early winter driving from Brady to Austin should be reserved for poets. In many places the trees are so near the highway that the feel of the countryside seeps inside a closed car. Over the hills near the capital there is breathless beauty in the great expanse of multi-colored hills and valleys. The road is a monument to engineering. The driver says the curves are "sweet."

Every Texan should see Congress Avenue in the capital city at night. My favorite view is from the top of the hill opposite the capitol. From this point it seems only a hand's breadth between the bridge and the State House—a jewel laden hand's breadth. The same scene in the light of day lengthens into such a long, busy thoroughfare that you'd swear some magic had been abroad the night before.

Out of Austin on the Houston road by way of Bastrop an unexpected forest of tall pines suddenly throws itself across the highway. For four or five miles there is the resiny, pungent odor of piney woods from the slim-bodied, reaching trees that seem to be trying to dust off the clouds. As suddenly, the pines are gone and the way leads through post oak and shinnery as before. The Lost Forest, it is called.

The Coggin fireside at Alvin held us pretty closely. The Gulf air, wet and cold, cut like ice. When frost gets to work down there, it finds plenty of material. So inches of frost and long icicles decorated the early morning scenery.

A day's shopping in Houston made me homesick for friendly Brady stores. Such a hurry of restlessness. Too much stock in the stores for my simple, country mind to get centered on one thing. I just gaped.

On the street I saw my first picketing-laborers carrying "unfair" placards in front of businesses, grimly walking up and down, up and down. To me it was dramatic, the kind of drama too close to tragedy. I didn't like it. Bugles blowing and flags waving generally mean that "we" are fighting "somebody else." Strike fighting is "us" fighting "us."

There were two Gypsies in voluminous skirts of rich brocades and velvets. To me these folks just ooze out romance.

In a shoe shop a traveling Jewish salesman was taking leave of a Jewish buyer. Seriousness marked their faces. And their leavetaking fell strangely in that busy, hustling, crowded, noisy city. "God be with you till we meet again," said the salesman. "And God bless you," the buyer replied. There was more than the matter of shoe buying between these two men who have not a where to call their country this holiday season.

Thanksgiving dinner was turkeyless on purpose. It was at a little restaurant overlooking the waves along the sea wall in Galveston. We had found the place a year ago last Thanksgiving and had made a rendezvous to have dinner this year at the very same place. "The Sea Wall" it is called, and it served the most appetizing trout dinners that can be dished up on a platter to a West Texan already stale on baked chicken and dressing. Besides, there's the whole of Galveston Bay spread out before you while you eat. Perfect food in a perfect setting!

Would you be interested to know that when the time came for us to return to our country home we found that Old Jersey and Old Legs each had a new calf apiece, so that now we are in the cream—and that Old Cat, cut off from backdoor relief, had kept herself fat on rabbits and rats, but was begging as piteously as of yore the next morning—and that a possum was averaging a fryer a night out of the hen house?

February 9, 1939

Beyond a doubt, February is gardening month for those who reap in the spring and summer. A few apron tails would hold the bulk of the edibles I've harvested from my gardens, but I've had some grand times putting seed into the ground. It's the happiest way in the world to sacrifice a manicure. I have scruples against messing up a half-hour's tussle with a tricky paint job, especially after I've coddled each of my ten digits into a show of what I, in fond delusion, believe to be crescents. To splurge the works on a kitchen full of greasy dishes makes me positively ill. To fling them into the pot with the family wash upsets my temper—but a good badger digging into moist soil in early spring—well, that's a different orgy. I haven't the divine touch with flowers and growing things that my mother has, but I have the itch of it.

March 9, 1939

"Sniff, sniff," sniffed Jane, as she came home a-visiting after a year and a week and six days of housewifing in her own right. "Mother," said she, "your house smells so countrified."

Now any housewife, even one who does her chores with a lick and a second-lien promise, wants a statement like that amplified or retracted. "Smells?" I asked, raising an eyebrow at the present generation.

"Smells good, I mean. Delightfully countrified. What makes it? Mine doesn't."

Together we sniffed to identify what made my farmhouse different from her hot-and-cold-water with fixings, punch-a-button icebox, radio, and coffeepot, slippery-slick-floors, and twice-a-week garbage-man job. But we were too familiar with the odors to single it out, so we took a walk down to the cow pen and sat on the baled hay where the sun came warmly under the shed. There's something soothing and relaxing in the clean barn odors, and we lapped it up while we got a lot of mother-and-daughter talking done.

With hardly more than a curious glance at us, the older hens went on about their business, but a pullet set up a hiccoughy cackling at our intrusion and finally persuaded us to leave. We circled back by the woodpile and loaded ourselves with a turn of wood. When we came into the house, our noses quickened by a dose of outside odors, we sniffed earnestly for the house smell. "Ashes," Jane diagnosed, "wood ashes." The smell is delightfully countrified—subtle, clean, and penetrating.

++++++++++++++++++++++

A headline in last week's *Heart O' Texas News* is a challenge to local wifehood. "Mrs. Elvard White," says the headline, "honors husband."

Is the practice becoming so rare that an observation of it ranks as news? Anyway, I think honoring husbands is a very charming, gracious thing to do and it makes better reading than state or national politics, or rumors of the latest war spot. So I contribute this instance from my neighbors: Zora Mooring is honoring her husband this week because, after a winter of hand-toted water, he brought home a barrel and now hauls the supply in the hoopie. In addition to being a personal news item, the above is also a report of rural progress not to be sneezed at.

April 20, 1939

For the past few weeks we have enjoyed a sense of security at our house that has been stimulating. The condition of the small grain, the chances of rain, the success of my neighbor's hatch, his rheumatiz, his garden, the best way to get rid of blue bugs, a new battercake recipe, and the kids' report cards have made up a good part of the conversation of the day. It's all because the wind charger is out of balance, so the radio is cut off; and in the rush of April chores, we've sort of slighted the dailies, too. It's a good feeling to let the world rock along without you as a chief worrier for a while—to be too busy to remember that a lot of folks we don't know are prodding us into a war, that distrust of our government is rank in the land, that unrest is everywhere. Separated from the radio and the dailies, we can generate a bit of confidence that begets a sense of security, and a sense of security, even though it be a false one, is becoming a treat.

War talk on the radio throws a bigger scare into me than war talk in cold print. I think it's the emotional effect of the voice. Emotion, the psychologists tell us, is the result of feeling, not thinking. Now, psychologists say further that folks do a more telling job of emoting standing than they do sitting. Here's my plan for a partial appeasement of war hysteria: all radio stations should be compelled to have all commentators, international newscasters, politicians, and, yea, even statesmen to sit while they broadcast. And since tumbling into war is such a childish thing, I'd be in favor of having them sit straddle-legged with the mike on the floor the way we used to play mumble-peg. It would be a while before one could get a lot of emoting done in such a position. At the same time, it's a calm, restful position for thinking.

+++++++++++++++++++++

It's been a long time since I've won a family argument. It's always a long time between wins for me. But last week I marked up a score. With the pens full of ewes and lambs for branding, docking, untailing, and marking the new crop, I fell to speculating upon the degree of lusciousness that could be cooked into a little, fat, milk-fed fellow, weighing, say, twenty pounds.

Recently I'd been investigating recipes for mint sauce to accompany roast lamb. Besides, we'd wintered on pork, baked hen and turkey, and as the Easter season came on, I developed a yen for milk-fed lamb—the kind you read about. You see, at our house we butcher a mature mutton or a grown goat from time to time, but to butcher a milk-fed lamb—well, that's quite out of the question, both economically and traditionally. Yet on this particular lamb-handling day, I chanced to be on the spot when there was a rush of ewes and lambs pushed into the crowd pen. Lambs tumbled under their mothers' feet in the dust, where trampled in the dust, and came up wild-eyed and bleating. When the dust cleared, one fine little fellow stood alone, shaking with a kind of ague. He'd been hurt, I told myself, in the rush. No need to bother with an injured lamb.

Right then and there I claimed him for my roast pot. There was an argument. Menfolk didn't have time to dress a sheep. That little thing? It wouldn't make a taste. Besides it might be sick of a disease. The lamb seemed to side with me. He was pretty well done in and was behaving convincingly like a recent injury case. Not to drag out the sweetness of my triumph, I shall relate simply that the animal was grudgingly dressed—it was about the size of four good hens.

Half of the meat I cached in the icebox; the other half I took to town for storage, mentally licking my chops over tomorrow's roast. I hurried home to try out the mint sauce recipe—only to be met by my countryman with a face full of concern and a voice full of ill-concealed triumph. After I had left, he said, another big, healthy lamb, behaving similar to my roast-dinner one had sickened similarly—and had died. A ride over the pasture disclosed another dead one. He had explained about them to neighbor Bratton, who diagnosed the fatalities as "clabber belly" cases.

Out of the icebox came my potential roast. The mint sauce was a loss without the lamb to go with it. I unmarked my score.

Still I doubt . . . . It could have been an injury, and I know it takes little effort for Charley Bratton to think up one as good as "clabber belly" for a brother Mason who has lost an argument.

++++++++++++++++++++++

Ewes have no need of fingerprints or blood tests for identifying their offspring. They know them by smell, which seems pretty awful to me, but has been quite satisfactory to them for the centuries. As a result of depending on this age-old method of identification, an instance of modern practice caused considerable consternation in our sheep pens the other morning. Following the generally recommended practice of curtailment of production, my countryman was clipping off the tails of the new lambs. With a little whittled out board pressed for protection against the lamb's hind parts, over which his tail was pulled, big, clumsy, dull scissors, previously heated over a bed of coals, slowly burned off the unwanted appendage, searing the wound so that there was no loss of blood.

It sounds terrible, but as a rule, the lambs offered little objection and were soon nuzzling at their mothers' udders and shaking the place where their tails used to be. Thus suddenly beset, the cautious mother turned a quick nose to the hocks of her sucking offspring. The acrid smell of burnt wool bespoke a thief in the larder. With a quick thrust of the head, she pushed the lamb away. Her nose, following to investigate away from the burned wool, proclaimed her own offspring. Over and over this thing went on. The puzzled ewe seemed to say, "The front end has the smell of Esau, but this back end is a stranger to me."

June 29, 1939

Hoar-hound, listed as an herb in garden catalogues but as an abomination on the Yeager premises, has fooled me twice this year. Once in a warm spell last February, I tenderly covered with grass its first leaves, which I had encouraged to come early through the earth's crust by watering a spot where I had allowed zinnias to seed last fall, fondly hoping for early blooming flowers. The cotyledons came through and, devilishly wise old weed that it is, simply stood there for weeks in spite of watering and pampering with fertilizer. It stood so till warm weather came. Then, where I expected satiny-smooth zinnia leaves, the darned stuff blatantly put out its creepy greenness in bunches! Another time I had lettuce planted under screen wire against sparrow thievery. Whatever became of the lettuce that was supposed to sprout, I don't know, but I nurtured hoar-hound for a fond week before its leaves came through to tell me it was not lettuce.

How I hate the persistence of that weed! I hoe it when it's small, grub it when it's grown, and pull it by hand after rains. Still it swamps me by mid-summer. Drought discourages it but does not deter it. One summer the road crew let down their scraper for a turn around the barn. They did it in the spirit of public service, to save us as a visible landmark to the neighbors. Too, there was a bribe of a chicken dinner.

I hope there isn't any hoar-hound in heaven, for I intend to live there some day; and I've never lived anywhere it didn't abound. When I've laid down my weeding hoe for the last time and hoar-hound has won its final victory over one more ineffectual combatant, I think I can hear the choir softly parodying, "Asleep in Jesus, no more hoar-hound, then death has lost its venomed sting."

August 3, 1939

Although tradition says that only fools and newcomers prophesy weather in Texas, nearly everybody has his favorite sign of rain. In our family we take our weather seriously. For instance, Arthur and Mackie Ma regard two sets of clouds at different levels as promising of rain. Raleigh looks out for rain pretty soon after a day of cloudless sky. Alvin, who mixes scientific study of government weather records with his sometimes spectacular forecasting, depends on the weather running in seven-day cycles, if something unusual doesn't upset the dope. "When you smell rain," says Roudel, "it won't rain where you are that day."

A "sundog" means rain within three days to the Elmer Davenports, and thunderclouds in the south at sunrise mean rain before dark to Tol Roberts. Doves cooing in the middle of the day is Jess Petty's favorite indication that rain is on the way.

My countryman was dour when I asked him for his sign of rain. "Mud," he said and stalked off to make a grim estimate of how much longer the stock water in the earthen tank will hold out.

August 10, 1939

It isn't true what the farm papers say about cows not being able to kick backward. Ours can—and does. She does it with such ease and naturalness, nay, with such apparent relish, that I fear backward kicking is a quaint old bovine custom, and your "bov" can probably do it too. I found out for sure about ours last week when I tried solo to put the kickers on the Jersey.

Now Cowpen Caperings have been a bit out of my line since, like a smart girl, I taught my menfolk the gentle art of detaching the surplus milk from bossy, but last week I was at it again, disillusioned woman. You see, my countryman fell off a plow.

Such a statement seems in cold print just a little item of local interest. But not to me. The fact is that my countryman isn't really a countryman. Oh, no. When first I knew him, he was a trainman, scaling enough cars in a week's time to shake hands with St. Peter, detaching himself with automatic precision and the swooping grace of a Texas chaparral from a rattling line of empties, hop-skip-and-jumping over the top down the long icy length of a freight train against a whipping norther in the days when freight trains had length. I mean to say the lad was grace and skill and agility. And he stole my heart away. For the likes of him I broke the hearts of the local swains in droves; mere clouts they were by comparison. Some left home and now sleep on park benches wrapped up in old newspapers. Others litter up the hereabouts landscape, sad-faced, melancholy old men who, editors suppose, get that way looking for a rain or a range check. For the likes of him I broke the heart of the man on the flying trapeze, for after all that was only an act. But my hero, in the good old days, grabbed himself a handful of freight train and made it sit up and beg! And he did it for a living. I mean—Wottaman!

Turned farmer, what did this Wottaman do? He fell off a plow. Alack for my pride.

To milk a cow, one which has confidence in you and one in whom you have confidence, one who contributes her share of the operation ungrudgingly, is a real pleasure. With your head resting in her flank, both hands whipping up alternating lacy frothiness of foam into a fast-filling bucket, pungent odors of hay and stored feeds, and the rich, earthy goodness of housed beasts, you get the feeling that this is, after all, a pretty good old world—not much wrong with it, that is, the world that is really important, the one that holds you and the flowing milk and the cow, munching contentedly on her rations.

August 24, 1939

August weather see-saws. There simply isn't such a thing as a typical August day. August may bring a tangy norther with a broad hint of winter. Or it may bring a day like today. Again it may bring a day all still and hot, full of wilt and cicadas' ceaseless rasping, while the kitty, sprawled dog-fashion under the milk cooler, searches its soul for a refreshing breath of air.

An August rain can come with the deep-throated thunder of a winter's storm, slow black clouds moving out over the land like a Paul Bunyan's paint brush, and leave the warm mud of a general summer spell. Or it can pile up thunderheads into fluffy dogs and bears and long-horned Texas steers, or perhaps into castles and cities and armies on the march or into funny old men and women. It can whip these about with a wind that doesn't know its mind, roll them into a wicked little mess garnished with forked lightning, and wired with the bottomless pit for sound effects, while it floods the back forty, drenches my neighbor's pasture lands, takes out a water gap, then skips over a couple of farms to let down again in a downpour which tapers off into a tantalizing sprinkle on a parched countryside before it whirls itself back up into the sky to go on about its business of fashioning make-believe castles and armies and grotesque figures.

After a day of thunderclouds and breatheless stillness, while the heat drove us from bed to chair to bed, vainly hunting a little coolness, sections of drifting clouds got together in spots during the afternoon; and thunder began to promise relief from the heat. There finally came a wind which had switched form cloud to cloud, banging the shutters on the east, rattling the north window, then slamming the west door. There would be rain, but it was an even guess whether it would come here or miss us. Everybody went about his business pretending not to notice the willful waywardness of the rainclouds, not to be edgy about how the best prospects ducked behind the hill or spilt out before they got here.

Sometimes we hoped, sometimes we were grimly sure it was all a malicious, tantalizing August threat. Then there was the sound of big drops and far apart on the roof. They spattered in wide-apart patterns on the awnings. One could count them. Such a prelude doesn't always mean a real rain. The patterns grew thicker; then suddenly they stopped quite still. As suddenly, there was a rush of wind and water. Nobody could count the raindrops now. The awning was a dripping sheet. Spray from the pelting rain blocked out the landscape in a beautiful fog. Wind-rippled puddles were everywhere, with a thousand "dancers" splashing into wet nothingness. And that's sort of how the August rain came to the Yeagers.

> "The rain it raineth everywhere
> Upon the just and unjust fellows;
> It raineth most upon the just
> Because the unjust steal the justs' umbrellas!"

Last week's rain was spotted, hitting only here and there. Uncle Walter Mooring says that he wishes it would rain good and hard on the unjust. Then, he says he'd carry water and pour on the just, giving the country a general rain.

October 5, 1939

Like tumbleweeds, Mexican cottonpickers are drifting across the land, from the Valley to the Panhandle. In every conceivable form of motorized contraption, one meets them. Are they allergic to flat tires? With what fortitude they attack them! It almost seems that they welcome tire trouble as an excuse for breaking the monotony of the turning wheels. Mexicans have time to take to do the repairs. Every stratum of poverty peers out from the endless bundles with which they deck their cavalcades. Indeed, affluence at times flouts its head from cotton-pickers' caravans on the highway. Yet, high or low, hardly a load that hasn't in its cavernous depths somewhere a guitar—and a dog. And babies.

Simple people, these, of laughter and love and song. Under the shade of a tree, in a ramshackle hut, under the shed of a farmer's barn they will stop, and within a little while coals will glow, a black pot of coffee brews, a pot of something savory smelling bubbles and the feeling of home is there. Mexican women sweep endlessly—with the stub of a broom, or with pulled weeds tightly bound together. A Mexican camp has a special smell about it—it lingers for days after the campers leave. It is a mixture of smoke, of garlic.

At the beginning of the cotton season, it takes a wizard of persuasion or very white fields to hold the Mexican in the Heart O' Texas. With something of the spirit of Coronado, they are lured onward by the dream of the unknown. With them it is whiter fields and better pay for the work of their nimble fingers. They must go on to the Plains. When the first norther of winter sweeps in upon them, they turn their engines south again. They've had their little adventure. There's money in their pockets. Stop them if you can for your second picking.

October 12, 1939

The unhappy droop of the shoulders, the sag in the once springing step, the hollow, melancholy "howdy," the lackluster look in the eyes of my neighbor—these are caused by the prolonged totaling of columns of figures—as belated accounting was made of how much that last clip of wool and of mohair would have brought. If— But my countryman wasn't glum about that particular "if." There wasn't enough weight in the Yeager clips to have disturbed the budget's balance anyway.

His glum is caused by the sudden realization of a man who wakes up to the fact that he has worked hard over a period of years to rid himself of a fortune. For after having fought cockle burrs, for two decades—pulling them, hoeing them, cutting them, burning them, unfleecing them from the sheep's wool—he reads in the newspaper about two lady tourists who carefully unrolled from sheaths of cotton for a garage attendant to see, two cockle burrs. "Look," they cooed, "porcupine eggs, just beginning to hatch. And a man sold them to us for only a dollar apiece!"

This story doesn't amuse my countryman. I don't think it has dawned on him that the gypped ones believed that they were buying possible porcupines. He read the story through in a daze, stared a while, then reverently murmured, "A dollar apiece!" Since then he has remained in a deep, brown study during waking hours, and in his sleep he mumbles feverishly, "Cockle burrs—at a dollar apiece!"

++++++++++++++++++++++++

It takes all kinds of stores to furnish the things people want to buy. A new kind of store has just made its appearance in New York, according to the papers. It's called a "sleep shop." If you are in New York and can't sleep, you just call up the Sleep Shop, and they will send out a messenger and a sleep-aid kit. The kit, according to the advertisement, contains "a herbal tea, a soporific bath powder, a soothing body lotion, stoppers for the ears, a sleep-shade to shut out the light, a telephone directory for disconnected reading, and the latest seven-pound novel"—just in case you're the kind who can't be lulled by reading names in a row.

No doubt that sort of service fills a need in New York, but a Sleep Shop in the Heart O' Texas would be as useless as a raincoat factory in an October drought. Most folks around here have devised ways and means of their own for dropping off to sleep. There's neighbor Carl Engdahl—he finds that ten or twelve hours behind four mules hitched to a breaking plow is just about the right dope for a good night's sleep. If, however, he finds that he doesn't drop right off to dreams as soon as his head hits the pillow, next day he adds a couple of hours behind the plow.

Naomi Stewart says a day spent in shadowing a highly suspicious turkey hen through the corn patch, athwart the cotton field, across the branch, down the highway, back down the highway, re-cross the branch, re-through the cotton field to her nest in the stacklot behind the house is conducive to slumber. Professor I.O. Sturkie finds three-fourths of a night filled with half a dozen boys and a couple of sharp-nosed fox hounds about right for dropping off to sleep in the middle of tomorrow's class period.

Ray Andrew woos sweet slumber by a day of lacing bundled feed into haystack architecture under a cloudless fall sky. My neighbor Sudie Allen doesn't have any trouble getting to sleep. Getting a chance to get to bed is her problem. Multitudinous Allens with healthy appetites, operating at the usual rate in the production of snagged pants, torn shirts, unbuttoned buttons, rumpled petticoats, and the customary contributions to the weekly wash; stubbed toes, sore throats, tummy aches, and growing pains; company or plans for somebody else's company; birthdays with special fixings—these things take up most of Sudie's regular hours. In her leisure time she rocks the baby, tells about the three bears for the jillionth time, weeds the garden, gets out a quilt, papers a room, does a spot of scrubbing, plants a four o'clock bed, rakes the leaves or churns. She wouldn't need the services of the Sleep Shop. Only veterans like Mackie Ma, who mothered ten of her own and a few odds and ends of other families, can comfort Sudie by pointing out that chimney-corner days lie ahead for napping—unless the grandbabies are too noisy.

Followers of the remaining threshing machines recommend sixteen hours of tossing small grain in the bundle for making Morpheus a pushover—even on a thin bedroll. Donald Lee Neal, who has made plans for getting on the Rochelle Eleven eight years from now, finds lessons and recess and thirty-odd playfellows enough to do a fellow in at the supper table. By and large, it would seem that local conditions do not encourage the Sleep Shop business in this section.

October 19, 1939

I wish I were more effectively helpful about things outside the house and chicken yard. For instance, I like to try to help with the sheep. They are just about my timber, and sometimes I get in some pretty creditable work at sheep-handling time. Goats, I've found, are a little too elusive for me—and considerably too fast. But cattle—if there are two ways to do a thing about helping handle cattle, I always pick out the wrong one. My countryman is very patient. That is, he is patient in retrospect, and explains to me afterward that I just don't think like a cow. Now what do you suppose he means by that?

++++++++++++++++++++++

"Ten fine two-year-old field-grown roses for a dollar. Let them blossom for you," says my radio, and I grow cynical. Twenty-five fine field-grown two-year-old roses have I offered the opportunity to blossom for me within the year. One-fourth of the 100 times has my countryman with pick and shovel made mighty incursions into the terra firma so that I could plant a rose bush there, and he says it's appalling how firma this terra can get between rains. He says a lot of other things, too, but the point is that he excavates according to directions.

I hoe and hose my roses, not too nuff nor too none, but just the way the experts tell me to. All last winter, through the spring and summer and into the fall I nurtured them. And what did they do? They died. Not all nor in bunches, but just intermittently. First the Sunburst, then the Radiance, next the Marchiel Neil, and so forth and so forth till the last one of them shuffled off. No, the ground's not too rich, nor is it too poor, for I've added all opinions of family and friends and mere onlookers together,

40

divided by something and come out with just the right degree of richness. "Ten fine two-year-old field-grown—"Oh, yeah?

October 26, 1939

I was reading *Man, the Unknown* by the eminent scientist Dr. Alex Carrel, the one who has been working recently with Col. Lindbergh on the mechanical heart, when I received my first jolt. Dr. Carrel, in not too scientific terms, said that there was enough evidence compiled in scientific research to convince him that there are a few people in the world who can sit at one place and see into the future and into the past, that these people eliminate time and space, that they are generally not complex people, and that, when questioned, they cannot tell how they do this eliminating and see events and objects in times and spaces other than the present. Dr. Carrel said that it would be the proper attitude of science in the face of such evidence to accept the fact of clairvoyance and set about trying to understand it. That, from the Rockefeller Foundation research professor, left me slightly agape.

It took only the fumbling confession of my domestic handicap that he had lost his billfold with our ten-dollar bill in it to turn my slightly agape into a gates-ajar agape. Now, ten-dollar bills are not sneezed at in our house, nor is the loss of one taken without much searching, sweeping, moving of furniture, raking of barnyard, clearing out of chests and drawers, and more or less patient questioning of when, where, and why it was seen the last time. This last course brought us only dismay, for it established the fact that the last time the billfold was in operation was on a day in town. That settled it. It was lost, eternally, unless it should be picked up by an Honest Man, and the Honest Man was now so many days overdue that we really had no basis for hope, but we just sort of kept on searching hopelessly and cleaning out more drawers and raking in some other hay.

Finally, I got back to Dr. Carrel. Clairvoyance? Well, why not go to Rochelle and see my neighbor Mary Griffay, I argued with myself. Now I know that Mary Griffay had been "seeing into the future and into the past—events and objects in times and places other than the present" for folks hereabouts for a number of years.

So I went to see Mary. She was about as impressed with my request for her to "find" the billfold with our ten dollars in it as she would have been if I had asked her for her sponge cake recipe. "No," she said quite matter of factly and without any mystery of mumbo-jumbo (I would have been impressed by mumbo-jumbo), "the billfold, and it is a brown one (it was), isn't stolen. It wasn't lost at town. It was lost somewhere about your place. It was dropped from the pocket near an opening that is not a real gate, beside a sheep trail. It's only a few feet to the side of the opening. Hunt for it."

The idea sounded familiar, so I asked, "Have you read *Man, the Unknown*?"

"No," she answered, "but I've read the Bible." Then she told me about an instance of "fortune telling" recorded in the first book of *Samuel* in the twenty-eighth chapter that might prove right merry doings in case the Rockefeller Foundation set about understanding the fourth dimension.

Back home, there is small need for me to tell you about how we threshed out the territory around about every "opening that was not a real gate," and that included practically every opening on the place. Never had I realized the things that can happen to gates that make them "not real gates"—a broken hinge, unworkable panels, discouraging sags—but that's another story. Nearly all of them had sheep trails pretty close about, but no billfolds, no ten bucks. We gave up—as nearly as folks who squeeze ten dollars as tightly as we do could give up hunting for a lost ten dollars, and the culprit, the careless one, the dropper of billfolds containing ten dollars, began a not-too-refined propaganda to make me feel like a fool for having gone to see a "fortune teller" about this thing anyway—the while he mended gates or said he was just hanging around them to sort of fix them up a bit.

Well, this yarn can have little suspense, for you knew from the beginning that I wouldn't be telling it if the thing hadn't been found "by an opening that was not a real gate, beside a sheep trail." It happened when Wayne came home and tramped the pasture for ducks. "I found it," he said, innocent of Mary Griffay's instructions, "in a little sheep trail over on the back line fence by the saddle gate."

We'd forgot the saddle gate.

Did Mary Griffay "find" the billfold with our ten-dollar bill in it? I don't know. I only know it was brown. It wasn't stolen. It wasn't lost in town. It was found in a sheep trail beside an opening that wasn't a real gate, just as she stated.

Funny, too, how telling this to my friends has brought me other similar stories about Mary Griffay—how she told my neighbor, Valire Engdahl, that she would find her lost engagement ring in a "dark place" near her, and Valire found it in the lining of her coat; how she told the whereabouts of purloined diamonds that were subsequently recovered; how she has helped locate stock that has been lost, strayed, and stolen; how she has told of "events and objects removed from her in time and space."

November 30, 1939

Innately clean—are you? I don't believe you know whether you are or not until you've had to drag in the wash tub from its nail outside, heated gallons of water over an oil flame that doesn't have its mind on its business nor its heart in the job, corkscrewed your nudity into a number five washtub in a drafty room, gone through the motions, shivered out all wet and half soapy, wrapped yourself cautiously in towels so as not to stir the icy air too much, hustled into clean ones, dragged the tub out, emptied it into the teeth of a norther, then come back and mopped up the puddles. At this season it is sometimes undaintily long between times at our house, and we don't know the term "innately clean."

December 14, 1939

At the present writing, this family is owned by two cats. We got Noble last summer from the M.E. Nobels family, when they moved away to Rocksprings. A right nice cat she is, too, on occasion. Part of her ancestry is plutocratic, and part of it is alley. The alley shows in physical characteristics, the plutocratic in her hoity-toity appetite. She won't eat my biscuits, she's snooty about gravy, and she demands her milk fresh from the cow—or else. Sometimes she's neither alley nor plutocrat, but just cat. Then she yowls. At times she's over-insistent about where she curls up. When she's good, we call her "Noble," but when she messes up the midnight welkin with blood-curdling and slumber-shattering yowls, or insists upon giving our duds a brushed-wool effect by sleeping off her hairs onto our favorite cushions, we call her Ignoble—and a lot of other things.

Now Blackie is a cat of another color. He looks like a polecat without a stripe. Blackie belies all that has been said and written about a cat's agility. He's the last word in feline awkwardness. He ambles across the reading table, swiping his great plume of a tail against the Aladdin lamp. Then there is a mighty smell of burnt hair in the room, but Blackie never suspects that the smell has anything to do with him. He never knows quite how far to jump to make it into our laps and on through into us as he lumbers trustfully onto us. It is the look of camaraderie in his big yellow eyes that keeps us from scattering him into Kingdom Come, for Blackie has the friendliest heart in the world. He strops himself on people, on other willing cats, on newly killed chickens, on fence posts, on the chair legs, or on the milk cow. Once we flashlighted him in the back yard playing with a baby possum.

In a cat romp Noble and Blackie sound like a freight train wreck. They scoot across the linoleum in a more or less Sonia Hejne way. They tumble through chairs like Admiral Byrd's snow plow through canyons. The other night as they tumbled through the hall, Blackie misjudged the distance from the serving table to the top of the ice-box, clawed trustingly at a basket of eggs thereon. He didn't quite make it. Down came Blackie with the Christmas eggs atop him. He was a repentant, black, raw omelet. The floor was a mess. My countryman was a sardonic I-told-you-so. Such is being owned by two cats.

December 28, 1939

Houses that aren't particular about themselves aren't so keen to live in sometimes; yet they have their compensations. There's this winter wet spell, for instance, and my hen with a brood of late chickens. Round and round the house they went, cheeping and crying in the cold of a winter's rain, while the old hen scolded and cajoled and scolded some more—but never found a dry, protected spot to hover them in. In the confusion of the unaccustomed wetness, she forgot about the coop, the henhouse, and the barn—but half drowned her brood racing round and round the house in a stupid frenzy. When she finally squatted for a distracted minute, I pried a plank loose beside the doorway. Under the house they darted to warmth and dry protection. "Thanks," says I to me, "for a comfortable old friendly house you can use pretty nearly any way you want to." A lot of houses I know wouldn't appreciate being made so free with.

After the rain, I tacked the plank back on and spent half a day studying floor plans and interior treatments in *House Beautiful*.

January 18, 1940

When cold weather comes and shuts me into the kitchen and the heater room, existence palls. I do the same few things the same way every day to the point of boredom. This Saturday morning, when the weather half-heartedly promised to be nice, I swept the heater room floor, beginning at the opposite side of the room from which I customarily sweep and aimed at the back door, just for the novelty of it.

I felt virtuous and high-chested like a crusader last Thursday morning, when I went into town in ten-degree weather to visit the early morning session of the Brady PTA. That is, I felt heroic till I saw Mrs. Houston Braly at the meeting. She had come in nine miles from Dodge, facing the norther—and had sat on an apple crate in the middle of the morning milk cans to get there.

Twenty-one years ago, to a day, I center staged an event in the middle of an eighteen-inch snow and the World War flu epidemic. It was on that occasion that I made the acquaintance of a squirming bundle of humanity we came to call Jane Yeager. The young medico who performed the introduction we yanked away from a flu case across the street, after we had called every doctor in town and found them out on calls. The doctor we lugged in by the nape of his neck and the seat of his pants, I never saw before, nor I never saw him since.

February 8, 1940

It was as exciting as the night before Christmas on the first fine Monday after the snow at Mrs. Hobbs' Helpy-Selfy Wash. Everybody with a two weeks' accumulation of dirties was there, including me and mine. The fellowship among the customers as we waited turns was as good as a tea party, and a lot heartier, because while sitting in the midst of a weekly wash, nobody tries especially to impress anybody. Wash day is more American than pumpkin pie, because it got a season's start on the pie. Nothing is more blue-blooded, for, according to the record, the first thing those illustrious, impressive grand-dames of the Mayflower did when they set foot on the American continent was to drag out the family wash and come democratically clean. Today we get the job done at Mrs. Hobbs' with a great deal less trouble, the same satisfaction, and we notice no loss of democracy.

Mrs. Hobbs says the fast way to dry washed things in freezing weather is to hang them on the line outside and let them freeze. Then bring them in and they will dry quickly by the fire. The program is a pretty good test of whether any of the Mayflower strength of character and pioneering spirit holds over to this generation.

++++++++++++++++++++++

Last week my cat, Blackie, paid a visit in the interest of vital statistics of the black cat population to Neighbor Engdahl's. A straightforward chap is Blackie, with a bunch of bad manners for which he feels no apology is necessary. Nothing servile about him. He puts up a capable paw and walks in at your door as if he has a right to anybody's door. So he visited the Engdahls'.

Instancing the truth of the proposition that while love is woman's whole existence, it is of man's life a thing apart (even in the cat family), Blackie deserted his fair charmer to investigate the wonders of Papa Engdahl's herring keg. He landed a nice one before Mama Engdahl landed on him with a fly swatter. Mama Engdahl says that Blackie, with paw firmly anchoring his herring, looked up in surprise at her and seemed to say, "Why'd you swat me? I like fish!"

April 11, 1940
Next week you can take your choice of weeks to celebrate or observe, or it may be that you can make them all. I see by the schedule that next week is set aside as Be Kind to Animals Week, Garden Week, and Good Foot Health Week. I never have been one to make a lot of celebrations, but I decided to do next week up brown. As my contribution to Be Kind to Animals Week, I decided to let my countryman dig up my garden—that would take in Garden Week, too.

I explained it all to him, showing him where I kept the weeding hoe, the spading fork, and the grubbing hoe. He got the idea right away, for he reminded me that I had almost made him a brother of the badger by this time last year, digging holes for twenty-odd rosebushes—all of which yielded up the ghost before the end of the summer. However, he thinks the week's observation is a good idea and has decided to observe for himself Good Foot Health Week, by taking the weight off his. So there we have it—three weeks and a good hole-digging husband all set aside.

May 2, 1940
Ah, summertime! Ah, henhouse! Ah, bluebugs! Ah, red mites! Ah, delousing! Only the fastidious who have upended a hundred hens delousing them with powders, then scraped the roosts and squirted anti-bug stuff into the present and prospective homesites of bluebugs and lice can appreciate the luxuriating rites of a bath and shampoo. Of course, the ardent golfer gets a faint idea, what with perspiration and chiggers, but she falls just as far short of the henhouse cleaner-upper's joy as sweat is dirtier than perspiration and lice are ugh-er than chiggers.

Nobody likes to kill a chicken at our house, and each of us studies to see how he can shoulder the job off onto another without the effort becoming too apparent. The other day everybody's rabbit foot worked but mine, and I found myself, target in hand, on the stalk. Of course, somebody should have cooped the victim days before, but nobody hearabouts likes to do that either. After too little search, I found the marked biddy, an over-fat "boarder" with a lovable disposition, sunning herself in an ash heap. I hid myself behind a live oak and brought her down. What was my dismay when I found my favorite Cornish game flapping and flopping, yielding up the ghost twenty yards beyond my now quiescent "boarder"? Since then, somebody else has done the butchering. My aim's too erratic, goody.

Last winter's trapping turned out surprisingly well for me. Aiming for a polecat that had broken up a setter three times, I put out two traps and poisoned an egg. Next morning, I found an exceedingly dead polecat, the rascal having eaten the egg and then got himself caught into both traps.

Last night's tragedy, though, was the worst that has happened in my chicken business. We came home from a school program to find twenty-eight baby chicks, the mother hen, and seventeen fryers killed by a double striped polecat, which we had the satisfaction of gunning to a nice finish. With carcasses to dispose of, today has been what Pa Joad calls "a heller."

June 13, 1940

It's only lately that I have been able to pick up one of those one-handed, hook-billed, single-action telephones with any sense of security. Now I've pretty well learned which is the talk and which is the listen end. It's a fact that they do snuggle up sort of chummy like for telephone visiting, an art I've never perfected even under the old system. But the dial gets me down. I simply can't ever get the number I have a yen for. And it's disconcerting to have the "central" who isn't there popping in on the line to straighten me out. "You can't make a mistake," the dial defenders tell me. But they have not studied my technique.

Now the kind of telephone arrangement I like is the kind Ida Cates has over at Rochelle. The customer twists up the crank and tells Ida in a friendly sort of way, "I want to talk with Mrs. So-and-So." Then you wait a minute while you hear Ida grinding out the number. If no one answers, pretty soon Ida's back on the line with something like this: "I don't think she's at home, Ethel. Old Lady Such-and-Such has been under the weather, and I think she went over there to take her some soup. She came by here about an hour ago going that way and hasn't come back yet. Wait a minute and I'll call her sister to find out." That's what I call service. Besides, it's a lot of other things I like.

June 27, 1940

My countryman now has a combine. To be more nearly exact, a combine now has my countryman. After a couple of weeks of bat-boying for it—chopping out weed-grown paths into fields; replacing bent guards, sheared pins, broken teeth, and similar fragile dingbats; falling out of bed long before the rooster's crow and getting back into it just before tomorrow has booted today downstairs; scratching chaff and chigger itchiness well nigh twenty-four hours out of twenty-four—this neighborhood's newest combine proprietor welcomed a rain, welcomed it all through a shower-punctuated night and well into the wet sunshine of the early morning. Awakened by the lowing of the unmilked milch cow that had grown impatient at having the sun lap up the dew from her pasture salad, I roused Himself with shoulder shakings. "Look," I chided, "see how the sun has already used the day." But Himself only flickered a heavy-with-sleep eye, snuggled more comfy between the sheets, soused his head deeper into the pillow, squirmed himself into a ball of bat boy weariness and mumbled, "I don't care. This is My Day."

July 25, 1940

Often and often I think nice things happen to us so frequently and with such regularity that, becoming used to them, we dull the edge of our appreciation. Once I read in a currently popular novel a thing that I resented; but recent events have set me thinking, and likely the book was right and I was wrong again. The item concerned the chore of milking, and the author, having beset her housewife heroine with illness, went on to say that the housewife's husband began to milk "for her."

I resented the "for her," taking the chore as a sort of a community responsibility in the family, and I told myself that the aforementioned husband was milking as much for himself as "for her," so should not be allotted any special credit for his "thoughtfulness." I held to that belief for several years—in fact until my countryman began bat boying for his combine. Throughout the grain season, this place has seen nor hide nor hair of him except by lamplight, during which time, I've been milking "for him."

Now, actually, I don't mind the job of milking. Once I get the hang of it, I find comfort and satisfaction in sitting down at the business end of a really good cow—one that knows what she's about when she sets out to collect an udder full of milk—and watching the frothy milk rise squirt by squirt, while the calf halves my chore on his mother's off side. I understand the poet who chants of the "sweet mellifluous milking of the cow." The warm, rich animal smell mixed with the fragrance that comes from the feed the cow crunches in patient rhythm as she lazily switches me and the flies, gives me a sense of well-being that lingers, even when I've loosed the cow to the pasture and bedded the now round-bellied calf for the day.

But milking has its drawbacks. It happens just when everything else wants to happen—the dishes want to be done, the beds want to be made, the floors want to be swept, and the dinner vegetables are crying to be readied. Again at night, milking comes when the garden wants to be weeded, the flowers are wilted for water, and supper is to be got. Besides, the chore comes around twice a day, 365 days a year, and an extra couple of times on Leap Year.

Now, milking has been going on on this farm for thirteen years to my personal knowledge. That means 4,745 days, not counting Leap Years; and every day has had both morning and evening sessions, totalling 9,490 milking times. Often there have been two cows; sometimes there have been three, and on occasions there have been midday sessions. So there's no telling how many times my countryman has squatted beside our milk supply. For every one of the times he did it "for her," I tender a belated "Thank you." Here they come, A.V.: *Many* thanks!

++++++++++++++++++++++

Living here in the country, regulating my days to suit my desires without a telephone, with few social obligations, I have often congratulated myself that I have, if anybody has, the highly touted and much coveted, often eulogized thing called by the name of "freedom." But the other day, when my clock refused to tick and I had to take it to the jeweler's, I got a jolt. I came to a sudden realization that I am the clock's slave. I look where it sat to see whether I am late or early with the chores. I look where it sat to see whether the butter came as quickly as it did last time. I look where it sat to see how much longer I must wait for the mail carrier. I look where it sat . . . . Well, I've looked so many times where it sat against the radio that I've worn a clock-face dial into the wood.

August 1, 1940

Now that August is with us, ants are too. And I do mean *with* us. The kitchen, hot with odors of mid-summer canning and cooking, is a day and night invitation to all tribes of sweet and fat loving ants—slow walking, persistent black ants; fast walking, highly flavored yellow ants; and big, lumbering winged red ones that sneak, roach-like, into the ice box in the quiet of the night and eat out the insulation if they don't first drown in the cream. For years I've warred on all the varieties, dusting powders into their runways, sinking half-filled bottles of water beside their holes with the fond conceit that they would get disgusted with themselves and go jump in and drown, tying kerosened garters around my table legs, and releasing cyanide eggs into their living quarters.

Never until recently have I more than temporarily discouraged the ants that have developed a fondness for my sugar barrel and my cake box. But this summer I am rid of ants. I want to shout it from the housetops, to tell it in Gath, and to publish it in this column. It is all very simple and very effective. I brought home from the Home Lumber Company a box of a commercial product labeled TAT and set it in the pathway of the ant tribe foraging in my kitchen. Into the box walked the would-be despoilers of my sugar supply, pinched off a shoulder load of

TAT, and hot-footed home with it. And, miracle of miracles, that's the last I ever saw of that ant horde.

The next day I took up the TAT box and waited for another attack. It came in a few days, this time a different species. Back went the TAT, and the whole comedy of errors was re-enacted. Now we take our ice tea in its virgin flavor. Go, thou, and do likewise, and the blessings of the summer be upon you.

My brother Arthur, whose practically fade-proof disposition can be turned a tattle-tale gray at his own birthday picnic upon the too-late discovery of ants in his pancakes, stayed home all day just to see his first box of TAT at work.

October 31, 1940

I welcome the first cool days of fall into my kitchen—not cold enough to have a fire just for having a fire, but exactly right for a half-cured oak wood job in the kitchen stove, just enough so that the stove seems to be busy about something. Maybe it's an egg custard, top freckled with nutmeg, or a pan of apples wrinkling up their hides and breathing of cinnamon. Sometimes it's oranges gently stewing against tomorrow's marmalade, or a fat hen baking. The ideal way to do it is to hatch up some small task for the stove, important enough to demand a fire, but so small it won't hold you in the kitchen. Then it's fun running back to the kitchen fire from a chilly job of bed making or a frosty outside chore.

January 9, 1941

All over the Heart O' Texas grain fields are a lush, velvety patchwork on God's footstool. Dun brown Jerseys browse the green grass and make it into white milk and yellow butter. Roly-poly sheep ankle over it, cropping blankets and woollen dresses, upholstery, and thick socks onto their backs, while bouncy lambs club up in the cool of the day and play games of back-out over the terraces and about the remnants of last year's haystack.

The perfect growing season conditioned in the ground should leave no room for a Heart O' Texan to quarrel with the weatherman. Mine is not exactly a quarrel. I love wet weather. It is just that during these days of alternate sunshine and shower our livestock have worn callouses on the gate posts, being driven into fields on dry days and out of fields on wet days, back into fields next day, and then it rains again.

Besides, look at what happened to Small Jersey, and think what might have happened. At Christmas time we were milking only half a cow. That is, production being what it wasn't, there was no inducement to go milking more than once in twenty-four hours. So when my brother said on Christmas Day, "If you had plenty of milk, I'd give you a baby Hereford calf we've named Anxious," my countryman and I went into a huddle and decided to share our half-cow with Anxious. "Anyway," I promised brightly, "Small Jersey may be fresh by the time we get home."

So Anxious was loaded into the back of the car on Christmas Day and romped all over the rear seat till we got home. And Christmas night how it rained—cold, wintry wetness, with a high, howling norther!

The next morning the grainfield emptied itself, animals seeking the shelter of buildings and brush. True to my prediction, we had a fresh cow. Small Jersey came in, hungry and bawling. But no calf was with her. All day she hung around the lot, hugging the shelter. We mourned that a calf should choose such weather to get itself born in. But Small Jersey wasn't nearly so concerned about the calf she had lost as we were. She seemed to forget the whole matter and busied herself keeping comfortable.

Just in case Small Jersey had made a mistake about the calf's being dead, she was rousted out from the shelter and driven into the teeth of the norther back to the wet field to show us where the calf was. But Small Jersey wasn't interested in the past. She only bucked into the wind and rain because she was forced to, and soon returned to hunker in the stall and munch dry fodder.

We closed the field gate till the next dry spell and set about introducing Small Jersey to Anxious. The mother cow wasn't cooperative, but Anxious didn't mind any lack of hospitality. In fact, Anxious was tail-pumping, nose-nudging calfdom come into his own at long last. With Small Jersey protesting at both ends, that program went on all through a cold, wet Thursday and

Friday and Saturday; and Anxious' enthusiasm grew in geometric progression at each feeding.

Then on Sunday morning the sun came out, it was a beautiful drying out day, and Small Jersey was missing. My countryman found her in the back of the field, though the gate was still closed and the fence is new and tight. With her was a moon-eyed, spindly-legged little Jersey calf.

March 13, 1941

In blurry mists and nipping cold and winds that howl like a banshee, March haunts the early springtime with the ghost of old winter. A new lamb lies by my fire on a gunnysack. Half an hour ago he had hunkered down in the cold, wet weeds and lost all interest in staying alive in weather like this. His coat now steamed and dry, he has wound himself into a ball and sleeps deeply, a gray, kinky little fluff of a lamb.

Lambing time: ewes with new lambs separate from the flock a little way. When they are in the open of a green field, they look like a maternity ward as they segregate themselves, each ewe with a lamb or two beside her. In the pastures, the old ewes seem to select cozy, protected nooks for lambing. Often ours choose the lee side of an algerita in bloom; then there are blossoms and sweet fragrance for the welcoming of the little one to the land of forty-cent wool (maybe).

When you come suddenly upon a newly dropped woolly lamb and its mother, the ewe faces you, ears atwitch, and stamps the ground with a sharp forefoot to frighten you. She will run a little away if you come too close, but generally she will turn and "baa" back at her lamb. I love the lambs when they are big enough to follow well. They run, all leggy and with too-big feet, beside their mothers, spanking themselves with their funny, long tails. They love to touch their mothers as they run, and must be an awful trial as they get awkwardly under-foot and shove about. My countryman says they use their tails for pumps when they suck.

I think the most poignant thing about lambing is the hungry little one that comes out baaing a steady stream of baas from a clump of bushes, ready to follow you or a car or a horse or another ewe or anything at all, its eyes begging. Then you know a little way back in the brush you are going to finds its mother dead.

I like to ride in the pasture at lambing time. I'm supposed to look for ewes that have lain down to deliver and have sunk into their wool so deep they can't get up again. They fan the air with their four feet in a helpless sort of way, head stretched out, and you can just tell when you find one so that she has made up her mind to die, and she will, too, unless you pick her up and stand her on her paralyzed feet till the blood comes back. Then she prisses off good as new, almost.

I try to look for them, but a red squirrel scampers up a tree; a whole draw full of robin redbreasts chattering and chirping fall from limbs in long, graceful swoops to skim their way under the trees, barely above the ground, in an ecstasy of wingspreads; a flicker flashes his tail light in sudden swift flight; a bunny cottontail hunches up beside a prickly pear with pink eartips aquiver; and once on a sunny day there was a tank full of mallards and teals. All these distractions and a hundred more besides make a poor sheep hunter out of me.

Our robins never come on the house side of the highway. Doves and red birds we have, yes, and too, too many English sparrows and field larks, mockers aplenty, and butcher birds, flickers and cunning orchard orioles, a few bluebirds, scissor-tails, and wrens in pairs—but never a robin. Yet half a mile away the woods are full of them all winter. They are a bird I never met except in books until I found them here. I suppose they have been here all the while, only I didn't see them.

July 17, 1941

Even in July and August the dry, hot earth cools off at the end of the day; and by sunset, Four-o'clocks, a bit off schedule, perk up their wilted leaves, open up their blossoms, and by twilight time they breathe a cool, clean, pungent sweetness into the air. I like Four-o'clocks. Somehow that flower is mixed up for me with revival meetings, starched dresses, new shoes, and thoughts of God, my soul, and eternity.

When I was very young and the world was simple, summers were made for watermelons, fishing trips, visits with kinfolks; and summers were climaxed by revival meetings. We went to all the revival meetings—every night. There was the Baptist meeting, which was "our" meeting because Papa and Mama "belonged." But we went as faithfully to the Methodist, the Christian (two varieties of them), as well as to a fervent session by a group we called Holy Rollers when there wasn't any of the sect in earshot. Willy-nilly, they all preached about God and love, the Devil and sin, heaven and hell, and a breathlessly unending eternity. So we went to all of them. It took nearly all summer and a lot of washing and ironing. But we went.

I used to love getting into a frock that smelled of Faultless Starch, stepping into a pair of new patent leather slippers so shiny you could see yourself in them if you got down really close, and with a sprig of Four-o'clocks for smelling on the way, walking alone to the tabernacle. Ah, sweet and terrifying were the thoughts I breathed in with whiffs of comforting Four-o'clocks—time without beginning—time without ending—an all-wise God who knows my most secret thought—a soul housed up in me that would one day be freed to live in that timeless forever—somewhere . . . And the only tangible thing in all my world, a sprig of soothing Four-o'clocks.

September 18, 1941

My countryman appreciates a benevolent government's efforts to make him secure by effecting a plan whereby he is able to insure the wheat crop. Cropping being what it is on this farm, he wishes the crop insurance plan included oats, barley, and row crops. Last harvest season, when wheat and oats were ripe for cutting, but couldn't be got to because of the wet in the fields, he aged considerably. Then one day it seemed that tomorrow would be dry enough to hold up the machinery. There were frantic doings around all day against tomorrow's early start. The last chore was finished, the last extra job was done, and we went to bed with that sense of anticipation dear to the heart of those who have made adequate preparations for a worthwhile undertaking.

About one o'clock in the morning a cloud came up out of nowhere. The rain poured like water out of a bucket. Even through the dark of the night we seemed to see the grain crop flattening to the high, shrieking wind. There wasn't any fortitude for that, so my countryman prayed. "Lord," he implored, "if you take my oats, take my wheat also. It's insured."

October 2, 1941

We who live in the country have mice, particularly at this season, and rats. John Brown plowed a wheat patch about forty-seven axe handles and a couple of wood-rat tails from my house, and the huge black ones darted into the weeds and unplowed stubble as he hemmed them in until, as he made the last rounds, a hundred of them, driven to the center of the field, scampered out over the plowed ground. Many were caught by the plow. Everett Salter said that where he plowed, so many were killed by the plow that next day buzzards gleaned in the field.

We drove by the John Brown plowing after dark, and the car lights caught a great granddaddy of a fellow perched on the top plank of the field gate, doubtless viewing the land for a likely nesting place.

A great many of them decamped to our cow barn and granary. Some have come into the house to abide with us. In two forays on my canary cages, they got the better part of my singer's leg, and now he seems about to finish the job by eternally picking at the stub. In the night we can hear them loping about on the housetop and in the loft, whipping and lashing their tails in boistrous rat glee.

Mice, too. We run our mouse-trap line every morning with the gusto of North Woods trappers. Our mice are more susceptible to trap gadgets than our rats. We usually have a nice catch in the mornings. Old Cat comes up from the barn about ten o'clock to clean up the night's take where we have laid them at the back door. She crunches them daintily, licks her chops thoughtfully, washes her face, and says, "Nice hunting!" The old sea cow!

When we country people get together, we talk unabashed about our vermin. We have a sprinkling of them all the year to poison, to trap, to cuss. But they come each year with the harvesting of the grain and the promise of winter, in Pied Piper hordes. "Great rats, small rats, lean rats, brawny rats, fathers, mothers, uncles, cousins"—gobs of them.

Mildred Williamson says that if she wakes up quietly in the middle of the night, it sounds like mouse recess.

Town people seem not to be harrassed with the "wee, sleekit, cowrin, tim'rous" beasties. Mildred Gainer said, "Once we had a mouse . . . ." I raised a skeptical eyebrow. "One mouse?" I insisted. "We don't have many," she explained. "We have eight cats."

October 16, 1941

Some folks sniff fastidious noses at the smell of sheep. My countryman says that on a low wool market they smell like the eternal abode of the unregenerate; but when it's going at forty cents a pound and better, wet wool on his sheep's backs makes glamor sniffing. On the other hand, we all agree that goats smell like profuse profanity on any market whatsoever, and seem to enjoy it.

Personally, I rather like sheep smells—in sheep pens. I must confess they're not alluring around the dinner table, and they would be quite out of place at tea parties, I should think.

But sheep driven to pen across the pastures stir up a nose-titillating symphony of smells on a cool, damp October afternoon. I love to follow along on foot after the straggling ones and lap up the smells their shiny hooves unearth. This year the bitter, penetrating odor of broom weeds follows in their wake. The flock brushes against a clump of prickly ash, and a clean, tingly pungency sweeps the air. Here they've trampled mesquite sprouts and left a green, lush freshness, tasting in the nose a little of bitterness. Bruised tansy assails me, clean and fragrant as a linen closet. The odor of sweet alyssum rises like incense from the altar. A hundred ferny weeds I've lived with all of my days and will likely die without knowing their given names or their family names, come up in fragrances from the earth with the bricky, dry, dusty smell that is forever with the white chalk shale of my hillsides, rain or shine. Late blooming mimosa is dainty under sheep's hooves, giving off a perfume like young girls going to the meeting house of a Sunday evening. Indeed, sheep are master chemists for nose mixings of sweet country smells.

++++++++++++++++++++++

It's true what they say about the country going in for chicken raising. The trouble with us is that the country thought about it before we did, so our chickens were a week late and a hundred short, in that order, and we can whistle to the wind for any more, says our chicken agent, until a few hundred others have had orders filled. However, the brooder house is now full of peeps and squawks and promises of pulley bones and baskets of eggs— perhaps, maybe, sometime, if we have luck, mayhap.

A couple hundred fluffy balls fresh from the eggshell, spread out on nice, clean brooder territory is an innocent sight and optimistic; but they can, and do, infest my natural laziness with a virus of activity that scurries me through morning chores slicker than a button, and keeps on scurrying me on and on and far into the night. Last week I didn't think to go to my Study Club till this week.

December 11, 1941

Last week I thought my house was little and mean and cramped. I thumbed old magazines for floor plans and found how with a change here and a change there and a room to the east with a sunporch and a bedroom . . . . But today I live in a big house. My feet clank loud on the bare floors. It's miles to the kitchen. There are echoes in the house.

This is the same house I had last week, really. It's only that everybody has gone except me. Last week Jane and Wayne took Nita Leah and Bruce to visit the Coggin grandparents in Brownwood. Yeager and I rattled around here like dried peas in a pod when they'd gone. Then yesterday my countryman went off on a binge with a passel of Masonic brothers to a convention somewhere, they said; so today I've been trying to find myself in my wasty surroundings.

This day I've heard no voice but my own, except when Zora came for a bucket of water and some greens.

Once one who loves us and comes happily to visit under our roof called ours the accordeon-pleated house. She said that it seems to fit whatever number of people come into it, that it spreads nicely to take in another and another, and that it folds gently back again when they are gone. But today I am lost in it. Maybe it hasn't shrunk yet to fit just one. Tomorrow, perhaps, it will be comfortable.

This warm Sunday the air is full of spider spinnings. The east-west fence row is a solid yard-wide wall of them, stretched southward in the gentle north breeze. Far up in the sky the sunlight glints off their silky, silvery strands. They catch on my coat and in my hair. I feel a strand across my face as I work. Yet all day long I never saw a spider.

I like staying here alone for a little while. I've had a nice visit with myself. I milked, tended the chickens, fed the hog, then turned on the windmill and watered the garden all I wanted. I wrote a little, mulled through notes on my desk, slept an hour, worked the cross-word puzzle, made some good resolutions about house-cleaning—sometime soon. Aside from breakfast coffee, I've not fired up the cook stove for five meals! Whoops! Dinner was cheese and a cold cut, with crackers, shallots, and winter radishes, buttermilk and an apple—and I ate it all by the typewriter.

I like lone nights here, too. I'm not especially brave. There are legions of things I'm afraid of. But I'd be ashamed of being afraid of the night after the bringing up Mackie Ma gave me. Last night there was an enthusiastic pounding and bumping out at the back. When I turned on the windmill light to see who was giving the show, three astonished cottontail rabbits sat hunched up in the driveway beside my turnip patch. The perky little devils!

I read the paper, too. The first two pages carried stories of three women who had shot their men. I shall save this one for my Mason when he gets back. Makes me nearly afraid of myself.

But why is it when He goes away, the milk cows lie out, Old Cat comes up sick, and the water trough valve sticks?

My countryman came home with a strange look in his eye. When I unpacked his overnight, I found among his things the pants and watch of a brother Mason. When I ask for explanations, he says, "I think Old Jersey's going dry, the way you milk her!"

January 1, 1942

January is a drab old crone in somber rags, but her petticoats are gay. After the glow of fall has faded, no month seems so dull. On the other hand, no month appreciates so much the color relief of green grain fields, spotting an otherwise brown and seared landscape. Tree limbs mark etchings, bleak and bare, against the cold January skies. Everyone should grow a winter garden, if for no other reason than to look at the greenness of it in January. My turnips, tendergreens, and Swiss chard are lush greenness, full of vitamins and pot promises. On any sunny day now I can cook up an incense in my kitchen that will make the most downhearted remember that God's in His heaven and the greens are in the pot. Nothing gives me the sense of security that comes from the smell of cornbread browning and greens simmering in a country kitchen. I've enjoyed, too, the leek, mildest of winter onions, and sweet smelling on the coldest days.

May 21, 1942

Wherever I walk these days, red ants are scurrying. When it's the time of the year that the sun takes over and the ground turns its face up for summer's baking, red ants begin to scurry. Scurrying is a thing red ants do with, to my way of thinking, greater gusto than any other creature. Of course, mice scurry when you open the barn door suddenly where they are enjoying a mouse social, and sow bugs scurry away from an overturned log (that is, those scurry that don't roll up into a ball and play possum); chickens scurry when a hawk dips into a flock; youngsters scurry when school is out; and grownups in crowds scurry at a sudden change of weather of whatever sort. But nobody nor nothing scurries with the apparent urge that a red ant scurries on a hot, dry day.

Last spring I foolishly told myself that I had put an end to red ants scurrying around this house. There was a man who came around. He said he could kill red ants so dead that they never came back again. He was right convincing, and the saga of the ant colonies he had done to death put him into the class with the Pied Piper of Hamelin as a pest eradicator.

It was alarming the number of ant beds we found encamped about us—all of which were to be cleaned of ants and eggs, which at seventeen cents a bed ran into quite an item. My ant eradicator seemed to be the sort of a person who makes sure of things. He made sure to get paid in full at the time, and he said it was his practice to return in twenty days for a recheck of the ant beds. Being plagued with ants the way I've been for years and years, it all seemed too good to be true. It was. Although my Pied Piper didn't forget to cash his check, he did forget to come back in twenty days. The ants and the ant eggs forgot to die, and now they scurry.

++++++++++++++++++++++

My country neighbors and I wonder just how much privacy we have left in our more or less splendid isolation. A historian, in writing of the spaciousness of the Southwest in pioneer days, says that it was possible in those times for the housewife to see the trail dust of her visitors rising against the horizon in plenty of time to cook dinner for them before they arrived. Times, to coin a phrase, have changed. We live closer to each other. Besides, there are the airplanes. Just how much does a Curtis Field unit, swooping down and zooming up again, take in of the goings on in our country place?

For instance, are topless outdoor shower baths really adequate? Or is it advisable for one to indulge herself in a quick garden-hose shower in the privacy (?) of her own back yard? Etc.? The other day I stepped into the yard in all too brief a getup to hang my sox in the sun to dry. A raucous whistle tied me into knots, then sent me into the house at a clip that should be an inspiration to Whirlaway. Once inside, I turned to see who had given me so ribald a salute. From overhead it came again, clear, jeering, tantalizing, scorching insult to the indiscreet caught unaware in her underwear, and a lone curloo bird floated lazily on the spring breeze.

August 6, 1942

We usually run two conversations at the same time when the Arthur Neals come to see us. "At the Young People's Retreat," I told Kitty when they came last time, "I am supposed to talk on 'Youth Facing the Future.'"

"If you'll get somebody to talk who knows what he's talking about," remarked my brother into our she-conversation, having driven a nail through his and Yeager's he-conversation, "and make it 'Adults Facing the Future,' I'd like to sit in on it." So would I, brother, so would I!

The Arthur Neals, along with a lot of other folks, are sleeping these rainless nights with one eye open, dreading the next grass fires. Twice in July they had to fight them. On one occasion there had been hurried telephone calls and excited reports of fighters going out to the Williamsons, the Richards, and the Gainers, and promises of help for the fire that was coming onto the Neals.

Then the Neals caught up wet sacks and rushed out to meet the fire line that was quickly on their own range. Time drags at a fire while you work and hope for help. A ruthless thing is a pasture fire. It closes in on you in spite of your efforts, jumping gullies here, creeping into that place you thought had been put out, leaping up beyond you, and playing a merry caprice with all your earnest efforts.

It is a desolate time while you look across miles of burning grasslands at a few impotent hands against the might of fire. It is a dreary time when you feel the need of neighbors' help—and the fire department. So the Neals fought the fire and prayed for help—and soon. Minutes dragged while the fire outraced their efforts. Finally Kitty spoke between sack flappings against the fireline. "Why," she asked, "do you suppose nobody comes to help us?" Between other sack flappings, Arthur replied, "I wouldn't know, unless it's because I've been a school trustee too long!"

But help came, loads of people—willing hands to an immediate job. Some had fought grass fires before. To others the thing was new, but the art and science of grass-fire fighting is simple, and the newcomers were soon sacking the fireline along with the others. Everybody worked. They worked a long, long time. In a lull a novice fighter looked up to see some men setting fire to a strip for burning out a fire guard. The tired fighter dragged a weary and sooty hand across his flame scorched face and swore, "Well, I'll be damned! Here I've been putting out fire all night. Now will you look at them nitwits starting another one!"

August 20, 1943

In the genealogical tables of fine cattle, my sense of propriety is mildly shocked by the habit cattle growers have got into of naming their dams Miss This and Miss That, like Miss Mischief, Miss Blanco III, Miss T-Bone Steak, and the like. At our house we call our milk cows all Mrs. There is Mrs. Lot, who got her name because when we go to drive the cattle "hame," to drive the cattle "hame," to drive the cattle "hame" across the scrubby hills, Mrs. Lot comes away from grazing reluctantly; and if we give her the least bit of time, she stops, looks back and lows, yearning after the fleshpots of her Sodom.

Then there is Mrs. Star, named without much imagination on our part, because she has such a pretty white star on her forehead. We felt that it would have been a waste of the creative urge to go thinking up any other name for her. Mrs. Star is a very matter-of-fact cow anyway. She comes at milking time (generally she does), mosies into her stall, is satisfied with a medium amount of calf-licking, eighteen per cent protein, and average attention. We thought her entirely without cut-up temperament until she dropped her calf last month. It was the usual trembly-legged, bug-eyed, satin-skinned number. That is, it was the usual until it flopped its ears forward. Then something happened. It took on a solemn, sacred look, uncalf-like as an altar piece. Somewhere in its family history, surely there ran the blood of ancient Brahmas. Mrs. Star took one startled look at her strange baby, bawled out a primitive, "My mistake," histed her tail over her back, and hied herself to the far side of the pasture, where she stayed until we had to drive her in. We kept them penned in the cowlot, and the calf had learned which side his bread was buttered on before Mrs. Star began to rationalize and reconcile herself to her position.

September 13, 1943

"When you go to select it," I wanted to know of Himself, "do you think you can recognize my pattern?" It's important, this matching of patterns. What careful housewife wants a piece of this and a piece of that in her collection? And many patterns are so much alike, unless one has an eye for design. I hesitate to trust a man's memory of form. Yet men have been the world's greatest silversmiths, artists, and sculptors—great masters of design. Yet I never feel sure my countryman has matched my pattern till he comes home and I go out to help him unload the cow feed. Sure enough, there it is, a cluster of small rose tulips with dainty green stems and wee tulip buds surrounded by little blue dots. Now we can finish Nita's dress, and the panties can be the same pattern.

++++++++++++++++++++

It's awfully hard in summertime for me to make butter firm enough to mould. If I leave the cream in the cooler overnight, the butter is sure to be soft and puffy. If I leave the churning in the refrigerator, it gets so cold I won't be patient enough to churn it without warming it, and there I am again, more than likely, with puffy, soft butter.

I am speaking about adding hot water to a cold churn. I suspect that I don't want to do it. From the first turn of the paddle, I know, almost, that I am going to do it, but I won't for ever so long. Not till I've whipped myself into a lather and got all prickly along the hairline. I won't even then, unless everybody is out of the kitchen. However, once I find myself alone with a cold churn, nine hunnert and ninety-nine licks done on it, and a kettle of hot water, the deed is done. Now, the soft, spongy butter is here, and I am disgusted and full of resolve never to do it again. But I will.

++++++++++++++++++++

This morning my house is waiting. Two small beds are ready for the night. Cottage cheese is dripping on the line, the cookie jar is full, and a sugar cookie-boy and a sugar cookie-girl, baked nice and brown, are lying on napkins on the table. There weren't raisins for eyes and buttons, so they have pieces of prune eyes, and a one-prune-piece button in the middle, in a sort of Dagwood effect. Nita Leah and Brucie are coming grandparenting this evening and stay two nights before their mama and papa come. Now that is what I call a social item.

October 15, 1943

One reason I hate to say goodbye to summer is on account of breadmaking. I respond to home-made lightbread, all of me. I bake it best in summer, when the yeast comes up from sun heat. That gives it the smell. Of course, it can be coddled into rising in cold weather if one is patient to keep it by the fire, neither too not nor too cold, but just exactly right, but I like my yeast grown in sun warmth.

It makes a lot of difference to me what sort of yeast I use in bread. I suppose I can't actually tell the difference in taste between bread made with commercial yeast and bread made with homemade yeast, but I enjoy thinking that I can. I make my own meal-cake yeast by working meal into the sponge that grew overnight. I do not know the recipe for making the original yeast. I wish I did. I've been told it involves some use of hops. Anyway, when, by careless management, I lose my start of cakes, I'm just out of yeast till I find someone else who will give me one. With so many housewives using commercial yeast, which is faster and surer, but without that extra something that makes all the difference in the world, it gets harder and harder to get a new start.

The first meal-cakes I ever saw were Grandmother Moseley's. She was the only person I ever knew when I was a child who made lightbread. I grew up on cornbread and biscuits, with pancakes sometimes for supper or for breakfast. When we went to visit the Moseleys or when there was preaching and dinner-on-the-ground, I got to eat Grandmother Moseley's bread. It was like manna, it didn't need any helping out, it was all sufficient. Mackie Ma tried making bread from Moseley yeast cakes, but it never came off right for her. So when I was the age for dreaming about growing up to become a Florence Nightingale, a George Eliot, a Carrie Chapman Catt, and a bareback rider in a circus, I set aside days when I simply longed to have a home of my own, an open fire, a checked apron with cross-stitching on it, and a jar full of high smelling yeast cakes that would make into bread like Grandma Moseley's.

I never got to try meal-yeast bread till I was teaching school at Lohn. Georgia Ryan and Marion Louise Lohn brought sandwiches to school, sandwiches upholstered with real, real lightbread. Their mamas sent me yeast cakes, and I eventually learned to make something that came somewhere within the neighborhood of Grandmother Moseley's bread. Not perfect, as hers was, but meal-yeast bread that didn't have to apologize.

Mixed up with a lot of other adversity, there were several years after leaving Lohn when I was without meal-yeast cakes. I'd lost the start, and I couldn't get a cake again. Not from the Ryans or the Lohns, because some unbelievable how these excellent cooks had become proselyted to commercial yeast. Then last winter while I was occupying a position that should have been held by a teacher over at Rochelle, I smelled that heaven-sent aroma that exudes only from meal-yeast bread. It was in the Kruckemeyer lunches. From that time on, my jar has been full of Kruckeyemer-started meal-yeast cakes. Since then, I've given away dozens. It is a downright pleasure, giving away meal-yeast cakes.

Unless company comes, we have simple things to eat at our house. Mackie Ma and I imbibe deeply of mush and milk. We also make a meal of cornbread and sweet milk crumble-in. All of us like our butter soft enough to spread on bread. We're sort of agin the consumption of icebox butter unless the bread is hot. I think the best dish in the world is freshly ground good steak broiled in a heavy pan on top of the stove with all the seasonings left out, even salt, until it is served with toast on a hot platter. Then eat it with salted lettuce and coffee. My coutryman prefers ham—baked, boiled, braised, fried, or whatever—but ham. I think he prefers it to me. Mackie Ma is only mildly enthusiastic about eating, but she speaks glowingly of baked sweet potatoes, cooked in ashes.

I read recipes of mixed food and drool. When I break down and cook them, they taste like the picture looks, smell like incense to the god of cookery, and give us all indigestion. We pay through the soda can for my off-brand cooking enthusiasms. My countryman has learned just this fall that gravies are lethal to him, and how that man can stow away the gravy!

Due to the fact that our digestions welcome only one or two things at a time, I have "goes-with" cooking troubles. What, for instance, goes with a pot of beans? Beyond pickles or relish and cornbread, beans seem to me to be, well, beans, and that's enough. There's turnip greens, too. What can one do about turnip greens except cornbread and buttermilk and a slice of crisp bacon? This is the way we dish it up at our house, except when there's company. And did you ever notice how company just eats cornbread, buttermilk, turnip greens, and a slice of thin bacon, and leaves the go-withs that you fretted over in the dishes to cool?

I eat radishes in the middle of the morning out of the garden. They give me indigestion if I eat them at meals. I eat onions that way, too, fresh-pulled ones, and get by with them. Onions backfire on me if I eat them under a roof.

Bright spots in my summer's eating: a gorgeous hunk of catfish, part of which I sliced and fried and part of which I baked in butter and lemon juice; a dishpan full of tomatoes from my neighbor's garden when she knew I was going to have house guests; a ribroast, fresh killed and not yet completely drained; and a platter of golden honey from Neighbor Woodford's.

October 29, 1943

It is eleven o'clock on a winey, still October morning when I shut myself outside my house to go to the mail box. All morning I've been pushed to go, not because I'm overly eager for the mail, because it's Monday and Monday's mail generally turns out to be the Sunday's and Monday's papers and we've had the funnies on Sunday. But on an October morning that is like honey on the tongue, I'm full of mellow melancholy and in veriest need of doing nothing. A soft veil of autumn haze abides in the valley and rims the earth where the sky rests on the haggled crests of the lazy, sprawling hills. It feels far away to the hilltops; yet airplanes that drone one instant above me are, in a few minutes, turning like boys' kites on the edge of the horizon.

One plane undoubtedly takes notice of the small speck that is me. It swoops earthward and banks and turns over me, and I can make out the toy-sized figures of the student and the instructor. I stop and wave at them, feeling that ageless uplift peculiar to womankind when the naughty, naughty masculine takes come-hither notice of her, be it with the raucous whistle, the sly wink, the tantalizing wave of the hand, or wing salute. The plane swoops lower, and in the rat-a-tat-tat of the upsweep, I remember what it's all about and wonder a bit whether I was for the moment an object of romantic interest to the flyers, or were they using me for an objective to see how completely they could splatter me if I were walking in the soil of the Fatherland?

Soon they were playing tag with another plane far across the country, and I am arrested by a giant sized brother of the doodle-bug loping lickety split across the path. I nuzzle him a bit with my toe and ask him what's his hurry. At my touch, he folds up for dead, possumming on me. I squat and turn him over. How dead he plays—dead and buried to the mere hull of a bug. I pick him up in my hand, and when he has lain still long enough, he cautiously wiggles a dead leg, then another. I lay him back on the ground and scheme to wait quietly and see him unpossum.

There's the rat-a-tat-tat of the airplane again, mounting above me. I look up from my bug and suppose the warriors have come back for another salute or to see how dead I am, not being sure whether this is an affair of love or hate. I take a long chance and rise and hopefully wave some more. Whatever I am to the flyers—and I certainly am something—they swoop and bank and rat-a-tat-tat bravely while I watch and wave.

Then they are gone, and I return to my bug again. But now he is nowhere and I can't find him at all. I feel cheated. Likely I was only being liquidated by the airplane. The bug would have doubtless been a more satisfying experience if I had devoted all my time to it . . . .

The postman is late again. The adventure has lost its flavor, and I hurry back to see if the oven is hot enough for cornbread.

January 28, 1944

My kitchen is finished, except I plan to put a geranium in it next spring. I've always wanted but never had a kitchen with a geranium in it. Now, that's silly, isn't it? It's not, I suppose, a Herculean task to wangle a geranium into a kitchen. Why I haven't done it years ago, I am at a loss to know. It is possible that I don't really, really care for a geranium in the kitchen. Perhaps I only think I want one. It won't be the first time something like this has happened. I'll find out.

When folks come into my kitchen and I say it is finished, they look it over dubiously, then ask, "Now, do you intend to keep those shelves open like that? And will you just leave the curtains on the bottom part of the cabinet? Or," hopefully, "will there be doors?"

The answer is, "Yes." I'll leave the dish shelves open, and no, there won't be doors. In the first place, I like to look at dishes. There is something about the shapes of them and the colors of them and the everyday friendliness of them that sort of fills out the corners of my soul. I will hardly part with even a cracked one. I'm not too tremendously respectful of germs, anyway; and for the pleasure it gives me just to look my dishes in the face, I expect them to be broad-minded and somewhat tolerant of the dust I allow to gather on them. From time to time, I will, of course, wash the dust off them, whether I use them or not. I want them to know this and be patient.

I like, even, to wash dishes. I like especially to wash lots and lots of dishes if the water is comfortable and lots of it and the suds are happy. I wouldn't give a whoop, or half a whoop, for somebody to help me wash dishes. Unless that somebody is good talking. In which case, I drag the dish-washing out interminably, for nowhere can friends get such good talking done as over a mountain of dishes. By and large, though, I am a lone dish washer. The suds sort of seem to lubricate my think wheels.

There won't be doors on my cabinet, because my kitchen is a sort of longish narrow thing, and open cabinet doors (they'd always be open and don't try to tell me different) would make a sort of low hurdles arrangement of my runway down the center kitchen, and I was never agile enough for track events. I can't always be picking myself up out of the floor.

I had all this out with my brother when he was carpentering in the kitchen. I think he wanted to show how he could stack 'em up and make 'em fit. Having been bit by the cabinet building bug, Arthur wanted doors. And drawers. And bins. Due to the narrowness of the kitchen, he finally conceded no-doors, but with a sort of "the-blood-be-on-your hands" resignation. Then the matter of the drawers hung fire for some days. "What, no drawers?" he opened the attack each day. "It wouldn't be a cabinet without them. A woman always wants a cabinet with drawers. Imagine one without them!" There are drawers, three of them . . . . If he were as right about the doors as he is about the drawers, I'm certainly missing something.

I remained adamant about the bins. I keep my flour and meal and sugar in crocks and cans—with lids. I know it's old-fashioned, but it keeps out the rats and mice, especially in my staples. I'm not a pessimist about them. Rather, I am a realist: if there are rats and mice, they come into my house. That's that. And I am convinced that any amount of doors and cabinets and artful gadgets to circumvent the little devils will not long deter them. My only refuge is un-gnawable containers.

You see, I learned about rodents from rodents. Once I had a beautiful boughten cabinet with drawers and bins and proof of rat-proofing all over it. It was a dignified piece of furniture. Even its designer had noticed that and had named it for the President of the United States. That cabinet had everything, including class. I had pride in my cabinet. I showed it off before my friends. I had confidence in my cabinet and loaded the drawers and bins to capacity. When my neighbors complained of a scourge of rats and mice, I sympathized, I pitied. Then I advised that they, too, try to get the furniture dealer to allow them to own a cabinet named for a President. Then I slept the untroubled sleep of the mouseless. This went on until one morning my nose whispered a suspicion to my ear. My ear was scornful, but my nose knows when it smells something. It enlisted the aid of my unwilling eyes. Then nose, eyes, and evidence not to be denied laid low my pride. My rat-proof, mouse-proof presidential cabinet was definitely infested.

No, the rats hadn't frolicked in my executive cabinet while I slept. Not they. Not in that super-duper joint. Evidence showed that they had been holding regular and solemn cabinet meetings, bogging themselves down in my flour and meal in order to establish precedent. There they had read the minutes of the last meeting, meticulously corrected them, and waited upon the report from the Secretary of Agriculture. That eminent one had brought out the latest bulletins on bubonic plague, poliomyelitis, and jaundice, which they studied diligently, apparently impressed with the enormity of their possibilities. Then each cabinet member, it seemed, rose in the order of presidential succession and did his utmost for ratdom and pestilence. Right into my staples. I don't like bins!

February 11, 1944

An armadillo rooted in our garden at night. He plowed up the greens and rearranged our fresh plantings. The next morning, Mackie Ma made the fence secure, stopping all the places where he could get in. Come night, we heard him digging under. When he had had time to let himself in, we turned on the 200-watt windmill light and lit into him with a .22. Armadillos can be shot in a lot of places without killing them. We must have hit all of those places first.

When he realized that he was hemmed in, that slow, torpid beast turned into a whirlwind of fury and pain. He zipped across the garden, hurtling into a tub and ricocheted into some potted plants. He hit the fence with shattering violence and climbed the small net to a height of three feet. He was here and there at the same time, all the while picking up more .22s. When we finally got him, we had to come inside and be counted to make sure none of us had been shot in the engagement.

April 7, 1944

Mackie Ma and I are not planning to get into the Easter Parade. During the winter we have pretty much confined our social and religious activities to attendance at the washateria. It is social because we meet the nicest people there—people who have come to the washateria to get a bit nearer to godliness. It is sort of religious because sometimes Sister Virdell is there, and she calls us Sister Yeager and Sister Neal. I always feel religious after she has done that. No, with gas rationing and Sunday overtime and new spring hats being what they are, Mackie and I will likely miss the parade entirely.

Yes, spring fooled us again. The early garden and fruit got set back on their heels. Boys flew kites too soon and had to put up marbles for mittens. Doves had to haul in their coos. Oak blooms were seared as if by flames and are a mess now. Algeritas took it in the buds. Mockingbirds had to postpone their night serenades and straw hats still look a bit silly. There was half an inch of ice on the house seventeen hours before the first day of spring. But it didn't fool the mesquites, except a few of the very young, inexperienced ones, and a few old, tough ones that didn't give a hoot.

Things I've learned of late about gardens: even for grade-A gardeners, it takes two weeks for carrots to come up, and five weeks for parsley. Most times mine have not come up at all. Beet seeds as planted are not simply seeds. They are pods of seeds, often several in a pod. That's why they generally should be thinned out. Nemetodes, say the books, are responsible for root knot (yes, "knot" not "rot"). And when you've got 'em, you'd just about as well pick out another garden spot. They cavort around in fields and orchards, too, it seems, with utter abandon. Nemetodes are also called wire worms and eel worms. I can't say I've identified a nemetode yet, but I've spaded up various slimy, wriggling beasts that I seriously suspect. Undeniably, some of my roots are knotted. Thrips (isn't that a cute name?) I hear are perfect devils with gladiolas and iris, as well as onions. I haven't met any of them yet so far as I know, but I'm of a naturally pessimistic nature—and I'm a-fearin'. This I know, because I've seen them—there are plenty of cutworms ready to greet the spring and your newly set tomatoes. I've interviewed them. They say they are hungry.

June 9, 1944

We went on a Sunday to Preaching-All-Day and Dinner-on-the-Ground at Camp San Saba. We went to bring Mackie Ma home, where she had been a week visiting Raleigh and attending the revival. Mackie Ma had fallen gently in love with Raleigh's Camp people and came somewhat regretfully home, full of fried chicken and salads and Lady Baltimore cake and good fellowship with fine folks. I stuck my neck out. I took food to Camp San Saba. I brought it back, too, because Camp San Sabans wouldn't eat it. I wouldn't either, not with their lovely feast spread out before me. The dinner bore no stint of rationing, and you should have seen the fragments! They would have made a bounteous picnic for a city crowd. There were steaks and salads—especially mine—and melting, crumbly Lady Baltimore. I mean left over!

Camp San Saba is an old community. Its roots run deep. The people are hospitable and friendly, not just politely, but sincerely. Friendship grows among them like yeast in kitchen warmth. I think I found part of the yeast that makes Camps so rich in living: three bright-eyed, work-inured, big-souled women, whose combined years totaled more than a couple of centuries. They were mothers Williams, Leifeste, and Appleton. With their generations filling the church and standing beside the river at baptizing time, singing, praying, ministering, these grand old ladies looked upon a civilization they had inherited and added to, a culture and a gentle breeding that they have made and that is the strength of our land, though to each the day was just another Sunday.

Mother Appleton was in a reminiscing mood, telling how she had fished the San Saba River when she was twelve-year-old Alice Simpson, remembering a girlhood companion, now long dead. Mother Leifeste, who resides in Brady now but plans to come back home in the good afterwhile, spoke of a dream to reestablish her home and her family in the home place. Her youngest, A.J., was enjoying a furlough with the family and friends. Mother Williams, a very wren of a small person, was enjoying the school vacation, because the daughter-in-law, Mary, had taken over the Williams' Voca place for the summer, and Mother Williams had begun her vacation, summer visiting among her children. In her lifetime, she has mothered thirteen, and so has a full summer ahead of her.

July 14, 1944

I warred the aphids on my melons today. I started in, turning each leaf and spraying a lethal dose into the midst of them. I had a good spray and so felt encouraged as I began. But the hordes of them! The more I sprayed, the more I found. Finally, with empty sprayer and rising doubts and sinking hopes, I came to the house, jumbling texts about the meek inheriting the earth and beginning in my canteloupe patch. For escape literature, I picked up a *Capper's Farmer*, and this is what I read: "Numerically the world is dominated by insects. It is estimated that there are more than five million insects in the air above each square mile. The total weight of the world's insect population is greater than all other land animals. A pair of flies, starting in April, would produce five trillion tons of descendants by August if all survived—this based on 20,000 flies to the pound."

Migosh! And aphids are numericaller than flies!

July 28, 1944

Tomorrow I shall be canning grapejuice. We got vine-fresh grapes from George Engdahl's young vineyard in the East Sweden community, just forty-seven axehandles and a plug of chewing tobacco from our own front door. We went in the afternoon and gathered most of them ourselves. They are mostly Carmens, nice, juicy black fellows, clean and tight-skinned. There are some Concords, too, winey, pungent, and sweet, and some tantalizing flavored, nearly black clusters that George told us are Spanish.

The Engdahl vineyard, orchard, and farm have been loved into being. This is the Engdahls' seventeenth year on it. They have brought it from native state into beautiful productivity, and by the labor of their own hands, building the fences, grubbing out the trees for plowing, terracing to hold the land and conserve the rainfall, setting the trees—all of it, even to the masonry of the beautiful tool shed and the carpentry of the very comfortable home. It is a sort of monument to the best of American living.

Mrs. Engdahl's son-in-law plans to climax his homecoming from overseas with a picnic under the oaks that nestle the farm house. Her son, a lieutenant in the Air Corps, got a short visit home once when he ferried a ship to Curtis Field. Carolyn and Beverly, daughters of the Engdahls, ride the bus from Rochelle school back to their home, where they grew up, like the weeds in the vineyard; and sweet, like peaches in their father's orchard. I like what they grow at George Engdahl's. I feel right tonight with the prospect of full-flavored grapes to bottle tomorrow and folks like the Engdahls to live over the hill and across the fields from.

I have all my canning jars full except three small-mouthed ones that coffee came in, which I shall fill with grape juice, and a few regular ones for pears and maybe a few fall peaches, if I'm lucky enough to find some I'll buy. Using up my fruit jars is giving me a mental and emotional set that I hope I can remember when processors go back to cans.

This year I've used every sealing kind that comes my way. The small-mouthed coffee kind I've used mostly for juices and things that didn't need to bother about keeping their school girl rotundity. I bless the manufacturer that made sealers that fit these containers. I saw stacks of little inner seals at Piggly Wiggly this week. But I am mad at the processor who uses the bald, flat-topped quarts (mostly for shortening) and half-gallons—the kind that comes with no screw-downs on them. That's just plain waste.

Then there's the manufacturer who puts fruit and choice vegetables into beautifully proportioned squat jars, which show the product to the best advantage—but which have no tops, lids, or screw-downs for me to seal my canning into. That processor I'd love to hold at twenty pounds pressure for thirty minutes and then see what he looks like. But the ones who put their wares into regulation-looking jars, with mouths the same size as my sealers, with screw-downs that look orthodox, but which, when

I've filled the jars with piping hot food and fitted the sterile lid and screwed down the ring, lack just one more round of screwdown to make the ring fit right against the seal lid—for that processor, Hell ain't hot enough!

People

I liked the world better when it was simpler. . . . I liked it after supper when we played until sunset in the dry bed of Deep Creek, filling our coattails with clean, white sand that was studded with quartz gems which sometimes caught the gleam of the sun and flashed like diamonds.

At times Yeager moved in for the close-up. The cameos of the people who filled her world round out the picture of rural life in the Southwest. Her elderly neighbors, especially, furnish a wealth of insight into the pioneer days they knew first-hand. There are details as intimate as bathing practices—and problems—in the days before water was easily available. These portraits not only speak of the personalities of their subjects, but also reflect the many social issues which come with "progress" and with adversity. For these people, a world war followed a depression, and the character forged from long acquaintance with hard work and demanding goals tempered them to meet the challenges.

o o o o o o o o o o o o o o o

September 11, 1936
The community has chuckled often and appreciatively over Fred Foster's homely philosophy clothed under a tangy humor, drier than cedar bark. This is the one I like best: says Fred, "I have a nice, agreeable family most of the time, and generally we get along better than average. But just let me run out of chewing tobaccy and the missus turns waspy as a nest of hatching yellow jackets and Santa Claus himself couldn't please the kids."
++++++++++++++++++++
Uncle John Waddill in speaking of cowboys philosophized, "A newcomer can learn a few things about tending cattle—he

can learn a right smart—get to be right helpful about the place if he's interested. But seems like unless he's been at it all his life he gets stumped when it comes to penning stuff. You know, there's a time—when you've got them up to the pens—there's a time to crowd them and push; then there's a time to be still and quiet. Well, sir, seems like the proper time for pushing and the proper time for being quiet is an art that is found only among dyed-in-the-wool cowboys."

May 7, 1937

Many are the Tommy Doran stories one can still pick up over his route. A favorite is of the time when he had spent the night at the home of Uncle Billy Gibbons. In those days the roads were mostly cow trails, and Tommy, eager to get through to Brady, but doubting his ability to find the town by dead reckoning in his van, agreed to follow Uncle Billy's buggy tracks through the pastures to the roadway.

Uncle Billy left half an hour before the Irish peddler, his buggy wheels marking a path through the grass, and as the way led by a newly filled earthen tank, that demon of mischief which has ever followed the cowman prompted Uncle Billy to drive down to the side-center of the tank as if crossing it, turn his team around the shallow edge of the pool, and on the side opposite his entrance tracks, straighten up the buggy, leaving the tell-take tracks, as if he had driven directly across the body of water.

Half an hour later the unsuspecting Tommy Doran was the very wet victim of the ranchman's "Jackpot."

August 3, 1937

A new conveyance has made its appearance in the neighborhood. It is a pick-up. That, in this motor age, is not in itself significant news, but what makes this particular pick-up news is a sign lettered on the door—C.H. Bratton and Sons. C.H. Bratton and sons have built up one of the prettiest businesses in the Heart of Texas in their flock of registered Rambouillets. Their local sales have been outstanding, and distant contacts are growing. One sale of a flock was to the

Russian government, which sent to the United States for superior grades of sheep for improving native breeds.

"And Sons"! What pride in "and Sons"! Pride for Wesley and Dick, who are still totin' school books from September to June, and pride for Charles, who has lived long enough under Texas skies to have learned some important things about boys as well as about breeds of sheep. Those who have seen the Bratton lads in action in the saddle and about the work pens will tell you that the "and Sons" was not a gracious gift from a doting father; rather it is the hard-earned reward of two youngsters who are coming ranchmen of this section . . . .

And have you seen the cedar picket fence around the Bratton ranch house? The old-fashioned flat wire topping the pickets, Mrs. Bratton says, is the result of a rather extensive search of the country. It was finally located in Mason County. Just another instance of the passing of an era.

Molly Davenport has something interesting in yards. To be exactly correct, her yard isn't a yard at all, for while she lives on one of the best farms in McCulloch County and while Elmer raises the best cotton, corn, and feed on the cleanest acres in our neighborhood, the Davenports suffer the inconveniences a tenant farmer is forced to endure in the case of absentee landlordship.

The farm is owned by a loan company far removed from Rochelle; so along with there being no front porch, few barns, and no windmill, there is no yard. But Molly has flowers—gorgeous, magnificent flowers—hundreds of varieties in the branch that hugs her little spotless house about in the crook of its arm. In June and July, she gathered loads of blue bells and couldn't miss them from the millions that grew almost to the door. Fragrant button willows bloomed then, too. In a little while waist-high goldenrods will paint the curving branch a brilliant yellow. There is never a time, even in the dead of winter, when flowers are not in bloom there. She and Elmer and Horace are learning the names of them.

No doubt the poet was right when he said that a rose by another name smells as sweet. But flowers, like friends, are more satisfactory when we can call them by their first names.

January 11, 1938

To walk through a Brady grocery store in January is an adventure. While our summer gardens are bare and brown, our winter gardens are brave with turnips, leeks, onions, and a few frost-free varieties of greens, while half a dozen grocery stores here flaunt bright fruits and vegetables without so much as a how-dee-do to winter. Besides the staples we have learned to expect, there are parsnips, Brussels sprouts, broccoli, mushrooms, kumquats, parsley, celery, cabbage, eggplant, romantic-sounding members of the avocado family, rhubarb, and frequently others as exotic.

In spite of the fact that custom now provides baskets for self-serve shopping, every foods shopper has a favorite clerk. But for an interesting tour through the mart of strange and stimulating displays of vegetables and fruits, I recommend as entertaining and informative guides Roy Tabor Holliday of Safeway and Cleburn Stanphill of Gilbreath's. They have few equals and no superiors.

++++++++++++++++++++++

It is rare indeed that Uncle Obe consents to leave the comforts of his own home and visit among the kith and kin, but when he does, it is an occasion. Cocooned in red flannel underwear, under which are pads of medicated cloth pinned over his chest until he sticks out like a pouter pigeon, layered with top clothes and underclothing, he appears someday surrounded by his apprehensive, super-attentive family, who are jittery about Papa's coming out, and he permits his host's household to revolve about him for a day.

He goes at once and unerringly to the best bedroom, crawls between the sheets, asks for more covers, has all the windows closed, demands that his hot-water bottle be refilled, shakes his head nervously in a gesture meant to be quieting so that Mama warns the children to play out at the barn and be careful not to make any noise. Dinner hour and menu are ordered to Papa's especial needs, and a tip-toe time is had by all.

++++++++++++++++++++++

Fin Petrie, ace country correspondent from Wyoming, gained a nation-wide following of reader interest in telling of rural simplicity. He says that people out his way hang the bath tub on a nail. Rural simplicity in these parts grows into complications when the neighbor borrows one off the nail to mix up the sausage in, another deserts the nail for the calf lot to be used as a feeder, and third and last springs a leak.

Mayfield Gibbs, ex-athlete and ex-athletic coach of Daniel Baker College, now country gentleman extraordinary of Brown County, has a solution. Mayfield says that God gave birds more sense than to bathe in the winter time.

A cold winter night setting in and a knock at the door. "Any place around here to camp out of the weather, mister? Our car's broke down." Their homes were in north Texas, and they were on their way back to their families for Christmas after five months' work on the range program in the cedar country. They made beds in the barn and came in to the fire to warm before turning in.

"They paid us a dollar and a half an acre. Gov'ment money. I heered talk the gov'ment was actually payin' more, but them others helt out on the pay. I heered talk . . . . What's the war news? We ain't seen a paper for weeks. I heered the gov'ment was askin' for volunteers and if they didn't get enough, they'd draft 'em. Yeah, I got one o' them cards—astin' if I had a job. I didn't put my name on it. Not me. I figgered if they got my name, I'd be in line for a job all right—a job o' totin' a gun. Not me, brother. I'd rather cut cedar—at a dollar an' a half!"

An old mother bent over her needle. "My boys won't sign it. They don't have work, but they're just the right age for the army. We don't trust it."

I talked with another very old mother whose sons now lie in the soil of France, where they have mouldered for twenty years. She never did understand. Her work-worn hands were a tremor of agitation as defeated old eyes bored into mine. "The President of the United States, he sold my boys to them warlords over there. He sold them for twenty-eight dollars apiece, and he put the money in his pocket. Hell ain't hot enough for Woodrow Wilson!"

Ignorance? Surely. But that does not lessen the fear nor take away the tragedy nor strengthen the "gov'ment."
++++++++++++++++++++++

Thunder, lightning, and wind leave my mother calm. She says, "Think the Almighty would miss me if He were aiming at me?" But I have never been able to rationalize nature on the rampage. God never seems so imminent nor so terrible as in an electrical storm in the springtime, with chain lightning stabbing here and there and God-knows-where, while the mighty thunder rattles the cups on the kitchen shelves and my little soul shivers in its corner with an unholy terror.

September 8, 1938

Here is a thing. For years I have known a little road that leaves the highway and trails off down toward the Corn Creek school house. All this time it's been nothing to me but the Corn Creek road. But the other morning, we followed it on past the Corn Creek School, and it led us to Margaret Moseley's house. Now, there's people, the Moseleys—friendly, glad to see you, and rapid-fire talk that skips about helter-skelter because there is so much of it to be shared.

And books on shelves. Books that need to be talked about, and kitchen business and talk of the doin's at Washington and Austin and Rochelle. Sakes! Why don't we visit oftener? Likely I'll not be going down that little road for months and months and months—even years—in spite of the fact that I know it leads to one of the friendliest, most interesting homes I've stepped foot into. But I'll love that little road every time I pass it.

It was Margaret's wedding anniversary, too. She recommends the state of matrimony and was quite radiant about the special occasion. And I think that's a good country commonplace.

October 6, 1938

The erection of chutes and effective gadgets on modern ranches for the working of cattle has simplified much of the work of handling ailing brutes and revolutionized, if not demoralized, the high calling of the waddie. However, in the absence of modern equipment, the time comes now and then amongst us po' white trash when heavy stock have to be handled in the raw. It is then that the scarcity of men trained to the rope and the saddle becomes painfully evident. I mean that the profession of cowboy is not a crowded one today.

At our house the other day it was an epidemic of pink-eye in cattle. Our own particular flock is scarcely more numerous than the ships of the Swiss navy. You could shuffle them up and lose the whole kit and bilin' in the rotunda of the courthouse we didn't get, but when one of the critters gets sick and must be handled, the little handful of cow brutes takes on alarming proportions. It is then the Yeagers wish again for simple, understandable things like an armful of school books and a handful of freight train.

But in our neighborhood there still remains one who has not forgot the art of cattle wrangling. A bit frosted by the years, Kidd Jeffers has lost nothing of the fast thinking and little of the lightning-quick sureness of hand that once made the cowboy the most romantic figure on the American scene. And he is training young Harry, a year out of school, in the vanishing art. A wide-awake boy on one end of a lariat and a half-ton of bawling cow on the other with a smoking double twist of the twine around the snubbing post between—there's an opportunity for physical, mental, and emotional development not to be found on any gridiron in the country.

Kidd shouts out the rules of the game: "Watch that rope, boy! Don't let it catch a hand. Careful now! Pull on her nose. Make her think you're going to tear it out! That's what makes 'em gentle!" Cowboying—Kidd and Harry dishing it out and taking it too when either's rope misses an aim.

And there was a funny little city slicker last election asking Texans to make him lieutenant governor of the state who angled for votes by saying that it didn't take executive ability to run a ranch.

Much has been said about the lack of opportunity the present industrial world offers its youth today. Industry in the city is unable to consume the man-power flowing in from the country; so in the terms of the economists, American youth is "backed up on the land." But the cattle country is a land that can stand to have a considerable bunch of fellows like Harry Jeffers, trained by a master in the old school, backed up on it.

October 20, 1938

The frankness of the very young is often penetrating and revealing. Often it is alarming. Throughout a long-legged, self-conscious childhood, I had comforted myself with the belief that I was the possessor of a set of blue eyes—or, if one must be exact, at least blue-gray eyes. But a small nephew ruthlessly blasted my illusions one day, when at the end of prolonged questioning, he asked, "Well, Auntie, if that little black hole in your eye is the pupil, what is that green?"

This story of childhood comes via Howard Payne College and the president of that institution. With his wife and small granddaughter, Dr. Taylor was driving in the night through an early spring electrical storm. Lightning cut the darkness into jigsaw patterns with machine gun tempo. Thunder growled and boomed about the speeding car and came inside to jeer at taut nerves. The Taylor grandchild sensed the helpless concern and the alien menace. She began a barrage of questions: "Does God make the lightning? Why does He make some lightning straight and some of it crooked? Does He make the thunder? Are you afraid of it? What does He make the thunder out of?"

Having whipped the grandparents down to the I-don't-know status, the youngster demanded, "Why don't your read the Bible and find out?"

Patsy Murchison's childhood furnishes me with the retort superb. When she was in the all-day-sucker stage, Patsy went from her home in Menard to San Angelo for an extended visit in the Alvin Neal home. It was Patsy's initial experience at spending the night away from her mother, and she sensed that many miles separated her from her home. However, all went merrily along until bedtime. Then a violent homesickness swept the child—a homesickness which grew only more poignant after long and vehement weeping. Her hostess exhausted all known adult wiles in successive efforts to bring comfort, but the urge for Mama and her own bed filled the child's soul. Finally, her hostess sank to self-pity in faint hope of quieting the child. "I thought you loved me, Patsy," she pleaded.

There were thoughtful sniffles on that for a minute; then Patsy exercised a child's privilege of brutal frankness in a new and more disconsolate outburst, "Oh, I love you all right, Neal," she wailed, "but I'm so tired of you!"

November 17, 1938

Observation of family reunions, Christmases, and birthdays cement family affections. Nowhere are birthdays more important than among the folks at Lohn. I found myself the other Sunday a guest in an assembly of a dozen families where several birthdays were being celebrated. The cake with sixty-odd candles on it that lorded it over a table full of home-cooked food was made for Mary Elizabeth Lohn by her son's wife, Mrs. Lincoln Lohn. Aunt Mary is still the most chipper little Irish lady that ever wived it for a sturdy German lad.

Neither her house nor her yard can hold all of her boundless energy. She spreads her personality all over the place. Cows with love-laden names and chickens that tag at her heels are Aunt Mary's. Sons and daughters and grandchildren by the house- and yardful wished her many happy returns of the day. Her hands are busy. Her mind is busy. When family and friends talk to her about slowing down, about giving up the garden or the cows, about taking things easier, she flaunts her good health, her clear eyes, her steady hands and quick step as evidence that life is good if one makes it so. Tucked away in her apron pocket that day I found the back torn from a garden seed catalogue. She said she had saved it because it expressed the philosophy of her living. I pass it on to you. Doesn't it sound like Aunt Mary to you?

"The search for happiness is presumed, by most people, to be the chief purpose of life. It is well worth while to pause in the hurry of everyday and find out, if possible, why people are happy. Also how we may find greater happiness.

"It has been pretty well demonstrated that wealth, power, and achievement do not always result in happiness. Neither is the key to be found in the dizzy whirl of pleasure, jazz, and modern high speed.

"Healthy effort in the daily work, with a reasonable amount of pleasure stimulus, followed by plenty of relaxation, preferably in the home, field, woods, and garden, brings happiness. Most people are supremely happy when they are working or resting in their own gardens; it is nature's own way of healing disturbed minds and nerves."

February 9, 1939

He was christened Vanuel, but because of the sprinkle of freckles across his nose that never lost all of its sunburn and because of an irrepressible twinkle in his eyes, everybody called him Van. And if he happens to want to come, a body doesn't have to call twice. On a January morning he arrived at school early. With a crisp, white letter in hand, a letter he juggled carefully, he sought out Superintendent Gainer. "Hey, Mr. Gainer," he bantered, "may I go mail this letter?"

Something about the boy, an undercurrent of importance, hinted of a more-than-ordinary occasion, a hint the boy-loving heart of Arch Gainer wasn't slow to recognize. Drawing upon a professorish air which was given the lie by a grown-up man's little-boy grin, Mr. Gainer pushed the question, "A letter, Van? Do you think it's important?"

"Important?" snorted the lad. "It ought to be. It's to the President!"

And, indeed, it was to the President, just a friendly letter on his birthday, because January 30 was birthday for them both, although there was a stretch of years between a bunch of other things that didn't greatly impress Van.

Van mailed the letter, and Franklin dictated the boy-to-boy reply that Van now treasures.

August 17, 1939

The last word has been spoken, the last report has been given, the last stay has been granted. This is the week set by the State of Texas for Francis Black, convicted for having pushed a boy over a cliff in the Big Bend a year ago, to start a life term in prison. It was two months ago that I talked to Francis Black behind the bars of the Alpine jail, where the condemned man was awaiting a report on the court's verdict that he should die for his crime. He did not believe that the state was going to take his life. He did not believe that he was going to die. His thoughts were in the future. For him, the present did not exist, and he reluctantly and vaguely reviewed with me the past. "I have not lived long enough!" he cried.

Francis Black grew up on a farm in the corn belt of the Midwest. He spoke with some bitterness of those early days. "There should be some easier way," he chafed, "to get our share of this world's goods than by hard work on a farm."

And in that cry of rebellion, Francis Black diagnosed the cancer that is consuming American youth today. "To get" is too often the aim of education. Who, nowadays, spends his time aiming "to be," and who spends his energies striving "to be"? Like Francis Black, youth on the campus, in business, in the trades, on the streets, and in the ditches, consumes itself trying "to get."

And so, leaving the farm, Francis Black went to his state's university to study electrical engineering, for such a course seemed to him to promise more for getting in this mechanical age. Still, the way was for him too long and the road too hard. It all seemed so slow. This is why he left the university to study in a trades school. But somehow, with all his striving, he missed his goal—ever "to get."

Fair means having failed him, finally it was an insurance policy on the life of a near waif that promised to get quickly for him his share of this world's goods. It seemed easy, too. An eager lad atop a bluff, a scuffle that seemed in play, a little shove—perhaps more of a shove than one would think as a desperate human being, even a gangling boy, struggled for his life. It would be all over before one could breathe twice. Black didn't collect on the insurance policy. And all of this world's goods that he finally held in his hands were the bars of a prison cell.

August 31, 1939

Was it yesterday that Maude and Winnie Smith, with pigtails flying, wound Rochelle around their busy fingers, while they glibly recited all the answers in the back of the book, wheedled a pack of very tall, broad-shouldered, very loose-jointed brothers into brotherly slavery (well, nearly did), giggled infectiously behind geographies, and took me home with them from school in a rattly old buggy when a sudden norther turned up in the middle of the day?

What a gay ride it was, the three of us tucked under the lap robe and an old quilt behind the dashboard, snug from the howling wind. You remember, Maude, don't you, who blossomed out of pigtails into a blonde with a gleam in her blue eye that made the hearts of the local swains go round and round and round and come out nowhere with a dull thud? Maude, who gathered up a few books and a lot of ideas and went away to the College of Industrial Arts, where she gathered up a young electrician named Teddy Pikuritz even there in that college designed for women? Then Mr. and Mrs. Pikirutz shook the dust of the Southwest off their feet and went to town. They settled down at 57 West 75th Street in New York City, and Mrs. does the shirts and bakes the clams for Mr. while Mr. regulates the sound waves at Radio City Music Hall.

Now I've often wondered while flip-flopping the churn dash or cleaning out the henhouse what living in a great city would be like, especially when I've let my imagination help itself and have had such a good time doing glamorous things in the great city that the flip-flop of the churn dasher has become the very pound of feet on the pavement and the butter came before I knew it at all.

Then the other day there came a letter from Maude. First off, she made me feel very puffy-uppy, saying her mama sent my column to her each week, and she didn't mention it if Mr. used it to swipe off his shaving lather from his razor. But instead of the glamor of New York and the gossipy, intimate details of house-keeping in the metropolis, of which I'm sure Maude has a goodly store of stories, her letter was concerned largely with the impression of an American woman into whose home the world's unrest, its insecurity, its distrust is being thrust. In short, Maude's letter was about things that make nations go to war when they are not sure why. She says: "There isn't a boat that arrives that doesn't bring at least a dozen or more writers, lecturers, etc., seeking fame through their denouncements of his (Hitler's) policies. Some of them are on their own, looking for publicity and a job. Others are paid by the French and English governments to stir up our resentment to the point of hate so they can count on our support in another war.

"To weed out propaganda is almost impossible, excepting in a few cases where we know they have personal interests. All in all, we are fed tons of propaganda by way of press and radio. I seldom turn on my radio but that I hear some person with a bla-bla accent, telling us just how dangerous Japan is becoming, etc., and how insane Hitler is. We get it poked under our doors, handed us in the streets, buses, and subways. We practically eat it for spinach. It is being overdone, and the majority of plain folks here are beginning to realize we are being railroaded into another war."

Now, New York is no more American than Brady is; yet it is just as much. It's sort of like the tongue when one gets bilious; it isn't, after all, the tongue that's sick—one is sick all over—but the condition shows itself in a coated tongue. What's happening to Maude in New York is happening to you and me here—only in a more limited way. It's in your newspaper because it's hot news and because some industry gets in a lot of plugs while we wait; it's in your magazines for the same reasons. Sometimes it has more reputable carriers. It isn't far to San Antonio, and a rash of it broke out there last week.

I'm sorry it's so. I liked the world better when it was simpler. I liked supper at Maude's house, when we sat, somewhat subdued in the presence of Mama and Papa Smith and hot biscuits and fresh spare ribs, when we didn't speak until we were spoken to, where we helped ourselves to the vinegar and the salt on the cruet caster from which dangled an array of spoons. I liked it after supper when we played till sunset in the dry bed of Deep Creek, filling our coattails with clean, white sand that was studded with quartz gems which sometimes caught the gleam of the sun and flashed like diamonds. Magic sand it was. We shook out our dresses, and not even Mama Smith could tell we'd been rolling in sand beds and making frog houses and "skinning cats" heels over head (a thing forbidden nice girls, and therefore so necessary to be done). We gleefully tumbled our bodies through our arms while suspended from the gnarled roots of mesquites sticking out from the steep banks of old Deep Creek. I liked studying tomorrow's lessons around the kerosene lamp on the dining table, all cozy and warm. I liked being tucked into bed in high-necked, long-sleeved nightgowns made of white outing. I even liked Mama Smith's gentle scolding us into quietness as we giggled, suffocating into the bedclothes. It never was effective, Mama Smith's scolding. But Papa Smith's deep-chested "That'll do now, girls" froze us into instant quietness. Soon we were snugly asleep, three in a bed.

Yes, life was simple in those days. We didn't have automobiles, steam heat, polished floors, bathrooms with hot water, nor electric ice boxes. But we had rest, a sense of security, an assurance that we were wanted. And it was all true what the teacher said at school, what the preacher said on Sunday, what Papa and Mama believed in; and the answers in the back of the book could be depended on.

What's happened? I wasn't looking, but I think somebody sold us short. Did you see it happen, Maude?

February 20, 1940

Today Granny Kyzar is having a birthday party. It is all right for her to have a birthday party, for in all her eighty years, she has had only nineteen birthdays on which she could have a party. The party is to begin with a family dinner at the home of her daughter, Mrs. C.H. Longley, and in the afternoon, Granny will serve coffee and cake and conversation to friends who come to see her celebrate eighty years of living. Born in 1860 in Livingston Parish, Louisiana, on February's extra day, she has had only nineteen birthdays in spite of the fact that four goes into eighty twenty times; for from 1896 to 1904 there is the century lapse of eight years when there was no leap year—a thing I am always forgetting.

Granny was married on the sixth of January the winter after she had had her fourth birthday. She says she has been married nearly all her life. Ten children she had and reared all but one of them in the pioneer country of Texas—all except one who died in infancy. Today she counts off grandchildren and great-grandchildren on each finger and toe, then has to start all over again. In speaking of her early marriage, she says that, though she was a girl bride, she wishes she had been married the summer before she was sixteen. This being a peculiar wish, she explains it by saying that when she and her husband celebrated their Golden Wedding Anniversary, they had to do so in midwinter, and many of the old-timers could not come on account of the cold weather. Now, she says, if they had been married the summer before, there would have been summer weather for the celebration.

When she had added two years to her four birthdays, as well as a husband and a baby, the young Mrs. Kyzar moved in a covered wagon, behind four yoke of oxen, in the summer of 1878 to Texas. The memory of that half-a-year's drive remains fresh in Granny's mind, and she can still call a lusty "hee-haw" that will convince her listener that stolid oxen ears have also listened to those calls. There was a company of four families, kin and friends, in the trek that ended at Mason Pond in San Saba County.

Here the four families bought a section of land at a dollar and a quarter an acre. Granny smiles with understanding when she explains that a dollar and a quarter in 1878 was hard to get hold of as the grocer's satisfaction is today. There was an all-weather spring on the section, and she recalls that during the drought of 1879, seven families "watered" at that spring.

As a pioneer homemaker, Mrs. Kyzar was known far and near. Her house was the shelter of the wayfarer. She remembers how travelers used to ride far into the night to share her hospitality. Some visitors became settlers and neighbors. The father of Emmitt Bratton spent the last night of his journey to his Texas location as a guest of the Kyzars. Always their house was the pioneer preacher's home away from home. Ten years ago, their family reared to maturity, the Kyzars sold the Mason Pond farm and moved to Brady. Four years ago Mr. Kyzar died, leaving Granny the watch-care of a growing tribe of Kyzars.

Although there is a pair of crutches upon which she has come to lean, Granny enjoys excellent health in her eightieth year, living under her own roof, doing much of her own work, with children, grandchildren, and great-grandchildren all about her. Last year on the twenty-eighth, which was as much of a birthday as she could hope to have on an off year, Granny baked a cake—not a birthday cake, but just a cake. There was no fuss or celebration planned for an off-year birthday, but as the afternoon wore on, Granny made a pot of coffee; and as neighbors and members of the family happened along, she asked them in for a bite.

First, there was her son, Houston, and a neighbor come to see about a chore. After she had had her visit with them and they were gone, she washed the two cups and saucers and called in two more guests. Like Noah's party, they came in twos through the afternoon, and it was the grandest party anyone could wish for, served in the same two cups, over and over.

Granny Kyzar reads her Bible without glasses, and takes it without dilution. Although she had only a matter of a few months' instruction in the classroom, a life of rich living has left her a woman of refinement and a student of life with a philosophy deep and satisfying. She was reading Dr. B.H. Carrol's *The Faith That Saves* when I called. In her eightieth year, she still had the faith into which she was baptized, seasoned with time and living.

To her the purpose of life is to glorify God, and although she says we sometimes make a pretty big mess of it, still, trying again and again is the abundant way of life. Her hands, busy with some infant clothes for a small one somewhere down the line, were steady and firm as the hands of the young. She hears as well as I do, and with more tender understanding. Thankful for the state of her health, the security of her home, the love of her family and friends, Granny Kyzar sails out into her eighty-first year, playing all her cloth to the winds, rich in the wisdom and tolerance of age, the healthy curiosity of youth, and the abiding faith of the believer. Power to her!

March 27, 1941

Today is MY DAY. It opened with a blustery, blowy March morning. I start if off with an early breakfast, which I sit down to still pajamaed and uncombed. (I read with awe and a little pity about lovely ladies who take coffee and ham and eggs, having tailored themselves to a turn before hand. Me, I love being sloppy. It comforts my soul.) There's a twenty-egg angel food cake to be spanked up, the cooky jar to fill, and sandwiches to make, for my Sunday School class is coming to see me tonight.

Before I have done the dishes, though, Edwin Edwards and Ted Harris are helloing at the front. They've been on their regular Friday morning trip to deliver the *Heart O' Texas News* to the post offices at Rochelle, Placid, and Mercury, and have dropped by to bring me the news while it is new and to snatch a cup of coffee after working all night getting the paper out. We have great kitchen visiting and coffee and buckwheat cakes mixed up with news about Ted's garden he is about to plant and the particular kind of small talk I love when Yeagers and an Edwards get together.

I don't know till they are gone and I licked the spoon after emptying the rest of the coffee cream into the churn that the darned stuff was sour. I try to comfort myself that maybe it didn't turn sour till afterwards or that maybe they didn't notice. But it keeps nagging me all the morning. A fellow may not notice when payday rolls around or when his draft number is called, but I think he'll always notice the state of his coffee cream.

I do the dishes and start the angel food, when into my kitchen, vivacious as the March morning, come Cleta Wallace and her guest from Brady, fresh and crisp in ginghamy school frocks. They have come to see if Cleta's mama needs to bake a cake for my Sunday school party. I think not, Sunday School parties being what they are, but isn't it a neighborly thing to do?

I always like to make lots, when it's an indefinite thing like a Sunday School affair, but mostly I know beforehand it will be given away afterwards. Now, when it's bridge, we hostesses know how many exactly—we have to.

In a little while the girls are gone, the cake is in the oven, the sandwiches taken care of, and I stir up some more cookies to fill the jar, for yesterday there were guests, and we sampled party cookies pretty freely. My countryman and I take two brooms, and pretty soon the house is redded up. (Emma Young says sweeping with two brooms in the same room is unlucky. I never figure it that way!) I get time for planting some Four-o'clocks and marigolds, but the wind whips the feathery marigold seed about so that I will hardly know where to look for them to come up. There is a smell of rain in the air, and I daresay it won't be necessary to send to Jewel Howard's for cups to serve in, but I'm always a fraidy cat, besides being a very poor weatherman. I send for them, just in case the wind lies down and the clouds go away and give us a fair party night.

I work in a nap and a clean-up. The chores are finished early, and the night sets in, no whit improved for partying. But lights over the hill argue that someone is coming to party in spite of the weather. Neighbors come in with the first spatters of rain. Soon there's enough to call it a party. Mama Irving brought a cake so as to be helpful. Nearly everybody says, "Happy birthday!" because already they have read in "The Heart O' Texas Wishes You" that today is MY DAY.

September 4, 1941

My Neal family never got around to genealogical tables, and we know little enough about what mixtures of nationalities resulted in the present crop of Neals. Not so my Yeager family, especially my Yeager women. They'll go to the mat with you any day for blood lines and ancient honorable ancestry. I've enjoyed a second-hand pleasure in knowing my offspring possesses some definite, tangible progenitors. "That is your Indian blood," I can say to her when she goes on the warpath. "Such frugality must come from your German ancestry." I confess goodly satisfaction in hazarding guesses on these definite racial characteristics in my child and sometimes wish I could climb my own family tree and play about in the branches.

Eating fiftieth-year anniversary cake with the folks at the East Sweden church celebration is about what brought on the above lament. Salt of the earth folks, the Swedish people are, respected the world around for love of home, their intimacies of family life, their dependability. Peace loving they are, asking only to be let alone. Generations of frugal, thrifty housewives pass the art of homemaking from mother to daughter; and although they are quick with learning new methods, the quality of Swedish homemaking is distinctive.

There was an old Bible on display on anniversary day, and pictures from old albums. Some were tintypes. They showed basques and bibs-and-tuckers and sashes and ruffles galore. The Carl Hendricksons were pictured in wedding finery, he in severe broadcloth, she in filmy veiling. Katie Engdahl stood in her prime before the camera in a dress that would be the despair of today's seamstresses, though the sleeves would be a lot of fun and very much in vogue!

George Irvin was there. What a wrench it must have given his memory to conjure up names after the years. But he was good at it. I was a puzzle at first, but when I went into action and orated, "Roll on, thou dark and deep blue ocean, roll!" with appropriate gestures, the way Miss Ethel Irvin, his sister, used to have us do it in elocution, he said right off, "Ethel Neal! Well, blow me down!" I would have been happy to, we were all so happy. My earliest speech teacher is now Mrs. Clem House, Fort Worthian. George looks frightfully prosperous, a mixed iron-gray handsome and still heart-warmingly friendly. We hadn't time to talk about Harold, but my mind did tumbleweeds in a high, rolling wind of the days when every Rochelle girl in pigtails was desperately in love with Harold. I guess I had about the best crop of pigtails in our crowd. I was very desperate.

Noble trenchermen, they! Plenteous dinner plates at noon didn't cut in a great deal on afternoon "coffee." No other place I have ever been for community eating covers the table with such uniformly superb home-prepared food. Their meats and salads are good, but Swedish sweets are like no others—they are good all off in a class by themselves.

My youngest brother had the good sense and the great fortune to win for a wife a granddaughter of the large and flourishing Dan Hurd family. Our own family being delightfully mongrel, we attach ourselves to our Swedish in-laws and our love for them makes us Swedes (if the in-laws don't forbid). We are very proud of it, especially on anniversary day.

September 11, 1941

When I was a young housekeeper, Iva Davis gave me a pitcher—a glazed piece of crockery, the inside done in hues of rose and deep wine. On its outside, embossed pansies and snubnosed fuchsias are worked out in warm hues and tones of green, yellow, and brown. Iva gave it to me, not for buttermilk or mint tea (though it is at home with either), but she gave it to me because there is an elusive quality of beauty about the pitcher each of us knows the other appreciates. It is not the kind of pitcher one would show to a collector, not yet the kind Keats would write a poem about. But it has a clumsy sort of honest beauty that would catch the eye in any company of pitchers and hold it for a space. It has been with me now for a couple of decades—a constant reminder of a treasured friendship. At some remote time I broke a sizable hunk out of one side of it, but I didn't discard it. I only set it farther back on the shelf with the broken part turned so it would hardly show. I'd never want to be entirely without it somewhere in my kitchen. It is, you see, my Iva pitcher. Sometimes a year goes by and I don't see Iva for more than a howdy, but the pitcher is there—and memories.

The other day Iva came by to see me. It wasn't a planned visit. It was only that the road to another place she was going passed by my door. We visited over tea cakes and buttermilk and cheese, and when she went too soon away, she paused by the shelf where the Iva pitcher sits. "What a pretty pitcher!" she said. "Isn't it!" said I. She said, "It's beautiful. Where did you get it?" "You gave it to me," I said.

Then how we laughed together over a broken pitcher, a seasoned friendship, a mutual understanding that has much of honest beauty in it.

September 25, 1941

It is four o'clock, and school is out for the day. I collect my family, for we are going to Annie Laurie and Marion Louise Lohn's for supper and an evening visit. Among the rich experiences I remember of my school teaching days are the times I went home with my girls and boys at the end of the day. No home was ever more open to me that the Marion Lohn home, and in no home did the hearthstone glow warmer for mellowing talk and laughter into ripe friendliness. It was a blessed place, that rambling old country home of the Lohns. Last week friends went with the family and put away into the earth the spent body of Uncle Marion, and now there is a lonesome place in the home and the community where for long, long years a wise and good man walked.

Uncle Marion came from a breed of men who loved their homes, the soil they tilled, and the liberty of free people. In France on St. Bartholomew's Eve in 1572, when ten thousand Huguenots were massacred, ancestors of Uncle Marion Lohn escaped to Germany, where they fond freedom to worship God as they wished. In Germany they stayed, sending down roots into the earth and becoming citizens with their fellow men until the Revolutions of 1848. Then, because home, liberty, and an opportunity to work were taken from them, they faced westward to the new land of America. Thus the father of Uncle Marion Lohn came to Texas and Uncle Marion to his own acres. With a heritage like that, Uncle Marion fathered sons and daughters with strong home loyalties. Hardly a visit I ever made there but that some grown son or daughter was home for a visit. How pleasant it was to sit beside his baggy old chair and listen to him croon little German songs to a grandchild on his knee, to gather for meals with quiet rows of us down each side of the long table bowed for grace before the meal, to look at pictures of absent ones, to listen to bits from their letters home, to watch the coals in the open fire sink into frosted rubies as the talk ebbed and flowed, then to say good night and drive away with his benediction resting on us!

Uncle Marion Lohn lived to be very old. When his body gave way, it did not go all in a heap, the way the deacon's one-hoss shay went. A good body it was, and it went slowly. So he was a bed patient for the better part of a year. That was a good thing, too, for friends and family had a long time for saying goodbye and for doing little friendly acts and big friendly ones to show their appreciation for a good life lived among them. At the Waldrip store there was a list made up of neighbors who took turns, along with the family, in the bedside care of him—a rich way to live, a rich way to die. God rest the friendly great soul of him.

October 2, 1941

The Bart Joneses live in a friendly house with the yard gate opening out onto the highway. It's down our road a stretch toward Brownwood. For more than twenty years we've been going past the house, but I never knew who lived in it. All last winter and into the spring, on my trips to Brownwood, I watched a row of turnip greens growing in the Jones garden. In the dead of winter, when the land was gray with last year's growth, the turnips flaunted greenery as if they and winter were in cahoots. In the spring they shot up tall into bloom and were a fernery of green and yellow for weeks.

In the heat of early August this year, when grocery store vegetables seemed listless and discouraged, I chanced to be going to Brownwood alone. All at once I realized I was driving by where the turnips had grown. "Surely," I argued with myself, "whoever lives here will have some sort of vegetables with the flavor of home garden about them." Then, because I was alone, and because it seemed the right thing to do, I stopped in front of the gate of the folks who grow winter turnips and was going in. A couple of friendly puppies had a lot to say before I got well up the walk to the house, and in the shelter of thick honeysuckle beside the porch, and old cat suckled newborn kittens. Madeira vines sent out a soft, sweet morning freshness into the air and sprinkled the porch with their feathery tassles. I had forgotten the smell of Madeiras.

It was easy talking with Mrs. Jones. She said her turnips and greens had traveled all up and down the highway in both directions in friends' cars when they had come to visit her. There weren't any turnips today, but she promised me some okra when I came home in the afternoon, though she never made a practice of selling garden stuff. Since the Jones husband and the Yeager husband are the grocery shoppers in our families, we were at a loss to agree on a price for okra. But I was assured of a mess anyway.

The Joneses, I found, live alone. A seafaring nephew had sent them coral and souvenirs from his travels. Mrs. Jones fashions things with her deft, short hands—hooked rugs, a complicated crocheted bedspread, a woven tray, and statuary from the mud she scoops up around an earthen tank on the farm. Old dishes interest her, too—odd pieces picked up and old ones handed down in the family. What goes on in the community interests her, and her pastor's problems are hers. Mr. Jones came in with his target from shooting rabbits that had been making free about the place. Both Joneses read the *Heart O' Texas News*, and we were friends already through this column.

The memory of the early morning visit stayed with me in town and lent a sort of special color to the day. In Woolworth's when I bought a thing for me, I got one for Mrs. Jones, too. Along in the shank of the afternoon I exchanged Woolworth packages with the Joneses for fresh-from-the-earth okra, and none of us ever knew what okra was selling at!

April 23, 1942

Men are funny about hats—their own and other people's hats. Or maybe it's just that men are funny. I shan't at this time go into the things men have said about my hats, though it would be diverting as well as revealing. This has, rather, to do with the matter of my countryman's Easter hat. For some years now he has been going up and down the land sheltered by a sort of headgear that looks somewhat like a San Saba River soft-shelled turtle (though it really isn't) with a cowshed effect for a brim.

He's been told delicately and otherwise that gentlemen occasionally renew their head coverings, but for years he has clung to his headpiece with the devotion of a zealot. Recently the fabric succumbed to the inevitable. That is, he wore a hole in his hat. Quite a hole. It not only showed, but let sun and rain in as well. So he bought a new hat. After the old one, it is a crowning glory. The family is elated with it. Even my countryman plans to love it in a year or two—he's no man of quick and fickle affections, not he.

So on Easter morning he wore his new hat to church. "Ah, such umph!" said the family. "Feels funny," said the wearer. But he wore it.

And the following Monday being Army Day and therefore dress-up day again, the new hat was called for. I brought it, all new and fawn colored and hatworthy, a thing to gladden the heart of a Ward McAllister. My countryman gave it a startled look, peered into its upsidedownness, and gasped, "Now look! That's not my hat! I swapped hats with somebody in church yesterday!"

June 4, 1942

When we went away last week, we left our oldest neighbor a patient in the hospital. The thought of his illness was with us all the while we were away. Sometimes I found myself telling my friends, who were strangers to my neighbor, that we had left Uncle Walter mighty sick. At night before we went to sleep and when we woke up in the morning, one of us was sure to say to the other, "I wish I knew how Uncle Walter is." And we stubbornly argued that he would be better when we got home.

But he wasn't. When we got home, Uncle Walter had died. On that account it doesn't seem that we are really at home. I mean it seems that early some Sunday morning he will come strolling across the little valley from his house to ours, helping himself along a bit with a yucca walking-stick he has picked on the way.

It was his practice to come around to the kitchen door, hail us with a lusty "hello." Then he would listen for footsteps. Before I could get the door open, he would follow up his challenge. There he would stand, framed in the doorway, a tall, gaunt, rawboned, loosely put together, weather-beaten old man. That is, all of him was old except his eyes. Up to the last, they retained the snap and fire of young life. It is the look of revolt and rebellion in them that colors my last memory of him. His ire had been raised by the bowls of soup brought to his bed on the dinner tray. "That," he said, indicating the offending pap, "is slop. I don't eat it when I'm well. Send it back, and I guess that makes seventy-five of the things I've sent back this week. If I eat, I've got to have grub!"

That's the kind of man Thomas Walter Mooring was. He reduced life to its essentials; he had small patience with its foibles. I have taught his children and his grandchildren. He was for a time my school trustee, and we made a team. Not that I always pleased him. There was the time I remember when he came by the playground at recess and observed that I had a youngster standing apart from the older children in a ring, not privileged to play with them. "What's that for?" he asked with a nod of his head toward the youngster. "He cusses," I explained. "What about?" Uncle Walter wanted to know. "Oh, I don't know, but he cusses," I said. My trustee gave me a disgusted "humph" through his nose and stalked off muttering something about a fool woman and a boy. Best I could get out of it was, "Ought to find out. Some situations just naturally call for a good cussin'. Wouldn't give a double blank for a boy that wouldn't know when a good dose of powders was called for and how to give 'em." He was a partisan community man. He took his politics earnestly and thoroughly, precinct, county, district, state, and national—and in that order.

Walter Mooring pioneered this section when life was hard, and he never forgot the art of living under difficulties. He was a native longhorn. Born in Rains County, he came to Mason near Katemcy at the age of twenty. At twenty-one he was married to Lindy Watts. Forty-one years ago he came to McCulloch County and has lived here in the same community ever since. He is the father of ten children, eight of whom outlived him. He was three-quarters of a century old when he died, and one of the oldest residents of the county. He pioneered in the use of harvest machinery. He was in theory and practice a thresher man. There was no arguing with him the relative merits of a threshing and combining a crop of grain. The thresher had been made, he believed, to separate the grain from grass and leave the grower a straw stack. That's what it was for, and that's what it did. No other device gave the service; and so, the Mooring fodder wagons continued to creak under their heavy loads and their harvest campfires glowed dull under the summer moon as tired field workers rolled themselves into their blankets after a long, hard day. Uncle Walter himself was with the camp the large part of the last season's run.

He never made acknowledgement of growing old. Easing up and letting down were things he never learned. Never tried to learn them. In this, his seventy-fifth year, he had more acres sowed to grain and more sheep on the range than during any other season since I have known him. When the drought and the green bugs took the winter crop, he pulled his belt a little tighter, hauled in his sails, and was scheming ways and means to see what he could make of the spring shambles when ill health and then death solved his problems for him. Though he seemed a bit grimmer this year, I hadn't worried a great deal about his grain failure nor how he would manage with the sheep. It just seemed to me that he would—somehow. He was the kind that bent with the wind, and the strength of old earth was in him. He was tough like grass and deep-rooted. He knew no failure, but he knew how to come back.

I shall miss him. In my home, on the streets, in the homes of my friends. Though he came to my house often and made long calls, he always left if he saw I was about to serve a meal. Our mealtime being somewhat irregular, he sometimes surprised us at table and would perhaps take a piece of cake, for he liked sweets, but he would never sit with us. Except one time. It was my father's birthday, in the dead of winter. There were sausage and eggs with biscuits and coffee. And there was sponge cake. Uncle Walter stayed for dinner, and both old friends were pleased as kids at a picnic.

I shall miss his colorful speech. Somewhere in my writings I have scribbled down pages of his phrases as I sat at my writing and listened while he talked to others. "I poled off the wagon," he once said, and I loved the description. "The sky scabbed over and it rained a-purpose," is the way he reported a sudden flood. Once during the drought he said, "If the good Lord will let it rain on the unjust in the next few days, why, I'll carry water and pour on the just, and we'll save this grain crop." He had an unbeautiful pet name for me that endeared him. With gruff tenderness, he called me "Old Haint." He was a tireless watcher of the weather, though I seldom heard him offer a guess as to what it was going to be. He walked the pastures and fields after a rain, and grudgingly admitted when the moisture went deep. Generally, his report was, "Just a splatter. I kicked up dry dirt with the toe of my shoe in plowed ground." If he just had to admit a satisfactory rain, he was likely to limit himself to, "Moisture met."

It doesn't seem as if Uncle Walter has gone. It seems that tomorrow or the next day or the next, he will be at my door, hailing, "Anybody at home over here?" He will come and lay his brim-rolled old white hat on the floor beside his chair, with his long fingers fish out a package of Bull Durham, roll a cigarette, spilling tobacco carelessly on himself, the chair, and the floor. I shall stop whatever I am doing and sit down and we shall talk. It seems that way.

Granny Cates

Life had been hard for Granny, but its hardness had made it sweet. She had been nurse, doctor, counselor, neighbor to every family that moved into the settlement. The very simplicity of life made of Granny's day a thing with tentacles that reached into every home, every life she knew.

The woman who served Rochelle as midwife in its early years ushered Ethel Neal into the world, and there was always a special affinity between the two. Granny Cates was for Ethel every bit as much as her own mother the model, the standard against which a woman should be measured. Her love for Granny came to fruit in some of her finest writing.

o o o o o o o o o o o o o o o o o

November 6, 1936

In November of 1936, Texans are especially thankful for pioneers that tamed a "brave new world." And in every Texas community a few of them linger. It is well for us to remember that in the November of their lifetime the years grow appallingly short, but ah, the days are long. Have you tried "going to set" with an old-timer lately? It's a quaint old American custom that has lost none of its charm.

Next to my own mother, I am thankful this November for Granny Cates, and last Sunday my mother and I went "to set" with Granny in her little cottage under the hill, where with the whirr of the old burr mill in her ears, she lies lengthening out the days. And because there is a Confederate veteran's pension and because all of the town of Rochelle stands ready to provide whatever Granny requires, she is tasting her last years in dignity and grace. Not that Granny is sick. She isn't. Disease that she battled with for her family and her neighbors has not dared to lay his ugly finger on her. Granny is simply worn out with the years, and from her clean, white bed, she is taking leave of life. Perhaps because she loved life so profoundly, the leave-taking must needs be long.

In season Othar Williamson brings Granny roasting ears, Arthur Neal brings spare-ribs and tenderloin, Joe Blout comes with a mess of river perch, and Troy Smith has oranges and a little something extra for Granny. Granny likes grub, and soup isn't grub to Granny. Then when the Texas winds play havoc with Granny's clanking windmill, Beanie Neal notices, and the bow-legged old cowboy mounts the tower and tinkers the pump back to work again. These and kindred kindnesses are Granny's "boys" laying their first fruits on the altar.

We found Granny among her pillows, for she has been lying in her bed for five years. Although November 7 is her eighty-sixth birthday, Granny is apparently without age. Like God, it seems that she always was and always will be. Her lashless eyes were closed, while hands, gnarled by labor, but strangely pliant, toyed with and folded the sheet hem as if hands so long used to toil could never be still while life is in them.

Mrs. Davis, the last but one of Granny's seven children, told Granny that there was company, but Granny only smiled. "Don't you know Mrs. Neal, Ma?" the daughter insisted.

Granny tilted her head back into her pillows as if peering under imaginary glasses, the better to focus her visitor, and in a voice that still holds a sort of singing quality she spoke to the orchestral accompaniment of cattle drives, fence cutting, circuit riding, and mid-wifery. "Well, yes, I used to know her," she said, "but that was a long time ago."

Indeed and indeed it was a long time ago when Granny's was the responsibility of the sick in the little struggling pioneer community. Historians would refer to her as a mid-wife; we only knew that if Granny got there in time, life might still be kept. And it was better than an even bet that Granny got there in time, for when a white-faced cowboy flung himself from his lathered horse and raced up Granny's walk calling for her, she was before him out of the house, flinging side-saddle on her stabled mare and giving house-keeping directions to her own brood. Leaving the spent horse and rider to follow, Granny, split-bonnet dangling from taut strings, hair flying in the wind, was lickety-split over the cow trails, flinging open wire gates and leaving them, hurdling those that sagged a little. She was a doctor, nurse, and apothecary. Too, she was a neighbor.

I remember Granny first as she sat across the aisle from my mother and me in the combination school-house-meeting-house on a drowsy summer Sunday afternoon. Her hair, straight as an Indian's, was wound in a low-loose, oily knot under her yellow sunbonnet. Held insecurely with ancient silvery hairpins, it threatened to break away from its moorings and creep down over her hard, straight shoulders. While the circuit rider droned on and on, I slipped away from my mother. Tired, sleepy, and miserably hot in unaccustomed Sunday petticoats, I edged over to the comfort of Granny Cates. A protecting hand reached out for me, and I lay face down in the multitude of gathers and tucks and ruffles that was Granny's skirt. "Please, Granny," I whined, "starch my back."

Granny smiled understandingly, and from a long, deep pocket cut into the material of her dress, there under her snuff box and her collection money and a curious old Indian charm piece, Granny brought a little muslin bag filled with starch and perfumed with dried rose petals. She slipped it somehow through the folds and bundles of my clothing and starched away the sting of heat and perspiration. Blessed Granny! Dangling there across her knees, my nose pushed down upon another pocket pungent with the odor of nutmeggy cookies, I slept. But not for long. An eerie shriek crashed in upon me, and I awoke to find myself plumped into the middle of the aisle in a heap. There was a whirl of yellow skirts, the pounding of many feet upon the pine floor. People were moving in their seats restlessly. I saw Granny's long arms lifted high above her head in weird gyrations. Her wild laughter froze me. Granny was shouting! Another one of her "children" had "come to the fold."

When I was old enough to be "told things," Granny used to sit in her rocking chair behind the morning glory vines and talk endlessly of her cases. I can hear her reedy old voice saying yet, "Honey, you are one of Granny's children! Yo' ma was mighty lucky that I wasn't over on the creek settlement when you come.

When I got there, you was just about done up, and so was yo' ma—and her all alone." Then she would lean mysteriously forward and peer deeply into my eyes. I was fascinated as her voice dropped to a husky whisper, "Honey, I always had a special feeling for you, cause you're like Granny. We can see ghosts! We was borned with veils over our faces. I had two!"

March 23, 1939

A lot of years ago this March, I was a wailing infant within the walls of a pioneer home. All things considered, I had a right to wail: no doctor, no hospital, no anaesthesia, no nurse to bid me welcome—not even a neighbor woman. In fact, there was no adult about the house when I decided to make my advent into this vale of tears, except my mother. Mackie Ma was always a pretty independent bundle and game as they come. Further, having staged a half dozen similar productions, she sent my father off on horseback for Granny Cates, and we set about the business of getting me born.

We did a very creditable job of it, Granny said when she finally flung the bridle reins over the head of her steaming mare and hurried into the house, surrounded by a huddle of awed children, the oldest less than fourteen, to my valiant little mother trying as best she could to wrangle a very new one. Granny arrived in time to give me my first grooming, and many a time thereafter her capable, work-hardened hands soothed and comforted me.

Today, these two women still live: Granny, after years of selfless neighborhood service, now a bed-ridden invalid; Mackie Ma, active and alert, spoiling generations of grandchildren and great-grandchildren, loving flowers into bloom, fashioning innumerable quilts. Small wonder that these women, inured to hard living, aren't easy to get fussed, that their ceaseless tolerance never wears thin.

April 6, 1939

Granny Cates is dead and gone. How many years she had, nobody quite knows. Some said eighty, some said ninety, while some are sure she could not have lived less than a century.

However many it is, it was too few for Granny, for she lived life with a passion. Weary years she fought grimly to keep a spark of it. But the other day it became too complicated for her failing strength, and so she ho-hummed it off. She had no fatal disease. She suffered no especial pain. She simply ceased living.

Then Granny, who had trekked the wilderness behind slow oxen, who had ridden down cow trails in a lumbering covered wagon, who had ridden in state of a Sunday in a rawhide-bottomed chair set in the back of a spring wagon to the meeting house, who had locked a sinewy knee about the horn of a side-saddle and raced with rolls of hair dragging anchor from silvered hairpins to be at the bedside of a sick neighbor—Granny took her last earthly ride. I think I can see how Granny looked at that last ride, her grudging smile breaking into a rich chuckle as she saw the solemn procession form. "Here comes Roy Wilkerson," I think I hear her say, "with his red buggy. Now after all the riding I have done in my days, I'm to take my last one in that thing! Oh, well, let's get it over with!" And Granny, rebelling at the funeral splendor so unlike anything she had ever experienced in living, I can see her compromising with this thing of small moment, the mere matter of the conveyance for tired old bones.

I shouldn't be surprised, too, if the whole thing pleased her a little, though she'd be the last to admit it. She was always a lover of things bright and showy. Why, when other women of her age restricted their clothing to blacks and grays and lavenders, Granny stuck to the braver colors, especially rich yellows and russet reds. And small attentions pleased her all out of proportion to the effort involved. I remember once I went to talk to her about pioneering. I told her I wanted to write her up for the paper. I shan't forget the twinkle in her old blue eyes, nor the humorous down-turned corners of her lips nor the lusty laugh with which she greeted the idea. "Write me up? Goodgawdlmighty, child, what for?" But I knew that she was pleased to be in the paper and to hold again for a little while the center of interest of her community.

Eight years ago, when Life was done with Granny, Life found that Granny was not done with it. So she crawled up on her couch and wrapped its drapery about her—to watch the thing out. Eight years she stayed in bed, tended by her daughter, Ada. Granny always called her "Ader," and Ader she is to me. Life had been hard for Granny, but it's hardness had made it sweet. She had been nurse, doctor, counselor, neighbor to every family that moved into the settlement. The very simplicity of life made of Granny's day a thing with tentacles that reached into every home, into every life she knew. Such living had given savor to Granny's existence, had made her grow in courage, grace, fortitude, and character. Then, Granny had seen civilization follow her into the wilderness. She had seen hospitals displace neighborliness, doctors outmode friendly recommendations of herbs and nostrums. She had seen the State monopolize charity, church programs pass current for religion. She was made to feel that it wasn't the thing to shout in meeting. In fact, Granny lived to see society softening the character of a people, but Granny didn't like what she saw.

It almost seems as if Granny deliberately planned to save her own from the decadence of a pampering world. At any rate, in her eight years of invalidism she gave her Ader what society had removed from her doorway, the ready opportunity for a life of service. Nor did Granny make what you'd call a "good" patient. Nobody does who works at it eight years. Better than being a "good" patient, Granny made a colorful one: she visited with callers when she felt like it and wanted to. When she didn't, she simply closed her eyes and shut you out, and there was no rousing her unless she wanted to be roused. Nonetheless, little went on about the place she didn't know about. She kept count of the passing of the old settlers with a grim kind of satisfaction, averring on occasions that she'd outlive the kit and bilin', and almost she did.

For food she demanded and always got "grub"—no soft, pappy stuff for invalids. In her last years, it pleased her to turn night into day and day into night, sleeping through the hours when Ader worked and demanding to be entertained when it was time for Ader to sleep. She became a veritable tyrant, but never without her old sense of humor, for she realized to the end how spoiled she was—and she enjoyed it. So for eight years

Granny saw her daughter grow in courage, grace, fortitude, character, till when Ader shall gather with the saints around the Great White Throne to measure wingspread or to compare the size of diadems, few wings will be so wide or few diadems so bright till Ader compares hers with Granny's.

"Granny was never one to let the grass grow under her," said my mother, when I asked her how soon one might expect Granny to get to the bedside in that long-ago time. Now the grave grass grows over her. But heaven is already too rich with kith and kin, and hosts of friends, for Granny to stay long under grave grass. Then, too, her husband, Sam, who helped to dig the first grave in the cemetery where we put Granny, and who himself sleeps in the second, must be seen about.

Granny will enjoy the New Jerusalem I've heard her shout about under a brush arbor. But after a while I think she will slip away from Sam and the children and the saints, away from the Golden Streets, out to a little farm under a hill with a spring branch running through it, like her old home place. I think she will walk the spring branch, turning over the yellow leaves with a crooked stick, picking up a last year's pecan here and there, left by the squirrels. I think she will drop them to the bottom of the cut-in pockets in her robe to surprise Scip and Daisy with. I think she'll twist off a withe from a sappy sweet water ell-um for her celestial "toothbresh," and I think she'll pick up a bright stream-worn rock to put around the hollyhock bed in the yard before her mansion. Then I think she'll take off her shoes and walk barefoot across the new-plowed field, the heavenly breeze whipping at her bright yellow robes and stirring the hair at her temples. I think she'll walk so, for so I once came upon her in the long ago in her field one morning, her shoelaces tied across one arm, a pretty rock cradled in the crook of the other, and she gave me three pecans from the depths of her cut-in pocket. She liked the feel of the soft, cool dirt, she said, against her feet.

Granny Cates is dead and gone—dead to the aches and pains and creeping age, dead to sickness and sorrows and heartbreak, dead to days that are long and years that are short, dead to the fear of the unknown. Granny Cates is dead and gone, gone from her narrow little bed to a newness and fullness of life. Granny was the first to welcome me to living. She comforted childish hurts for me. Without saying a word about it, she taught me the blessedness of living in the lives of others. When it's time for me to go, I want to go where Granny is.

Two Essays

Share the first fruits of a life of service, for such sharing never lessens, but always multiplies the store.

Ethel Yeager's writing is seldom didactic—or at least not ostensibly so. Much of what she wrote pointed from the specific to the general, from recognizable and homely humans and human events to moral or philosophic principles implied, but rarely does she *teach:* she nudges, hints, cajoles, suggests. But on occasion, she prepared essays which tell a lot about her and the way she saw life. The first here was the prize winner in a 1938 contest celebrating the fiftieth anniversary of the Texas State Fair. The second was in "Yeagitorial" as an envoi to the old year.

o o o o o o o o o o o o o o o o

September 28, 1938

What the State Fair Means to Texas and the Southwest.

On October 8 Dallas is going to put on the vestments of the high priest while Texas and the Southwest lay upon the altar the first fruits of the hands and the brains and the hearts of a great people. The festivities are advertised under the title "The Fiftieth State Fair of Texas Golden Jubilee Celebration and Eighth Annual Southwestern Dairy Show." For sixteen days, the best of the products of this section will be on display to challenge the wonder and imagination of all who come to see.

Community fairs, county fairs, state fairs are as American as Plymouth Rock. After all, that which we in reverence call the First Thanksgiving, where a pilgrim band with dust on their feet and sweat on their gallus straps agreed to lay aside their day-to-day labors and meet for a few hours with their Sunday clothes on, is in its final analysis, nothing more nor less than a community fair—a coming of people for thanksgiving for harvest and a dedication of the first fruits of the earth to man's use: the biggest trout, the bluest-headed turkey, a stalk of Indian corn, if it be the best of one's labors, is enough for an American fair. The fact that the Pilgrim fathers and mothers and their Indian guests ate the exhibits makes it none the less a fair, for it had the fair spirit.

Now the Golden Jubilee Celebration State Fair of Texas and Southwestern Dairy Show at Dallas, October 8 - 23, is a fair that is differently American because it is the handiwork and brainwork of a people that is differently American—the people of the Southwest.

True, the leveling influence of rapid transportation and communication, of the press and the screen, grooms Farmer Corntassel's daughter and the sons of Ranchman Quickdraw on the campus of the state university so that it takes an iodine test to tell whether or not they are in the Social Register; and Sam Acheson's "35,000 Days in Texas" gets a sassy review in the New York *Herald Tribune* before the printer's ink is dry. Yet the people of the Southwest are different from the people of the East, because history has made them so. When they left the slopes of the Appalachian Mountains and fronted the Great Plains, necessity compelled them to make a new way of life. They were challenged by a virgin land. They went in and possessed it. They dressed it with farms and ranches and cities, with railroads and highways and six-lanes, with big and little churches pointing fingers to God, with schools.

All this they did for the virgin land in a new way, with wire and windmills, with broncos and six-shooters, with irrigation and crop control. The frontier woman came in fear and distrust, repelled by the unknown, yearning after luxuries she had loved and left by the river fords, eaten by loneliness. Dressing a new and untried land was not her idea of a wonderful time. But she came! Because her man felt a zest for life in the saddle, where Colonel Colt made all men equal, she followed. Her man was coming into the new land to make a home. What he made, she would keep! And today's gracious homes throughout the Southwest are monuments to these immigrant women and testimonials that today's Southwestern women have kept the faith with the pioneer mothers.

Verily the civilization of the Southwest is not simply an extension of the civilization of the East. It is, more fundamentally than any other, the American way of life, made by necessity of adjustment; and no exhibit in the great State Fair of Texas holds a specimen a fraction as important to the development of this country as the *man* and the *woman* of the Southwest.

The products of the new way of life are on display in lots and pens and booths at the State Fair of Texas for the fiftieth time, greater and grander than they have ever been before. To the producers they say: "Sons and daughters of the Southwest, behold, here are the first fruits of your fields and hills and homes. Your minds have imagined them, your hearts have loved them, your hands have made them. They are good. But remember, these are the *first* fruits. In the midst of your plenty there is poverty. There is illiteracy. There are slums. There is death. Let these words before you challenge you to achievement that will make the future point to you with more pride than glows in your hearts as you behold the fruits of your labors!"

To the 4-H'ers they say: "See how you have built on the works of those who have gone before you. Plan magnificently. Saddle yourself with untried responsibilities!"

To the farm lad, his untamed feet hot in the confines of new shoes, they say: "Here is your beginning. Others made it for you. The future depends upon you. Be a master farmer. There's a big job ahead. Live to feed the world!"

To the women and girls, they say: "Strong women mothered the Southwest. The world still has need of that kind of mother. Build better homes. Raise up sons and daughters who will call you blessed!"

To you and me and to all, they say: "Share the *first fruits* of a life of service, for such sharing never lessens but always multiplies the store!"

January 4, 1940

"Ring Out the Old"

Far and wide over the world, Old Man 1939 went out with a swift kick in the pants. Folks of every tongue were glad to see the last of him. Pretty generally, the world was fed up with Old Man 1939, said he was lousy with man's inhumanity to man, broken faiths, smashed traditions, bloodshed, war. These folks gave the raspberry to Pippa's God's-in-His-heaven and all's-right-with-the-world song and dubbed the singer a sentimental Pollyanna. They said Old Man 1939 was a mess.

But I think these folks are wrong about Old Man 1939. I think he was a pretty nice old chap. We ushered him all new and full of promise, a year ago, and honesty compels me to confess that he did a fairly representative job of his 365 days. One at a time, he brought out the days, some sunny, some full of rain. He did an average job of sorting them out. In due season he brought the seed time and the harvest, and unrolled the seasons in their accustomed order. The age-old laws of nature he kept in force, punishing the offenders and rewarding the observers. He kept the laws of health functioning during 1939 as well as they did the year God spoke and said, "Let there be light." To the very last day of 1939, he kept alive the sparks of hope in human hearts. When you come to think of it, that's about all Time's business. The rest of it is our doings.

As a member of the well-known and over-advertised human race, I have a conviction that we didn't do as well by 1939 as 1939 did by us. The fact is that we piled up a right un-nice stack of failures for the Old Man. As a world, we failed outstandingly during the year in humanity and humility. Nor have all the failures occurred in the region of the Maginot Line nor in the vicinity of the heathen Chinee, nor on the battlefields of Poland. My friends and I did not do right by Old Man 1939. For instance, a lot of charity we used to minister unto ourselves, we formed a nasty habit of passing on to the government. The fear of war has made us intolerant of folks not like us. The fear of loss of social security has made us suspicious of our neighbors.

We have taken Sunday for our day—a practice that, according to history, has always cost a people dear. There've been a lot of other ways, too, in which we have failed Old Man 1939. But you know as much about them as anybody else, because you've been working at this failure business about as hard as the next one.

Yessiree, there's been a lot of failures during 1939, but they have been ours, not the Year's. And unless we take our moral and spiritual selves out to the woodshed, we'll be as sick of 1940 a year from now as we are of 1939 today.

"Ring in the New"

Little old 1940 is already here. How do you like him? Promising chappie, don't you think? He promises we likely won't go to war, at least during his 366 days. That is, if we follow our long heads instead of our willful hearts. He promises to let us in on the story of the year—whether FDR will do it again or not—and won't that be fun? He says that in July we shall learn what sort of biscuit substitute Pappy will be passing around, if any. He dangles the prospect of a cotton market and dares us to get out of debt. (Who isn't in?) With a rainbow round his shoulders, he tantalizes with hints of four-bit wool. He promises a grain crop, but threatens with drought, just to show that he's not all peaches and cream. He gives us today and promises us tomorrow—maybe.

Doing anything about it?

Yeagitorial

About the time I make up my mind to be true to a candidate, he ups and makes a speech. I find that I care less and less for the people's would-be servants who stand like Gibraltar for the Constitution, who were born in a very loggy log cabin, and were kind to their poor old mothers, . . . the while they beg for the privilege of serving me.

When Yeager's first column, "Country Commonplaces," proved a hit, her editors asked her to write a second one, this time pitched not to community news but rather to her view of the world beyond. She called it "Yeagitorial" and filled it with her consideration of events around the world, much of it no doubt the distillation of conversations with her husband who was as avid—and acute—a news reader and commentator as ever drew breath. Its wide ranging scope shows her a woman intensely connected both to history and to the turmoil which surrounded the years of her writing—and it certainly gives the lie to any notion that those days were "a simpler time."

o o o o o o o o o o o o o o o o o

August 3, 1937

Have you chewed over the President's reasons for the veto of the low interest rates to farmers? It seems that he considered that the farmer of 1932 with $5,337,000,000 income was in a spot but that the farmer of 1936 with $9,530,000,000 income was sittin' pretty pretty. From where I sit, I haven't been able to see a lot of difference in the situation.

Some things like the price of things the borrowing farmer has to buy must come in here somewhere; and when it comes to balancing reasoning by "the things the farmer must buy," figures, of course, won't lie; but liars will and, I'm afraid, do. Farmers that I know who are using the Federal Farm Loans live pretty much as they did in 1932. Living in rain-barrel simplicity is less frequently a figure of speech than a rough reality. And the farmer, debtor to the F.L.B., who buckets the literal water from the realistic barrel into a round wash tub on Saturday nights for the weekly ablutions—well, his name is still legion, just one of the many Legion boys. A hot August week in the country as the guest of the F.L.B. borrower might change the President's idea of the 1936 farmer's ability to pay. If it wouldn't a February visit would.

But then, with the election coming up pretty soon, I guess he couldn't get off anyway.

January 11, 1938

House Majority Leader Sam Rayburn didn't let his Texans down when asked to comment on the President's message to Congress. Said the Texas countryman with the terseness that characterizes him, "The message was assuring to everybody who wants to be assured." Laconic speech still has its power when it finds a body who is able to use it.

++++++++++++++++++++++

Must be election year. I see by the last issue of *The Brady Standard* that commissioners Snearly and Edmiston are already scraping their wings at the public. But the fact remains that it is more important to you and to me who sits in for us on the Commissioners' Court than it is who gets Jimmy Allred's chair or F.D.R.'s.

July 14, 1938

Such a choice for governors and things! About the time I make up my mind to be true to a candidate, he ups and makes a speech. I find that I care less and less for the people's would-be servants who stand like Gibraltar for the Constitution of these United States of Amurrica, who unconditionally endorse the alphabet, who were born in a very loggy log cabin and were kind to their poor old mothers, who will lower the taxes and raise the wages, who promise the aged a bunch of blue ribbons to tie up their bonny brown hair, and who toot loudly on their bugles and beat the drums resoundingly as they point to the medals jingling on their manly breasts, the while they beg for the privilege of serving me.

Really, there ought to be a law that all politicians should make their speeches sitting down. The posture would curtail some of the effervescent oratory. Besides, that is the position they will occupy most of the time after the election.

I don't know a lot about politics, but I understand that a platform is made up of planks and that its chief purpose is to hold somebody up. I've begun to suspect that that somebody is me.

++++++++++++++++++++++

Ma Gainer spoke the way out for producer and consumer. She gave the answer in the back of the book when she said, "Right now I could use a bale of cotton in my home if I had the money to buy it."

Multiplied by America, what she said was: "Why are crops curtailed? How can there be an actual surplus when the standard of living is below comfort?" We could use more towels, sheets, pillow cases, mattresses, bed spreads, dish towels, aprons, dresses, shirts, trousers, under clothing, hose, rugs, curtains, shades, and dozens of unguessed cotton products if we had the money to buy them. Such a program would put the producer, manufacturer, distributor, and consumer to work. The natural way to regulate production is to work toward raising the standard of living in the home. The brain truster who can solve the problem and show the economic world how to get Ma Gainer's answer will be another Moses leading the host out of bondage.

July 28, 1938

This is a good week in July. A lot of very tiresome people have deflated their balloons of the hot air of personal ambition, and the country can now twirl its radio knob in search of Gracie Allen or Charlie McCarthy without having to turn through a "The next quarter hour has been bought and paid for on a political basis." Never before has it been so plain how much better for the digestion of a nation are the nit-wits and fun-making blockheads than the Hitlers and the Mussolinis and grim Texas politicians.

When an office seeker begins to talk about the Alamo and Texas and keeping the faith, something seems to tell me that I am in the presence of mine enemy, and the hair on the back of my neck begins to rise. After all, the job of running the government of this state is a job of running a some-million dollar business. And business is best attended to by thinking and not by feeling—your business and mine and the state's.

If it won't stretch your imagination completely out of shape, suppose you owned a million dollar business which you were going to delegate to someone to operate for you. In that case, how would you warm up to an applicant who handed you a line like this: "Mr. Thus-and-so, if you will let me handle your business, I promise to live up to the traditions of the Thus-and-sos. Their glorious past thrills me with admiration. I stand uncovered before them. I look back to the time when they branded mavericks while nobody was looking and then beat the sheriff to the state line. The Thus-and-sos were the backbone of the nation, and if you will hire me to run the business of the Thus-and-sos, I promise etc., etc., etc. and any number of other etcs. Besides, I was born in a log cabin and was ever so kind to my poor old mother. And I sold newspapers on the street."

Tut tut. Oratory is an appeal to the way the listener feels—a fine thing in its place—but it has no part in political speech, where the listener needs to think, not to feel.

September 1, 1938

Lesson I

Uncle, what is that bell in the college ringing for?

Well, Nevvie, this is September, and that's the school bell.

School bell? Hotcha! Take my shovel and gimme my football! I'm rearin' to go!

Keep your shovel, laddie. You won't be going back to college for this year.

But why? I like to go to college. It's fun.

Yes, I know. But American youth is backed up on the land now. Only thirty percentum of the crop will be going to college this year.

Only thirty percent? Why, Unkie—

Yes, I know, Nevvie. It's the smallest percentum since the Civil War. It's just the way things are.

Lesson II

Hey, Unkie, what am I going to do with this shovel? All the family men are digging in the ditches. There's no room for me.

Well, Nevvie, you might move over to one side and dig ditches and then fill them up again.

What for?

So 'twill give you practice. You might be a family man one day.

Lesson III

Look, Uncle, it seems sorta silly digging ditches and filling them up. 'Tisn't any fun. How about going to the city? I'm young and strong. I could stand the night life in the hot spots, and I understand traffic signals, and . . .

No doubt, Nevvie, but what do you plan to use for money in the city?

Oh, I could get a job in a factory.

Steady there, boy. The factories, that is, those that are running at all, are not running at capacity and so are holding a long waiting list of trained employees. They couldn't use you. Better practice with your shovel.

Lesson IV

Or, Uncle, I could get a job in an office.

Just what was your IQ up at the college, boy? Offices don't need help with factories closed. Where's your shovel?

Lesson V

Well, I could sell. . . .

Sell? Who to, Nevvie? With factories and offices on the blink, who's got money to buy? The trouble with you is . . .

Yes, I get the idea. I'm backed up on the land.

Lesson VI

Say, Uncle Sam, I know I'm backed up on the land, all right. But tell me, how'd this thing all get started anyway?

Well, Nevvie, you're a little young, but it's the modern practice to explain the Facts of Life to youth, so I'll try if you will listen closely. You see, Nevvie, the industrial world had a depression and it had to curtail production. Manufacturers had to . . .

Yes, I know about that, but why?

Why? Because the consumer had ceased to buy. Of course, when the consumer can't buy, the manufacturer can't continue to manufacture. He doesn't any longer need the country man's raw . . .

But, Uncle, begin at the beginning. Why did the consumer cease to buy?

Exactly as I told you, he ceased to buy because his income had been reduced when the factories closed down. One can't buy when he has no income, you see.

No, frankly, Uncle, I don't see. You're going around in circles and somewhere you've missed the beginning. Who started this thing? It seems there's a missing part in your explanation. How'd you get in the picture as the check writer for shovel pushers and crop cutter downers and everybody's banks—even the banker's banker?

Smart boy, huh? Arguing with your elders. Shame on you! What'd you do with that shovel?

Lesson VII

Backed up on the land, huh? Dig a ditch, huh? Then fill it up, huh? So I'll be in practice, huh? Uncle Sam's sort of funny if he thinks that's getting anywhere. Shovel? I'll spade in Ma's garden with it. I'll try inbreeding some seed. A guy up in Ilinois did it with corn and is on the way to a million dollars on what he learned. And he hadn't finished the eighth grade.

I'll see what I can learn. Nobody's found out how to control the pink boll worm, but someday somebody will get the idea.

Or somebody ought to solve the problem of the loco weed that kills sheep. A fellow out at Menard just the other week found a way to control the horn fly that's been pestering cattle for ages.

I'll make a set of books for this farm and see what's paying off and what's not, and maybe we can all together figure out the why and what to do. I'll get a hobby, a hobby that will teach me. Then, too, I'll see what I can do to take that little mob of snipe-sucking street waifs off the pavement—social something-or-other we call it at college. I'll read. I'll read a heck of a lot. And I'll see what I can do about being a member of my own family—try out some of my company manners and charm on the dog.

There's a lot of things that's not been done before. I'll learn. Radio's new. Science is barely scratched. Farm science is so new it still smells. And medicine . . . I'll shine up my thinker so slick somebody'll need what I've got—or I'll need it myself. By cracky, I'll even go to church and see if I can find out what makes folks so sleepy when they go.

Ma! Oh, Ma! Care if I try some leaf mold on this petunia bed of yours? OK. And while I'm gone to the creek for a load, how about you making one of your own especially individual apricot pies for dinner? Nobody in miles can hold a candle to your apricot pies. Then after dinner let's you and me . . . Say, where's my shovel?

November 3, 1938

Poor Mr. O'Daniel! He seems like such a good man, but forever tumbling out of the frying pan into the ashes. A lot of tumbles. There's the Great Tumble, of course, when he was scooping up advertising for Hillbilly flour and found that he had scooped unto himself the redhot governorship of the State of Texas. I can but faintly imagine his surprise.

It must have been like unto the surprise experienced years ago by 'Fessor Gualt when he was one-room school teaching the sires of the present problem children of Rochelle. Between 'Fessor Gualt and his Moseley-Neal-Cates-Williamson-Short-*et als*, a game—well, a sort of a game, anyway—had been pretty well perfected. It was the indoors continuation of "Keeps," in which 'Fessor Gualt, in awed and awful silence, permitted surreptitiously handled marbles which slipped through too eager fingers to roll ominously down to the front of the schoolroom, where he, with baleful look at the dropper, impressively stooped and picked up the offending sphere, letting it fall significantly to the bottom of his cavernous pocket, from whence no marble was ever known to return.

One winter's day, a resourceful lad was absently reading from his history book about the ancients' "trial by fire," when he conceived an idea for varying the one-sided game of dropped marbles. So before "accidentally" dropping his next one, he pretended that it was an ancient receiving his trial by fire through the coals in the apron of the stove. When the big chalk "center" was glowing like one of the coals, the inventive one "accidentally" dropped it from the apron to the old pine floor, where it rolled toward the unsuspecting 'Fessor, leaving a scarcely perceptible but drama-laden trail of smoke in its wake.

That was the marble that 'Fessor Gualt stooped to pick up—not as a matter of marble gaining, but as a part of the regular routine of disciplining the lads and lassies under his care. Only a diligent flour salesman, carrying out the regular routine duties of advertising, who finds that he has scooped up the governorship of a rollicking state can really appreciate the sudden and hot surprise that was 'Fessor Gault's that winter's day.

Then there was the original Pension Tumble, which glued the hands of the "have gots" to their bankrolls and the cautious eye on the flour man, and the Race Track Tumble with its "open mindedness" that was such a shock to the Bible Belt constituents.

Newest, as the paper goes to press, is the Capital Punishment Tumble. In this case, Mr. O'Daniel reached for the Decalogue, only to find that Moses' medicine is too strong for Texas politics, for according to Columnist Landrum of the Dallas *News*, eight of the Ten Commandments carry capital punishment as penalty for failure to obey them.

I'll bet the only fun a fellow gets out of being governor of this state is when he dresses up to welcome a delegation or to lay a cornerstone or to open up a new bridge. Poor Mr. O'Daniel!

December 8, 1938

That something is wrong for and with the cotton farmer everyone is agreed. Even on the net results, everyone is agreed: the little yellow basket that the cotton farmer lost had the world market in it. And if he doesn't find it, it's plain that he will die—or that which is just about as uncomfortable—be forced on the relief. And while theorizers are hunting for it, the cotton farmer, tenant, or landowner is having the hardest pull he's ever had to keep the kids in school, the family warm and fed, and the wolf out of range.

The local grocery stores have already felt the tug of a hard winter in increased sales of molasses, an infallible sign of lean living. Last year's suits, hats, coats, and frocks are going to be the vogue this winter regardless of chic. Indications are that waistlines will be slimmer. The school kids' list of must-haves receives a closer parental scrutiny than usual and evokes some sour remarks into the whiskers about "free schools."

But just why did America lose the world cotton market? Ah, there's where everybody on the sideline has an answer. And the Texas farmer who plowed up and down cotton rows ten years ago, raised four and one half million bales of cotton and sold it for fifteen and a half cents stops to learn the why of the eight and a half price. His straightforward mind that has been taught to reason from cause to effect becomes hopelessly muddled with a jumble of terms—Old Farm Board, Bankhead, Triple A, parity price, parity income, Smoot-Hawley, poor staple, debtor-credit nation, round-hog buying, market control, production control, the gov'ment. He turns away from the explainers, his mind lost in a maze of words. The only sure thing he can tie to is the feel of the gov'ment check in his jeans. Where the money came from, why he got it, who finally pays the bill, the how, well—he leaves those things to the explainer, too. He reckons that he'll vote for the bunch that's in. That check sure came in handy for molasses and such.

The menacing element in the situation is not the lost world market; that might be recovered or circumvented. Nor eight-cent cotton; that might be endured. Nor yet the molasses; that might be eaten for a time. The menacing thing about it all is that the system is making of the American countryman an apathetic acceptor of checks and ideas—a peonized "brother of the ox." Our danger is that we stand to lose another little yellow basket, this time with the American way of life in it.

January 12, 1939

Not all country commonplaces happen outside the city limits. For instance, Grandma Roosevelt's big boy made a speech upon Capitol Hill the other day the effects of which will be felt over in the back forty at least up to the time it's all straightened out about who'll be driving Baldy in 1940.

Funny thing about that speech. Everybody heard the same words, but different folks got different ideas about what Mr. Roosevelt meant. It was sort of like the game called "Gossip" we play at parties where everybody whispers something in his neighbor's ear, like "Betty Brown's got a new beau," and it is whispered on down the line till it comes out at the other end something like "Molasses and sulphur is good for the croup." Only this speech of Mr. Roosevelt's wasn't whispered. It was broadcast over the wide, wide world. Seems there'd be no call for folks not agreeing on what the man was saying. But, take us Democrats: we said the speech was the sound utterance of a statesman, a state paper to proclaim the savior of his country to posterity. That is, that's what we Democrats that talked said.

On the other hand, the Republicans felt sure the speech was the last squawk of a fowl whose tail feathers had been plucked in the last election.

The British said the speech was the real mustard, and Mr. Chamberlain tucked a copy of it in his hip pocket to pull on Mussolini when he goes over to play in Il Duce's back yard, provided that gentleman gets nasty about who slides down whose cellar door.

Over in Paris, the French dittoed the British attitude. In fact, the English ditto is quite the mode in Paris now.

Italy must have thought Cactus Jack wasn't muttering through his sombrero last summer when he opined, anent the elections, "You can't beat four billion dollars," for they said in the land of the Caesars that Roosevelt's bugaboo about the danger "from without" was just a very dead herring dragged across the trail to keep the American public's nose off the stench of her own election scandal.

And Germany was sad about the whole thing. They seem awfully afraid that Mr. Roosevelt intends to make a dictator out of himself some dark night—not a nice, comfortable dictator like their fuehrer, but a mean old nasty one without Herr Hitler's "spirit of peace."

All this diversity of opinion calls to mind the funny little verses about the six blind men and the elephant. You remember, the blind man who felt the elephant's side and said it was like a wall, while the one who felt his tail thought the beast was like a rope. Then there was the tusk, the trunk, the leg, and the ear feelers, each of whom interpreted the elephant as it was revealed to him. All they got out of it was an argument.

I can't believe there is as much bad eyesight in the case of the President's speech as there was in the poem about the elephant. Rather, it seems to me, an old text is fitting: "There is none so blind as those who will not see."

As I listened to Mr. Roosevelt's speech, sitting in my tax-covered chair before my tax-plastered radio, warming my feet before a free wood fire in my tax-wrapped stove, I noticed that the wildest cheering followed the announcement that no curtailment of spending was to be considered. Which means that the store-boughten things around these diggin's will continue to be tax swaddled—with my income. The thought got to fretting me about where my practically theoretical income was coming from. Of course, there's my gov'ment check.

As Kay Kaiser says, "Isn't that silly?" Besides, I never could see any net gains on a cow that sucked herself. In theory, it looks like a good idea, but considering the nature of a cow, it just won't work out to pay a profit in practice.

There was one fellow up on Capitol Hill listening to that speech who either didn't think Mr. Roosevelt was very cute or who wasn't feeling good that day. Anyway, he got his name in the papers because he didn't cheer the President nor his speech—just sat there real close to Grandma Roosevelt and the President's wife, too, and looked glum through the whole thing. A lot of people looked at him during the speech, sort of the way a sneak peeks at the town's blackest sinner or biggest hypocrite at revival meetings when the preacher "pours it on 'em." The uncheerful uncheerer was named Hans Thomsen, and his home address is Berlin, Germany. He's over here on something about his country's business—nobody seems too certain just what.

February 2, 1939

The governor has come in for something of a horselaugh for jacking up the help about eating dollar meals and sleeping in two-buck beds as they go about over the country tending to John Q. Taxpayer's business. The governor, in making his criticisms, did what critics should always, but seldom, do: he suggested a substitute plan—in this case, thirty-five cent meals and dollar beds.

Ruffled gentlemen come back with hot words about "greasy spoons" and third-rate hotels, countering that the whole amount spent for meals and hostelry by the government would amount only to a something-itty-something of a fraction of one percent of the total cost of government, and then they pulled the old saw about straining at a gnat and swallowing a camel.

Now there seems to be a strong sentiment against camel swallowing; but practically everybody old enough to pay taxes had seen gnats that needed a good straining at. Having walked through the Looking Glass only two weeks ago, Mr. O'Daniel possibly hasn't been able to get a good perspective of the governmental camels yet. As self-appointed spokesman for John Q., I'd say the state is lousy with them—visible only to duly elected representatives of the Peepul—and, frankly, we are considering what Mr. O'Daniel will do when he stumbles upon them. Will he let out yelps loud enough to be heard back on John Q.'s side of the Looking Glass, or will he, following tradition, be struck cautiously dumb? We are wondering, and there be those who hope.

Now as I view the situation from John Q.'s side of the Looking Glass, I am left wondering what is a "greasy spoon" and to whom? After all, the folks who are privileged to sign the State of Texas to dinner checks are only the hired help who carry on the business of the state, and I am acquainted with a fairly representative number of Texans whose tax receipts make it possible for the aforementioned dinner checks to be honored. Most of them are farmers, stockmen, employers, and employees in small businesses, and school teachers, the majority of whom would be stepping high, wide, and handsome if they ate and slept up $61.50 in thirty days.

Based on twelve months' salaries, the school teachers would have considerably less than a ten-dollar bill left, and a lot of the other folks take it that the teachers—who are also government employees—have it pretty soft. Now I'm not sure how far down the scale of living my acquaintances and I belong, but it seems a slice of Americana to support hired help on a scale of living that is better than the average can afford for themselves.

Of course, folks whose expense accounts are being limelighted may have million-dollar stomachs and bell-hop complexes. So thirty-five cent meals and dollar hotels may be slumming to them. It doesn't exactly stretch my imagination to think there are possibly camel drivers to whom dollar meals and two-dollar hotels are "greasy spooning." Yet I can't figure that a something-itty-something of one percent of my tax receipt pays off the damage; so I'm all for the governor's gnat straining. It might sharpen the eyesight for camel hunting. Besides, he wouldn't swallow no camels if there ain't none, I betcha.

May 11, 1939

At school census time it hits us in the eye that our rural population in this section is decreasing. It somewhat startles us that the farmer has packed up his wife and kids and moved out of the dell. His exodus started when motorized horsepower put old Jude and Beck on a pension—or sold them for fertilizer. At that time the bright and early tenant farmer equipped himself with machinery. Then, with less expenditure of man-hours, he was able to multiply greatly the amount of labor he and his wife and kids and Jude and Beck formerly turned off. The less efficient tenant was forced off his acres by this machine farming, and he and his wife and kids pretty generally ended up in a shanty on the fringe of town where the head of the family took on odd jobs when he could get them; and when he couldn't he added to the town's unemployment problem. Then, as the efficiency of farm machinery was increased, the machine-owning tenant could take on more and more acres; and it was necessary for him to work to his own and his machinery's limit, because with the slump in farm prices, the cost of the machinery, its upkeep and its operating expenses, he was kept scratching to realize even as much for his own "take" as he had formerly realized with Jude and Beck while he had a two-figure market.

Things rocked along for a while with the farm owner under the new arrangement, yet seldom daring to saddle himself with the risky business of equipping himself with costly machinery in the face of low prices. The equipped tenant was treading debt water up to his chin to meet payments on split-note equipment. The ex-tenant became the town's "pore," instead of the country's "pore." Then came a crop of Government Lettuce—crisply green government checks paid on the land for crop curtailment. To the landowner, the checks were a sort of insurance against crop failure. Now he could afford to take the risk. He did the logical thing—he began to buy his own equipment, hire part-year labor, raise his own crops, and cash his own government checks. And the bright and early tenant? Too often he was forced to follow the beaten trail to town. Now he gets up bright and early to get to his WPA or PWA or other alphabet job. So at census time the country finds itself short of scholastics.

Who has benefitted? What slumped farm prices? Where does the Government Lettuce germinate? Where do the alphabet checks come from? Darned if I know, but it does seem to me that the whole kit and bilin' has its living cut short and its taxes cut long, and the country is a lonesome place since the kids have moved from the old swimming hole to the pavement.

June 22, 1939

The most significant story for this country last week did not concern itself with royalty dining out of golden goblets nor with the gracious hospitality of the nation's leaders. It came out of McKinney, Texas, where 200 families of uprooted farmers, camping on two filthy city lots at Princeton while they labor in the onion harvest—packing onions at six cents a sack—muttered sullenly when a newspaper man and a Farm Security worker came to the camp for data and pictures. Some of the campers handled pocket knives and sticks in that sickeningly significant way you see it done in pictures of the French Revolution, when you whisper to quiet your fears, "It can't happen here!" One hurled an onion at the visitors' car as it drove off. The things that rankled with the harvesters were "necktie" people taking pictures of their poverty to parade in newspapers and thin-worn promises of governmental alleviation of their living conditions.

It is estimated that there are adrift in Texas 150,000 such migrant laborers. They are, as a rule, family people who remember a feeling of security they left behind them with the land, which no longer sustained them. Their recent kinship with the soil has left in them a fierce pride that resents charity and pity. Shuttled back and forth over the country, following the citrus and spinach crops of the Valley, the onion harvest of North Texas, and back again to the cotton harvest in the Valley, following it north again as winter set in, this growing army of laborers is causing sleepless nights for those who hate change and revolution. "Human tumbleweeds," they have been dubbed.

Now, a single family uprooted from its home and turned out onto the highway is lonely and bewildered. Squatting along the roadside by the campfire, the puzzled father knows the bitter taste of failure, and fear sits with him. "I was driven from the security of my home by a tractor—by a system—by the man higher up. A piece of land was once my home. A roof was over my children. Now I am alone, without a chance to work for bread. How shall I fill the mouths of my children tomorrow?" The mother grows desperate with despair . . . .

A day's travel, two days, and the single family comes to the camp lot of the uprooted. Here another man comes to sit with the lone man beside the campfire. Two men. It is significant. The story now is, "We were driven from the security of our homes by a tractor—a system—the man higher up." We, us, our. It is the seed of revolution, and it multiplies like yeast set in the sun.

In Europe, years of dealing with the disconnected have taught rulers how to control this dangerous thing. The method is simple: rulers keep these two men apart. They implant in their hearts fear, suspicion, and hate toward each other so that they are eternally at each other's throats. A workable system for Europe, where people have forgotten the taste of liberty and security. It wouldn't, I think, work with the onion harvesters of McKinney, Texas, for the memory of another day is still poignantly fresh in their minds and hearts. The strength of the soil is yet in them. Together they are neither so lonely nor so bewildered as when they first hit the highway. They will be reckoned with . . . .

There is another side of this same picture. While harvesters pack onions at six cents a sack under conditions where one man and his four children were able to earn $4.08 in a day and a half—their first work in two weeks—the grower markets his crop for 42½ cents per bushel. These figures show that one-seventh of the grower's "take" goes out for the harvesting. His other crop expenses include seed or "slips," planting, cultivation, labor, sacks, transportation, as well as initial investment in land and machinery—and his taxes. If there is an optimistic side to this onion business, it has to be still another side. The big difference between the packer and the grower is that the grower still has a roof over him.

September 14, 1939

Men make peace at council tables? Men with hates and fears, men with ambitions, with suspicions, with distrust, with selfishness, men with memories? Even good men have them.

And it helps to understand things when we remember that not all men who sit at council tables are good men. Too, both good men and bad men who counsel for peace know they are doll-ragging when they go gallivanting off in airplanes to shiny seats at long tables.

Then why do they go? Because the fat's in the fire and folks expect them to do something about it. Thus the circulation of the umbrella, the razzle-dazzle of reporters, the blare of news bulletins, lots of headlines, racy stories of poundings on tables and stevedore name-callings. When it is over, the fat's still in the fire, but the folks have sort of got used to the stink, and the world bumps along as it did, or with new bumps.

No, peace, when and if it is made, will not be made at council tables. It will be made in cradles, where children learn to love and appreciate—not patronize—Little Black Sambo, Little Brown Koko, and Little Yellow Lin Tu Fu, where mothers echo the song of the shepherds about an Asiatic baby that slept in a manger because there was no room in the inn. Peace will be made in supervised sandpiles, where selfish natures learn respect for the rights of others. It will be made in woodsheds where parents with ideals and razor straps will teach the proper respect for authority. Peace will be made in schools where teachers aim at educating emotions and shaping attitudes.

But, truth to tell, peace likely won't be made at all; and in the end of time there will be wars and rumors of wars—because it's a lot of trouble to be intelligent, militant parents every day in the week. Besides, readin' and writin' and 'rithmetic is such an endless job one bogs down and doesn't get around to the business of emotions and attitudes.

May 30, 1940

Today's country commonplaces are about polly-ticks. I can think of nothing more commonplace in the country at this time. Besides, that's what comes of being "talked of for Congress." The fact that readers of this column saw in its homespun ideas some indication that I might be of service in representing them in federal legislation had a series of effects on me. At first I suppose I was mostly stunned with the audacity of the idea. Then, remembering how completely I am nobody, I was amused. But the persistent sincerity of the originators of the idea sobered, impressed, honored, and humbled me. That day I began my political education; and if, when I have groped my way out of my present abyss of political ignorance, I can be of service to my neighbors, I shall be happy "to make myself available." I believe that is the generally accepted phrase for saying, "Sure I want to run—who doesn't?"

And it's more than a good idea, in spite of what you think when you first hear about it. Farm people, country people should learn that it is important for them to have full representation when it comes to dealing with all public questions. Editor Clarence Poe says, "Hasn't the time come when the right thing to do is to put more farm people (farmers, farm women, rural teachers, preachers, and doctors) into positions of authority? Why not let's put more of them on our county governing boards, in our state legislatures, in Congress, and in all governing boards, commissions, and public bodies?"

I didn't know how right Editor Poe is till the other day when I went to see Judge Cobb about a divorce. There I learned that while, in the eyes of the State of Texas, the marriage contract is a simple civil contract between the state, the husband, and the wife, yet, when that contract is broken, the party seeking redress will find it necessary to employ a lawyer, at a healthy fee, to "draw up the papers." "To draw up the papers?" I remonstrated. "Why can't I draw up the papers? Why can't anybody who can read and write 'draw up the papers' if the contract has been broken? Seems to me, as many papers of that kind as have been 'drawn up' in this courthouse, the papers ought practically to draw themselves up! Isn't there a form to follow?" The judge smiled in a bored fashion. "No," he said, "there isn't a form. And while I wouldn't say, in the course of time, you couldn't draw up a set that would meet the legal requirements, I do say you'll find it cheaper to employ a lawyer—and quicker."

Now, who do you suppose made the "legal requirements" so involved as to require the services of a lawyer to "draw up the papers"? You guessed it—it's that bunch of very clever lawyers we have been sending places to "represent" us. They are really clever fellows, and that's what's the matter with them. Still, by the time we got a cowpenful of country people elected to represent us, I suppose we'd have to use political pull to milk the cows—human nature being what it is.

No, I didn't get the divorce. It's cheaper this way.

In days gone by, the office seekers had to be able to call all the constituents by name, kiss the babies, pass out cigars. Now it's different. The modern office seeker calls everybody "darling," makes the babies kiss him, and takes cigars from the voters, just to get the voter accustomed to having things taken from him.

But the modern successful politician must have a band. However, that isn't an insoluble problem. There are ways, it seems, of getting a band.

A hangover from the old days, though, is a platform. Politicians still have platforms. I don't know yet exactly what for, because they all sound alike. For instance, they all endorse the alphabet, and with reservations, the Ten Commandments, together with the Constitution, the log cabin, their mother's knee, selling newspapers on the street when they were boys—and Our Old Folks.

Against the time when I have fitted myself to answer my country's call, I have started working on my own platform. I think I shall string along with the others in raising no objection to the alphabet, the Mosaic Law, etc., etc., etc., on through to Our Old Folks. Here I think I shall branch out, shall blaze a new trail, shall seek a new horizon. In short, I shall originate a new plank. It begins like this: "For all the Old Folks who have been good, I shall advocate a warm, well-lighted, comfy chimney corner, a tolerant philosophy, a reputation for wisdom and plenty of grandchildren." All of this, not as the just deserts of old age, but because the loving, tender care of the young, the old, and the helpless deepens and broadens, strengthens and blesses the home life of a people and builds a nation strong. For the irrepressible oldsters, those who have accumulated years without aging—I mean folks like Jack Crew and his sisters Blanche and Grace—I advocate in addition to the above a key of their own so they will have to give account to nobody of their comings and goings. God bless them—and keep a weather eye out for them!

In this talk about running for Congress, I heard a lot said about $10,000. So far, I haven't been able to find out whether that's what it costs to run or that's what you get for running. I've given it a lot of thought, and it seems to me, considering the amount of effort I put into a job of work, to translate it into folding money, the $10,000 must be what it takes to run. Nobody's services could be worth that much money.

August 1, 1940

After the humiliation of France, Adolph Hitler, taking a page from the old caesars' notebook, returned to his capitol riding into the city over flower-carpeted streets, while his people hailed him as triumphator—the title used by conquering caesars when they rode in triumph through the streets of ancient Rome. Now a lot of detailed news comes out of Germany nowadays, and small embellishments of the hero's triumphal entrance have reached us. So I have been guessing just how Romanized the recent triumphal entry was. According to history, in ancient days the triumphator, robed in royal purple, crowned with laurel, flanked by prisoners and surrounded by spoils of war, rolled in his chariot through the streets amid the cheers of the spectators. It was a grand affair, and to prevent the conqueror from becoming too conceited, a wretched slave was perched on a high seat, and it was his duty to bend down, from time to time, and whisper in the conqueror's ear, "Remember, you are nothing but a man."

Then, too, a little bell was hung under the chariot, in such a way that it tinkled all the time. This ringing was to remind the conqueror that he must always be good or he would again hear it when he was led to prison or to the gallows.

Likely the herr didn't go in for the details of the ancient practices, and it's probably of no consequence anyway; for in spite of the whisper and the bell, the old caesars forgot, and so their memory is dust.

++++++++++++++++++++++

Have you heard that the folks got back home? The Federal Bureau of Agricultural Economics reported in July that on January 1, 1940, there were 32,245,000 folks on American farms—making the largest farm population in twenty-four years and edging very near to the all-time high record of 1916, when the count showed 32,530,000 folks in the country. Although the report came in mid-summer, somebody must have been watching the moving vans headed toward the cabin in the corn, for both Republicans and Democrats made a bid for the rural vote by selecting Senator McNary, veteran former of agriculture laws, and Secretary of Agriculture Wallace as vice-presidential bait for the forty-odd percent of the population now living in rural America.

This return to the soil raises a lot of questions; it's likely to raise a lot of cain before they are answered. What are the Joads going to do, now that we have them back home? Why did they come back? Do they remember why they left? Is the tractor still tractoring tenants off the premises? With the world market shot to smithereens, what is the forty-odd percent of the population living in rural America going to use for money? How abundant is the crop of Government Lettuce that comes out from Washington in crisp green checks for the horny handed tiller of the soil? Well, I admit it's all past me, but I'm glad the folks are back. There's still the cow, sow, and hen, and none of the tombstones in the Rochelle graveyard records the fact that any of my neighbors ever died of starvation.

September 5, 1940

We went to visit our grandchild and her parents in their trailer-house in Beaumont. When we got there, they had company. Jane was as calm as a crock of clabber. She said finding room in a trailer-house is a matter of technique and company is never any bother if her guests are *narrow*-minded. We stayed a week and were quite comfortable. Jane says to compress her housekeeping, she buys *condensed* milk, refuses *double*-yolked eggs, and that they run to *narrow* and *pin* stripes for their wardrobes. Wayne is experiencing a little more difficulty in fitting his six-foot-something-or-other into the seven-by-twenty foot home. He has been teaching the dog to wag his tail up and down instead of from side to side, and in order to fit the cat into the trailer-house scheme, they have employed a pucker-string operation, taking him in in the morning and letting him out at night.

My countryman and I went fishing in the Gulf with Wayne, the kind of fishing where you throw a reelful of line out and bring back funny looking things on your hook. It's the first time I ever fished without a cork, and if our fishing places here were snag-free, I'd go in for that kind of stuff.

We Fifth Columned the State Republican Convention while we were in Beaumont. We sneaked in like suck-egg dogs and heard the Governor of Colorado tell how Mr. Willkie is going to beat Mr. Roosevelt and take all our government checks away from us and give them to the Republicans. Republicans, in a close-up, are an awful looking lot. We saw Clarence Ousley. He looks as if he'd enjoy taking nickels out of babies' banks. And that Creager fellow—why, all he lacks is a wicked black moustache to twirl, and he would be the spit image of the villain that hisses, "Marry me, my proud beauty, or I'll foreclose on the mortage on the old homestead!" They talked like politicians.

Finally, I heard the speaker saying that Mr. Willkie is going to put electric lights in all the poor Republicans' houses when he's elected. That is, I think that's what he said Mr. Willkie's going to do. You see, I couldn't listen very well, my conscience bothered me so. It's just not in me to lead a double life like that—good, honest Democrat that I am. I kept sitting there brooding over my election pledge to support the nominees of my party—or whatever the pledge is. I got to thinking how Jim White, editor of the *Banner Bulletin* and watchdog of the Democratic Party in the Heart O' Texas, would grieve if he knew I was trifling on the party, way off down at Beaumont. I thought of all the nice, crisp checks, too, that Mr. Roosevelt has sent us, and we needed every one of them. As I sat there, I declare to you, I felt downright mean and terribly out of place—like a love-child at a homecoming. Though I suffered, we stayed all the way through and shook hands with the governor along with the rest of the folks. But I gave my hands a lysol bath, washed my mouth out with lye soap, and said my prayers when I got home.

They have big mosquitoes in Beaumont. On the way back from the Republican Convention meeting, I heard a conversation between two of them that had caught a big, fat Republican wardheeler and were about to eat him. "My, my," gloated one mosquito to another, "ain't this fellow prime? I thought these blue-bellied Yankee Republicans would be wiry, tough devils."

"Don't be silly," the other mosquito replied. "This is not a blue-bellied Yankee Republican. This is a Texas Republican, just an ambitious Democrat that voted for Hoover. They are all juicy—they taste like post-offices and pork-barrels!"

November 7, 1940

Soon it will be Armistice Day again. Twenty-one years have passed since the signing of the Armistice, that historical document that ended the four longest years in history—twenty-two years since American youth rallied to the call to "make the world safe for democracy." Was it futility? A heroic, but empty gesture? A wild, impractical dream?

With the world in the mess it is in today, short-sighted thinking might so brand our part in World War I. Just so, short-sighted thinking branded Lincoln a dreamer when he begged that "we here highly resolve that these dead shall not have died in vain—that this nation, under God, shall have a new birth of freedom." The same kind of thinking would call Dr. Jess Lazear's a heroic but empty gesture when he allowed a mosquito to suck blood from the back of his hand and died a few days later of yellow fever, a martyr to science. A wild, impractical caprice must have been the way Florence Nightingale's wealthy friends characterized her journey to the Crimea, where the sick soldiers called her The Lady of the Lamp, the Angel of the Flaming Sword, and kissed her shadow when she passed. And what of the angels who sang Peace on Earth and Goodwill to Men, and the Man of Galilee when He said, "Turn the other cheek. Resist not evil. Love thy neighbor. Bless them that curse you"?

It takes time to place great acts, great deeds, great events in their proper perspective. It is only today that we can see

American's part in World War I. It is only today that the American Expeditionary Force begins to fit into what went before and what has come after. This Armistice Day is the most significant anniversary of that glorified dip we took into the stink-pot of Europe. Today, even the nearsighted can see it as a signal, warning men that worse may come if they do not act promptly and plan their society consciously—instead of letting it "jest grow up" like Topsy.

January 30, 1941

Have you bought at the January white sales this year? Today I went into town and laid in a supply of sheets, pillowcases, and towels. I bought this year, not in order to hoard, but because twenty-odd years of wear and tear was beginning to tell a tattered story in my "linen" closet. Now, since I've bought mine, I'm glad because, though I'm no seer in things political and economic, I believe this is the year to fill up the gaps in your cotton supplies. Not that cotton prices promise to be appreciably higher—the lost world cotton market and today's surplus don't promise the cotton grower a rosy future.

Sure to goodness, though, cotton prices won't be lower. However, all the seers tell us we are living in a period of "easy money." That is, while money may not be coming to us in sluices today, yet just ahead there lies a time when it will be harder to get. So even if cotton goes lower (and I cross my fingers), we shall have less money with which to buy. That being the case, the prudent thing for a housewife to do seems to be to budge some cotton goods onto her budget while the budging is good. Besides, my sheets were nearly three percent under last year's prices.

February 6, 1941

A question without the answer in the back of the book has been lying on my desk since last September waiting for me to Yeagitorialize on it. I still don't know the answer, but we'll all probably be in on the solution together, so here goes!

The question came to me when Maude Smith Pekuritz, once of Rochelle and now of New York City, wrote me that her now defeated Republican Representative, Bruce Barton, had asked her if her Texas folks knew they were being sold down the river for next spring's wool crop. The Honorable Mr. Barton based his premise on the August and September negotiations of the National Defense Commission, which was at that time making itself furtively busy about plans for storing a quarter of a billion pounds of Australian wool in New York warehouses. The NDC got the arrangements beautifully complete along with the approval of their agricultural member, Chester Davis, who stuck in some pretty flexible ifs and ands about the Australian wool not being sold in the domestic market unless the President declared a national emergency or we got out our guns and went to war.

Then on the first of October, before the story was in the news section, Paul Mallon's "The News Behind the News" gave the story a going over. By the middle of that month, small stories of the plan began to make the inside pages of the Texas newspapers—oh, very casually.

On November 26, A.K. Mosely of the Texas Sheep and Goat Raisers' Association at San Angelo replied to my query after this fashion: "Our people are very much concerned with the effect of the 250 million pounds of Australian wool. If government orders continue and it should be entirely used for that purpose, it may not have such a detrimental effect as it would have if the war should end soon. The sale of this wool is to be handled under the direction of the RFC. As we understand it, the present arrangement is not to release it for any purpose other than for defense."

Then on December 10, the *Star-Telegram* carried this story: "The State Department announced that strategic reserve of Australian wool totalling 250,000,000 grease pounds would be established in this country immediately as the result of an exchange of notes between the British and American governments . . . . It may be sold in the United States domestic trade if and when the United States announces that an emergency exists."

Since that date the wool has reached New York and is now under lock and key, where sheep raisers hope it will remain till the American crop is marketed in the spring.

I don't pretend to understand international horse trading. This storing of Australian wool may be the cat's whiskers. I hope it is. However, if the thing is done in good faith, with no idea of artificial control of the domestic market, it seems to me that the August, September, and October arrangements might have been made with less shush-shush to the newspapers and with far less tender solicitude for the goodwill of the American sheepmen. The sheepmen, as I have known them, are a sheep pen full of adults, plenty able to take it on the chin and out of the pocketbook if the circumstances justify. They are a patient, longsuffering, philosophical, understanding bunch of Christian gentlemen—else they wouldn't be in the sheep business. In the past, in matters political, where the dollars of sheepmen have been needed, it hasn't been necessary to sugarcoat the pill, nor give him a shot in the arm to get him to part with his roll. Space doesn't permit a resume of his long and inspiring history as a dollar and a doer patriot, but it makes interesting history and wonderful whittlers' bench converse all over the Southwest. I only wish that governmental agencies could learn to treat the American wool grower with the open confidence his illustrious history deserves.

And I wish I could be taught to repose the same brand and earmark of trust in my governmental agencies that I place in the men of the sheep pens.

Right now I'd feel more nearly satisfied that everybody concerned is in for a square deal out of the 250 million-pound wool storage proposition if the Defense Commission would send the key of that New York warehouse to Abe Mayer or T.A. Kincaid. And that's not all myopia.

February 20, 1941

I suppose everybody's governor has a movement all his own. Oklahoma used to have one who dunked himself into the nation's notice. Michigan has one who teaches Sunday School, a singular thing for a statesman to do. Louisiana has one who stays out of jail, and that's something in Louisiana. Then the governor of North Carolina is supposed to have a famous cue which he gives to the governor of South Carolina. But ours has a Sunday morning broadcast.

We got up early enough to go to one the other Sunday. As we drove over the bridge on Congress Avenue, we were following a Ford full of folks of assorted ages. "We can just follow them," my countryman observed. "They are headed for the governor's broadcast." I never know what makes him that way, but he is. So we followed the Ford, turning left out of the traffic and in a few minutes parked in front of the governor's mansion behind the Ford and followed the Ford's people up the sidewalk to the broadcast.

We registered at a pedestal on the front walk, then hunted out a protected place behind a column out of the wind to wait for the door to open. Pretty soon there was quite a huddle of us, clothing a bit awry from early morning toilets and long rides, or both, in varying stages of travel wrinkles—a good average of early morning Americana who go in for governors' broadcasts, visits to the morgue, steam shovel washings, and similar curios—a group about one degree from what the ancients termed "motley."

Presently we were joined by one who was with but not of us. Tall, gray, distinguished, handsome—he strode into our midst as one to the manor born. He wasn't an out-of-towner come to see the show. He wasn't a prospective pensioner come to behold. He wasn't a cutie from the University, out to get an early morning audience for his wisecracks. Nor was he an average townsman come to see what he could see. He was a gentleman correctly and carefully groomed, set purposefully about investing a Sunday morning. That was a thing that set him apart from the rest of us—that, and a blob of breakfast egg on his lower lip. I saw the blob in the midst of this masculine perfection with sorrow.

I looked up at my countryman, the way a wife will when she helplessly witnesses tragedy. I saw that he saw. But I also saw that he wouldn't do anything about it. The others saw, too. You could see that they saw by the looks in their eyes. A dumpy little squirt of a fellow engaged him in conversation and gave his own lips a thorough going over with a not too clean linen as he eyed the egg, the while he talked. He called the elegantly egged-on Brother Something-or-other. So he was the preacher. I hoped the dumpy one would tell his friend about the egg, but he didn't. He seemed to think he'd done his part when he wiped his own mouth. I looked again at my countryman, and though he didn't exactly shake his head, I knew he hadn't changed his mind about telling the man. He's that way. He wouldn't have told him if a couple of boa constrictors were playing hoop-la around his neck.

"Very well," I said to myself (I notice that I only say "very well" when things are not very well). "Very well," I said to me, "I shall tell him myself." And I knew by the look of dumb horror in my countryman's eyes that he knew I had very-welled myself into doing the job.

And why not? If a grandmother can't offer a helping hand, what's the good of being a grandmother? Folks are supposed to forgive a grandmother her *faux pas* by saying, "It's her age." So I would do it. I would lay my hand motherly on his beautifully tailored arm, smile gently, and say, "Are you a minister? I love ministers. My favorite cousin is a minister. Will you please wipe the egg off your lip before going in to see the governor?"

I'd be discreet about it. I'd wait for the confusion of the opening of the door. Then everybody wouldn't be looking at the egg blob. It would all be simple.

And it was working out that way, too. There was a rattle of the door, a sudden hush, the screen was pushed back. In the confusion with just the right degree of reticence, I laid my hand on the stranger's arm. I gave him my best Mae Robeson smile and began, "Are you a minister?"

But a lot of other things began to happen at the same time. The egged one looked down and yes-yessed me in a bored sort of way, as if to say, "Another neurotic she-Nicodemus come to talk about her soul . . . "

At the same time, at the door someone was saying, "Any senators and representatives will please come first. The governor wants to see you."

It was the clarion call. My egg-blobbed one was not only a minister but a senator or a representative as well. He was such a one as the governor would delight to honor. At the call, he oozed from my gentle grasp. He simply melted and poured from under my hand. Head high, feet firm eye single—he marched as if to an invisible band in to see the governor—with the blob of egg clinging chummily to his well-turned lip.

My countryman sighed deeply. The dumb-horror look in his eye turned into a twinkle of husbandly relief. "Don't worry about it," he comforted. "The governor will likely pass him a biscuit."

October 9, 1941

This October Secretary Hull had a birthday. It was his seventieth. Newspaper men brought him a birthday cake, gay with candles and pink frosting—and the secretary talked to them about liberty!

On first thought it would seem the secretary chose a trite subject for talking to gentlemen to whom the story of liberty is a twice-told tale, and it seems he would be hard put for finding something new to say anent liberty. And though the subject is as old as the first time two human beings inhabited the earth in the same community, and though the secretary is old, what he had to say about liberty seemed new enough to the secretary that he pushed aside a birthday cake, a present from the country's most influential group of men, and took time to say it. It seemed new enough to Washington newspaper men that my state paper gave it a two-column headline on the front page. What the seventy-year-old secretary spoke about was the terrific responsibility of liberty.

With forty-nine years of government service behind him, he said, "One of the most important lessons that has occurred to me out of this long contact and experience has been that statesmen and peoples everywhere must recognize the strong responsibility which liberty imposes on those who enjoy it. This terrific responsibility is not realized today, either here or anywhere as it should and must be recognized. Today we are living through a dark period. We cannot lose hope that the lesson which so many of us have learned as I have learned it will be learned by all."

Now, I have read text books on the social sciences; I have studied them in schools and have taught them to boys and girls in years gone by. Yet little, indeed, have I read until recently, precious little have I studied about, and pitifully little did I teach about the "responsibility of liberty." After Hull's birthday talk, I looked back through my text books to see whether, perhaps, I had overlooked a significant lesson. Only its ghost was I able to find in my dusty volumes. I found much about rights and privileges and prerogatives of liberty; but the responsibilities of liberty—it has taken a world cataclysm to point out to the Secretary of State, the American press, and to me.

"The terrific responsibility of liberty" is a new-old lesson that the Secretary of State was forty-nine years learning, yet that responsibility is as old as liberty itself. How strange we waited so long to learn about it. Tragic, too, that we learn the lesson in the school of experience. Yet the bright spot in the situation is that when free people learn the new-old lesson, as free people must learn it if they survive, then seventy-year-old gentlemen can talk about cakes with candles on them and pink frosting when they have birthdays.

December 4, 1941

In a public address to the American people, a Virginia mule breeder donated a valued collection of hoss sense about the gentle art of running this nation. George Washington was the mule breeder, besides being a surveyor, army man, first President, and a proud citizen of the United States. The oft-cited advice to which I refer is found in his Farewell Address, composed when he retired to private life after forty-five years of public service.

It was a better than run-of-the-mill bit of advice, and folks have been quoting and misquoting it ever since. Any time we peep over into our neighbor's yard across the pond, somebody warns, "Remember what Washington said in his Farewell Address about foreign alliances!" People have been saying it to me in conversations, and I've been hearing it over radios for a good while now. I see it in print at least once a week. I suddenly work up to the fact that if my life depended on it, I couldn't say for sure what Washington did say about the feasibility of nations making alliances.

So I began asking people, "What," I asked, "*did* Washington say in his Farewell Address about foreign alliances?" I asked two teachers, one farmer, three school kids, and a hoss doctor. All were as indefinite as I. Some were even more so—which was considerably indefinite. Most used the words "beware" and "entangling alliances." Finally I dug out a dusty school book to see. Nowhere did I find the word "beware," and if "entangling alliances" is in the address, I'll eat my copy. I found that George did offer some practical advice, logical and long-wearing, about running the government. Since today marks exactly 158 years since the address was made public, I think it not inappropriate to tell you some of the things I found in Washington's Farewell Address.

Well, in the first place I found a stupendous collection of polysyllables. It seems the austere old dear never used a simple word when he could fish up a dictionary-sounding one. I found much of dignified modesty. I found a patriot with an inspiring faith in the future of his pioneer country. I found a calm, cool, logical thinker. Whittled down to my size, the address says in part: "Goodbye, folks, it's been nice knowing you. But before somebody else takes over, let ole George tell you how it looks from here:

1. Stick together like glue. Don't get all hot and bothered about sectional or party politics. Such doin's use up your steam.
2. Don't change the ABCs of our government every whipstitch. Think!
3. Mix some religion and morality with government. Otherwise it stinks.
4. Keep folks learning. Ignorance embarrasses a republic.
5. It takes money to run a government, but watch your pennies and keep your credit respectable. Pay as you go. Don't saddle debts onto babies yet unborn.

6. Get along with your neighbors. Be slow to get your back up. We have big oceans all around us, and they are deep and wide. Let folks who don't like us jump in 'em. Tend to your own affairs. Don't go around pulling other fellows' chestnuts out of the fire. Don't love any foreign nations too 'nuff; but be sure you don't love any foreign nations too none. Paddle your own canoe insofar as you are able, but if circumstances force you to club up with any other nation, make the session short and sweet, and try to do better next time.
7. Well, that's all for now. As I said before, thanks and goodbye."

January 29, 1942

Doctors grimly told young Franklin Roosevelt that medical science knew nothing more to do for him, that he was a victim of infantile paralysis, and that he must adjust himself to the idea of life in a wheelchair. They told him that he'd never be able to move his leg again—not even a toe.

When the doctors were gone and the man was left alone, he faced the tragic verdict. Then he set to work to move his leg, and he began with the toe.

That he brought back life to his toe, that he made his leg carry him again all the world knows. That he had it in him to fight when there was no hope, to try this way and that way and fail and begin all over again; that he had the will to see the thing through; that he pitted his courage and patience and strength against an insurmountable obstacle and surmounted it; that he brought his toe back to life when it couldn't be done—those are the things our world can be thankful for this day. They explain why he goes to war to get peace, why he cuts red tape and ventures untried ways. They explain why, when he fails or errs or meets a blank wall, he backs up and begins all over in a new way.

For years I puzzled to see him quoted this way at one time and that way at another on apparently the same question. That doesn't puzzle me any more. Now I know when I see such evidence that it's just the toe-wizard trying another way and another and another, backing up to go ahead again when some plan has failed to attain whatever was his objective. In such cases he is brave enough to be wrong.

I am thankful on his sixtieth birthday that my President has the stuff in him that makes him wiggle his toe when it can't.

July 30, 1942

At breakfast on Sunday morning after—I mean after the election—I asked the also-ran for commissioner of precinct four of McCulloch County, to wit, my liege lord, one A.V. Yeager (often referred to in these columns as my countryman), what, if anything, he had to say to the voters of his precinct. "I do," he said, "have a thing to say, and I'd take it mighty kindly if you'd put it into your column." So here it is, as nearly as I can remember it after I got the dishes done:

"The 120-odd votes I garnered out of nearly 600 give me a great deal of pleasure. You see, aside from the relatives and near friends of the other two boys, all of the *best* people of the precinct voted for me. That left the other two fellows to share the good, the bad, and the indifferent votes, and there always was an awful mess of them in any election. I have found, too, that it is not true what folks always say after an election about there being a big bunch of liars who go to the polls; ten times more people voted for me Saturday than ever promised to support me. I am impressed.

"I had a good time electioneering. I met and talked with people I'd otherwise never have known, and the experience was worth what it cost me and then some.

"I have had some awful mud holes pointed out to me this summer, and they had the hang-dog look of having been pointed out to a couple of other candidates—mud holes, deep mud holes, holes needing bridges, holes needing pontoons, holes to ditch, holes to drain—a terrible lot of them, each one worse than the last. I got so I dreamed about them at night and muttered about them in my sleep. I'll likely be a better man, now that they are the district's again, and Commissioner Smith's. It was gratifying though that precinct four's mudholes had no political mud in them. Thanks, neighbors and fellow candidates.

"To the 400-odd voters who so forthrightly returned me to private life, I wish to say I never meant any harm. Sure enough, I'm no professional politician, and I hereby put away my fiddle. It was nice knowing you, in a discouraging sort of way."

That was the gist of my countryman's post-breakfast talk. It made good listening to me. Yes, I voted for him. I did it because I figured ever and ever so long ago that he was *the best man*. But I think he wouldn't have been happy as your commissioner, and I think he would not have made you happy. You see, he has such old fogey ideas—like paying debts, living within one's income, running on a cash-or-can't principle, keeping your desires within your ability to provide, and getting 100 cents' worth to the dollar on purchases and investments. And he thinks you ought to pay debts with money. Silly, isn't it?

Anyway, that's not being a gov'ment man, and I thank you a lot for sending him back to me. I'll keep him busy performing the above services for me the rest of his natural lifetime—and oblige.

July 30, 1943

Funny things get into the mail box: letters, papers, catalogues, bills, box-holders' notices, wrens' nests, stinging scorpions, spider webs, neighbors' notes, congressmen's speeches, and what-nots—lots of what-nots.

Last week we got one from Claude R. It was a honey. We've had several from Claude R. before. He is a tireless letter writer, and you can't blame him, considering that he doesn't have to buy any stamps. But this last one out-Wickarded Wickard. It is printed in red, white, and blue, on crackle-pop paper with a border around the edge that looks sort of like treble clef music signs, only they are run through with a couple of heavy marks that suggest, in an absent-minded sort of way, dollar signs. It suggests to me that the designer might have been humming a catchy version of "Bountiful, Bountiful Texas" as he gaily sketched the design.

On the white field surrounded by the dollar-marked treble clef signs and cut bravely across by a beautiful blue V, Mr.

Wickard said, "Certificate of Farm War Service. This certifies that this family is enlisted in all-out farm war production, 1943."

In a nice letter along with the certificate, Mr. Wickard said he was sending out these pretty certificates to all the farm people, because they had met the goal the country had asked for in food and feed.

Now, wouldn't you just love to sit in on a session up in Washington when the idea of one of these certificates was getting itself born? I can imagine Claude R. calling in the Jones boys, Marvin and Jesse, and all their cronies they are not fencing with at the time, and drawing up for a good spit-and-whittle session with an opener like this: "Well, lads, how's fences in your neck of the woods? Laid any cornerstones lately? Haven't laid any more eggs, have you, boys? How's the Post Office crop? Slim? Maybe we'd better send out some Dear Constituent stuff. Don't you imagine Ole Miz Yeager and her man would be tickled pink if we'd fix 'em up a cute little 'Certificate of Farm War Service'? Sure they would! Could frame it and hang it with the enlarged picture of Uncle Hezekiah. Or put it in the Bible by the album on the stand table along with the family death notices, marriage write-ups, and Cradle-Roll Certificates. Better than a good idea, I'd say. Ole Miz Yeager hasn't had any fun in a long time, I imagine. Let's fix her up. She'll love us to death for it!" Then they solemnly draw straws to see who'll get to send it out, and Claude R. wins again.

Well, all right, Claude, dear, I got it. It is a dinger. Gives pause for thought. And speculation. How the heck can you know in the middle of a dry Texas July what'll go into Texas barns and kitchens and into the world markets this fall? From the way the sun glints off my dried-up garden and the hot winds rustle through the seared stalks of what I thought a couple of weeks ago was a feed crop, the chances are you'll be wanting this certificate back in your office before snow flies.

On the other hand, how'd you like a certificate from me to you for a change, like this: "Certificate of Political Doll-Ragging. This certifies that, in my opinion, the good old Department of Agriculture, created in eighteen-hundred and something for the purpose of acquiring and diffusing useful information on subjects connected with agriculture, would garner a better crop of respect from folks in the forks of the creeks and come a sight nearer earning the money they are paid if they would sort of hunker down to 'acquiring and diffusing' instead of using time and money and energy trying to ingratiate the Department against the next election. Signed by me and anybody else whose ego wasn't especially ministered unto by their 'Certificate of Farm War Service' and who thought the popple-crack paper smelled a lot like the paper we burned up gas and used up tires collecting to save the world last fall."

December 3, 1943

"Save paper!" says Uncle Sam.

Who is the greatest publisher on topside of earth today? He is our own Uncle Samuel. And he is expanding. Within the year, while commercial publication has cut down, combined, and folded up, our own Uncle Sam has brought out three monthlies and two weeklies; nor have any of his other regular publications found it feasible to fold.

"Save paper!" says Uncle Sam. "Tons of it are needed in the manufacture of ammunition!"

Today our Uncle Sam publishes these: four dailies, eight bi-weeklies, eight weeklies, 110 monthlies, fifteen quarterlies.

"Save paper!" says Uncle Sam. "We've got to have it to win the war!" So in order to guarantee paper for winning the war, the OPA decrees that civilian publishers may use only eighty-five percent of their 1941 consumption. That saves a lot of paper. So Uncle Sam goes right on publishing seven periodicals on South America and five monthlies and one weekly on *labor*. Seems each departmental agency has to have a paper to toot its own horn in. So Uncle Sam takes six percent of the paper production of the nation. With plenty of paper on hand, the great old publisher steps right into competition with private publishers, and in his new magazine, *Victory*, a baby of the OWI designed for foreign circulation, there appear some ads at about $3,000 a page.

"Save paper!" warns our Uncle Sam. "Each new battleship requires sixteen tons of paper for plans, designs, and blueprints. The building of a Flying Fortress takes twenty thousand drawings." Yet the government's publication "Federal Home Loan Bank" weighs alongside of *Harper's Bazaar* and *Rural Electrification News,* straight from our Uncle's in Washington, hasn't shed a page since December 7, two years ago.

Please to note, gentle reader (and remain gentle), that this information taken from the *Reader's Digest* of November concerns only our active Uncle's publishing of civilian (not army) periodicals and makes no mention of the immense bulletin business that has been going on for years and continues.

"Save paper!" demands Uncle Sam. "Commandos need it for paper overcoats that are ripped off and discarded as soon as the fighting men land!"

Listen, Uncle: there was once a haunted house. Spooks walked in it. No one would stay past the stroke of midnight within its walls. Its reputation grew. A purse of money was raised and offered to anyone who would, one hour after the town hall clock had struck twelve, drive a nail to its head into the floor in the center of an evil bloodstain that marked the place where its ancient owner had died, the victim of an assassin's knife.

Many tried. Terror caught them. None stayed. Then there came one in great need of money. He would stay past midnight in the haunted house. He would drive the nail into the bloodstain. He went alone at dark into the house. One hour past midnight, listeners stationed across the street heard the hammer slowly pounding, pounding. Then silence. The man had done it. But he didn't come to claim his reward, and when the curious went in the sunlight of the morning to see the nail, they found the poor man dead on the floor. In the darkness he had nailed his own coattails to the blood spot and died of terror when he found he couldn't rise.

Read a lesson, dear Unk. We love the United States. We want to serve. We'll save paper. We have saved it. We'll stack it by the trainloads into boxcars. We want to build ships, to build Flying Fortresses, to make Commando coats, to make a billion cartridges. Our publishers will cut their periodicals to the bone, combine similar ones, fold the unnecessary and the unprofitable, use the margins and get them out in squint-eyed print. We want to win the war. We want to get the thing over. But, Unk, it looks as if you'll have to help us in this paper business. From where we sit, it seems you could do a lot if you'd cut out the waste, the duplication and fold up a lot—fold up *all*—of those unnecessary departmental horn tooters. It is not sympathy we feel, but chagrin, when we see you *nailing down your own coattails!*

May 12, 1944
In her autobiography, Eleanor Roosevelt devotes some time to her teenage visit to Europe, on which occasion an acquaintance asked her to explain details about the division of state and federal powers of government in the United States. Eleanor confesses with charming naivete her complete ignorance, at that time, of the fact that the governmental powers of her country are divided into state and federal duties and responsibilities and explains that she had always considered (if she could have been said to consider at all) that the American system is composed of one governmental unit. She intimates that she later corrected that blind spot in her education.

If she did, she could now perform a valuable service for her country to putting Mr. Roosevelt wise to the fact that the Constitution, which he promises to enforce each four years, recognizes state as well as federal powers of law making and law enforcing. As it is, the way our party leader leads us, Jim White and all us other Democrats are finding it increasingly difficult to explain what is a Democrat.

July 21, 1944
At the Democratic shindig in Chicago this week, a lot of guessing will be going on about how much various factions of the party can get Mr. Roosevelt to compromise. This guessing blossomed in the press in the VP Wallace rebus, which brought string-pulling Democrats almost to the hair-pulling stage, their own as well as other people's hair, with "letters" and

"statements" and "acceptable substitutes" and "dark horses" galloping all over the premises. There will be other guesses about Mr. Roosevelt's tendency to compromise as the convention grows older and hotter. How much will Mr. Roosevelt be willing to compromise on his beautiful bureaus? How much will he be compromisable on Federal Powers vs. States' Rights, if any? On Paternalism? On Directives?

On the surface it would seem that Mr. Roosevelt might be a good prospect for a compromiser—if he takes the notion. He seems to have been on both sides of practically any question with which he deals, from "peace at any price" to "war to the hilt," from Farley to anti-Farley back to Farley again, if Farley is willing, which Farley isn't yet. The *Saturday Morning Post* and other Republican-minded publications used to make great glee reprinting excerpts from Roosevelt utterances and writings, quoting him on both sides of any question, and then tossing in a Roosevelt statement down the middle.

Through the years, however, Republicans as well as Democrats are learning the psychology of the Compromise Rooseveltian. We are learning Mr. Roosevelt will compromise any small point, even a large one, if he can, by so doing, get what he wants. He'll demand Wallace and no backing out if Wallace is the only answer to his need. If, however, he grows himself a nice little crop of Wallaces to choose from, he will loose Wallace to the great out yonder and lay the mantle of approval on his "compromise," who is to him a Wallace in all but name. So with bureaucratic government, he will sacrifice this bureau or that, if the public must, so long as he can still get what he wants through a new or different bureau. He compromised on the NRA, and, lo, the New Deal. The New Deal was scrapped for the Square Deal, which got lost in the tumult of war, the while the Roosevelt administration marches steadily on to a new day, harkening ever to the pipes of the same distant music: paternalism in government, concentration of federal powers, strangulation of states' rights and powers and responsibilities, heralded by the clinking of many federal dollars, innocuously accompanied by federal authority—for "we have planned it so."

The Rooseveltian Compromise, by which the party has functioned the past dozen years, has all of the wisdom of Tze Ch'i's "Three in the Morning." In fact, it *is* "Three in the Morning" as recorded in *The Works of Chung Tze,* an oriental scripture:

"What is 'three in the morning?'" asks Tze Yu.

"A keeper of monkeys," replied Tze Ch'i, "said with regard to their rations of chestnuts that each monkey was to have three in the morning and four at night. But at this the monkeys were very angry, so the keeper said that they might have four in the morning and three at night, with which agreement they were well pleased. The actual number of the chestnuts remained the same, but there was an adaptation to the likes and dislikes of those concerned. This is called 'using the light.'"

And, citizens, has that man used it!

The Coke Stevenson Story

Governor Stevenson's has been a life built on faith: as a banker, he rested his faith in his fellow man; as a ranchman, he rested it in the weather, in his own ability as a herdsman; as an office holder he rested it in the people. Today as governor, he will need the bulwark of his faith to guide him at the helm of a mighty state.

One politician who satisfied Yeager's definition of a public servant was Coke Stevenson. She followed his career as he progressed from Speaker of the House of Representatives, to Lieutenant Governor to Governor (when O'Daniel resigned to run for the United States Senate) to his election as governor in his own right in 1944; and while she would have been the last to claim to "know" the governor, they did have a leisurely visit together in the McCulloch County countryside, a visit recorded here.

o o o o o o o o o o o o o o o o

April 12, 1938
As one tops a rise coming into Doole Valley from the east at dusk, there is something that gives the feeling of the sea—the vastness of the valley, slightly sunken below the rims of the hills; the smoothness of the enfolding uplands like a giant soup bowl; the dome of the sky coming down in an unbroken horizon, unbroken, that is, except to the southward, where Old Father Time has taken a snaggle-toothed bite out of the bowl itself, leaving the gap. It was toward the gap that pioneers aimed their herds of cattle trailing the long, slow miles to Abilene, Kansas. Through it went the first trails. Today boys find arrowheads there.

Doole has a lagoon, if you have imagination. After a good rain it stretches forty-seven happy thoughts and a flight of fancy along the highway on the south side. It elbows past Lu Cursia Porter's little cafe, where Dema and Papa Porter have bordered it with a snatched-back bit of old-fashioned flower garden, tea-apron in size. Here phlox, hollyhocks, petunias, zinnias, verbenas, and cornflowers bloom in its bank. Of course, mosquitoes and crawdads and myriad gnats foregather there, but then, frogs croak in its grasses with the same savage crescendo that their brothers do in the romantic Galapagos. Then in mid-month it dips up the moon and stars.

Open roads beckon to the adventurer, allured by promises of something different beyond the next hill. Closed roads, too, sometimes bring pleasant contacts. State Highway 23 had ribboned itself across the country from the river to an obstinate ridge of rock on the Kidd Jeffers ranch, where the power shovel had rooted and bucked and snorted and pawed the ground between charges of dynamite for a solid week. There my country gentleman and I drove, lured by the miracle of machinery. As we stood watching, travelers came from the north over the new highway, asking the way by detour to Brady.

My countryman introduced me to Mr. and Mrs. Stevenson and in neighborly parlance directed the two "by Kidd Jeffers and the Fairview schoolhouse." Neighbors, I surmised, lost in the maze of progress. Then the talk fell, as it commonly does, to the condition of the country, the beauty of springtime—and politics.

While the menfolk went into a huddle as a committee of the whole on the state of the union, about equally dividing honors as to wealth of suggestion concerning what should be done to save the nation, I got in a bit of first-class woman visiting with my new acquaintance. We found mutual interests in a three-member family and the problems of what mother should do when the one hopeful had made its own home. She spoke with a glow about a grandchild for whom she had crocheted a bedspread, this as her contribution to bedspread heirlooms of four generations in her possession, dating back to the hand-spun, loom-woven bedspread of a great-great-grandmother. "I made mine to pass on with the others," she explained. "I wanted to do my part by the generations."

She listened to my saga of housewifing and schoolteaching and in return told me that she was spending part of the time away from their ranch, traveling with her husband—a duty she had at first promised herself small pleasure from. "What shall I talk about to the people I meet?" she had remonstrated to her husband before setting forth. "Why, I am just a plain country woman. I don't smoke. I don't drink. I haven't had an operation. I haven't even a hired girl. Nobody could possibly be interested in me." But the sparkle in her eyes said that she was finding her life good. "People," she explained, "have been stimulating to meet, and I like to go with Mr. Stevenson. It is a grand feeling to know that one is needed."

A series of blasts in the road ahead broke in upon our visit. Mr. Stevenson, whose keen eyes squint half-shut in a manner peculiar to men who have spent long days in the saddle under dancing heat waves of Texas sun, released a satisfying grip on a wicked-looking underslung pipe and estimated the measure of the charges and went on to explain that he had fenced his ranch, blasting out the post holes himself.

When I commented on the accomplishment—for I have big-eyed respect concerning the handling of explosives—Mrs. Stevenson laughingly elaborated, "Yes, he can do a lot of things! He's even a pretty good barber. He learned how on a cowboy on the ranch who had a grudge against store boughten haircuts. Coke," she confided, "can make good coffee, too."

I have always liked a woman who recommends her husband. The Stevensons were not in a hurry. There is something about the two of them, something patient and philosophical, something friendly and real that gives the impression that they have time for the luxury of living.

When finally small talk had dwindled and they told us goodbye, laughingly promising to meet us in Austin at the inaugural, they drove away, down the little Williams lane, on by the Jeffers ranch and the Fairview schoolhouse, with Mrs. Stevenson at the wheel feeling grand at being needed. Then I turned to my country gentleman and said, "Your friends are what I call really neighborly country people. I wish we could see more of them."

Then he turned on me a smile meant to be withering (only it doesn't really) and explained more or less patiently, "We might even at that, because, you see, that ranchman has been Speaker of the House of Representatives as long as the law allows; he's now a candidate for the lieutenant governor and he'll get it, too. After which this state will have a wrangler to ride herd, and nobody'll need to worry about the top hand being big enough for his britches!"

Rather solemnly, I took off my sunbonnet and straightened up my back hair. I looked critically at my faded house dress, a snide thing, I thought. Then I laughed in spite of myself, for I'd had a good woman folks visit, and for the life of me, I couldn't keep from feeling that Mrs. Stevenson had too!

August 11, 1938

And now comes the *Pathfinder Magazine* all the way from Washington, D.C., to tell us that our governor-elect "is the biggest politician of them all." My head aches. What is a politician? What a natural this would have been for Will Rogers! But now he'll never know.

The other day I heard a candidate asking for an office in our state. I had to listen several minutes before I knew that I was hearing a candidate. The line was different. There was no beating of drums, no blowing of bugles, no banner-waving oratory. The fellow was asking listeners to think, to reason and to judge—a different approach than the kind that marked the late election.

But then, I learned that the speaker was, himself, different. He is a country man with town connections instead of being a town man with country connections. To me there is a vast difference. He runs on a platform backed by a record of public service.

So much is he a country man that he has never worn a watch, simply squints up at the sun or reckons back to "gettin' up time" for the hour of the day. That is Coke Stevenson, ranchman of Junction, asking for the lieutenant governorship of Texas on a plea of better government, with a record of better government services backing his request.

Time is the stuff of life, but too many of us count it by figures on the face of a clock. So we make ourselves slaves to routine. I'm for the sun-squinters. I count on them to reckon human values.

January 26, 1939

Along with 59,998 other folks, my countryman and I went down to Austin last week to see the final wave of the wand by which a flour salesman is made into a governor. Under tons of decorations, miles of flags, and behind phalanxes of parked cars, we found the capital city in a dither. Daylight slowed the way for a few early comers to cinch rain-drenched seats at the stadium in the chill of early morning.

In the capitol building, employees on their way to work brushed past gaping school children, their escorts, and constituents from the forks of the creek. Back of the Senate Hall we found the Coke Stevensons getting ready for breakfast in their apartment, which adjoins the lieutenant governor's offices. The apartment is magnificent in height and in atmospheric dignity, but decidedly cramped in floor space, being a living room, a bedroom, and a kitchenette. Can you imagine a kitchenette with walls twenty feet high?

It was family day at the Stevensons', with Mother Stevenson, young Stevenson and family, and assorted relatives as guests. They had slept on couches and cots and pallets and beds all over the place in order to be ready for inauguration day. Mother Stevenson was a pattern of subdued excitement. To her the day was a full one, but her life has been made up of days that were full. She recounted pioneer times, how she had come as a child in a covered wagon to Brownwood when that town had only two houses, how her father's wagon had followed a plowed furrow from the Colorado River crossing to Brady, which was a town by virtue of only one building. She relived the growth of a virgin country as epitomized in her life in McCulloch and Mason Counties—the one-teacher schools, the unfenced ranges, neighborly "sitting up with the sick," all the romance and realism of log cabin living. Today she was to ride in a great pageant before half a million people to see her son take the oath of office as lieutenant governor of the state she had seen grow into a mighty commonwealth. A great day for a great little lady—a great day because an army of such great ladies had made it possible.

Listening to her, I got the idea that the Stevenson tribe was well able to weather the inconvenience of cramped sleeping quarters. They've been a bivouacking people, sleeping in security behind the walls of the State House or snugly in home-made beds of a pioneer country or deeply under the blue of the open on a Tucson bed—a Tucson bed being explainable in Southwestern lore as the bed of a cowboy caught by nightfall out on the range without his bedroll, when he unsaddles his horse, stretches out under the stars beside his campfire and sleeps on his back and covers with his belly or vice versa.

Out at the stadium the good-natured crowd piled in all the morning. "Many a human," once said a Texan as he marveled at the mass of humanity spewed out on the streets of New York at the end of a day, and "many a human" echoed when 60,000 people sat under a bright winter's sun to see the pageantry accompanying the inauguration of a governor. One section of the stadium was reserved for the brightly uniformed bands, and other bands, occupying places on the playing field, painted up the scene for color. In their somber winter coats, topped by hats and scarves in splashes of variegated hues of reds, blues, golds, and greens, the crowd was a spectacle of color, like a late-blooming bed of old-fashioned zinnias on a bright morning after the first frost. The brilliantly colored bands were sprays of fresh sweet peas set in the frost-bitten flower bed to brighten it. Here and there a band instrument caught the light and sparkled like dew.

Photographers—they were all over the place. They oozed through the walls, sprouted from the turf, came up through the cinder path, and crawled out from under rocks. They snapped the governor smiling; they snapped him frowning; they snapped him speaking. They clicked at Molly and Pat and Mike, and they clicked at the governor's lady. They didn't overlook the Stevensons. They got the judges and they got Scotty Gale. They took in the crowd. They got everybody and everything—

got them coming and going, and they didn't ask anybody anything. They took—they took before, after, and during everything—even prayer. Hoyle or Emily Post or Queensbury or somebody ought to write some rules for the game.

Another thing that should have rules written about it is the intricate procedure involved in presenting a billy goat to a governor. The Mills County delegation had the goat and the idea, but not the information about how to turn the trick. So they sought out Senator Penrose Metcalf as the only man in Austin who really understands the soul of a goat, and pretty soon the Hillbilly governor was fraternizing with his own individual Billy from the Hills of Mills.

Caught up in the glamor of the most brilliant spectacle of state the Southwest has ever staged was Kitty Williamson, almost yesterday a school girl at Rochelle, now grown into Texas Rose of the throaty voice. The only feminine interest in the famous Hillbilly Band, Kitty keeps her head, does her job with poise and charm, like the good trooper that she is.

Following the Highway Patrol escort, the entrance of the governor's party climaxed the drama of pageantry. Roman triumphs of ancient days could not have been more colorful. Roman triumphs—they had a trimming left off the O'Daniel triumph that might have been useful. You see, in olden days it was the custom to have a slave ride along with the conquering hero in the triumphal car, a common slave, dressed in the coarse, rough cloth of the menial. It was the duty of this humble person, unkempt of body and stupid of mind, to tap the C.H. on the shoulder and whisper remindfully from time to time into his ear, "Remember, thou art mortal." It is possible that such a reminder might not have been amiss last week. Too, he might profitably have added, "And don't forget, the public is as fickle as Texas weather in early spring!"

Presently the governor and the ex-governor, their wives and families, together with miscellaneous gentlemen, were little figures seated on a raised stage before the sea of faces. Forgotten were vituperations and old hates. Governor O'Daniel was no longer "a Yankee from Kansas." Governor Allred was no longer the "little boy in the big britches." Political bedfellows were miraculously Texans. Then a Lilliputian O'Daniel stood before a gray-haired judge, and in a voice made Brobdingnagian by amplifiers, hoisted a Brogdingnagian load from Mr. Allred's shoulders over to his own, and if he staggered it wasn't noticeable where I sat. Nonetheless, there'll likely be a new avenue for sedative sales in Austin before the moon changes.

Mrs. O'Daniel was cool, calm and beautifully alive to everything. Pat and Mike were alternately grave and gay, now and then indulging in bits of horseplay to show that they were still the O'Daniel kids and that this wasn't exactly their funeral.

Then there was Molly. Vivacious, laughing, friendly—her Irish face framed in a cloud of black hair, her heart in her eyes. Her happiness in a full-skirted white satin dress with a long red cape spilled over for all of Texas to share. Sixteen, with gardenias in her hair; sixteen, with an itch to slide swoopingly down the balustrade of that dignified old mansion, making it ring with young laughter. "No, no, Molly. No more balustrade sliding. You're a big girl now!" Poor little colleen. There'll be hurts and bumps and bruises and hurts, but they won't be in places that can be rubbed. Yet, trust the Irish heart of Molly— she'll take them swoopingly.

We'd like to have gone to the ball. We had our invitations, the first we ever saw. We were impressed, and we'd left our pastor at home. We'd have gone, too, only we couldn't find a parking place.

July 4, 1940

Up from the South Llano country to ride in the Jubilee parade and to speechify on Texas politics comes Lieutenant Governor Coke Stevenson. A more colorful rider or chewer of the political fat the committee would have been hard-put to find, even in this country of picturesque saddle-sitters and leather-lunged viewers-with-alarm. The lieutenant governor rides the lead horse in the parade that officially opens the Jubilee, and the way Coke Stevenson forks a horse and makes his loosely put together bulk a part of the animal is a vote-getter without equal, wherever Texans congregate. The manner in which he sits the saddle is not a polished study aimed to catch the eye of a holiday crowd. He learned the art of cowboying in his youth on a Texas ranch, valetting the cows, sheep, and goats of the Hill Country, and he still takes on any of the chores that show up when he is at home on his own ranch down near Telegraph.

Though most of the year his bunk house is the red granite capitol, Coke Stevenson remains a man of the wind-swept hills and open spaces. Even our other hired hands we have loose-herding our interests down at Austin know that while they have corralled him, branded him for the enactment and execution of law, and inoculated him with the sweet discontent of public service, his earmarks still stamp him an outdoor man, rooted in the soil of Texas. In recognition of this fact, the members of the Legislature, when making the usual courtesy gift to the retiring Speaker of the House, didn't present him with a watch, as is the custom. Coke Stevenson doesn't use a watch. He tells time by squinting at the sun. So the legislature made his gift a saddle. He uses it.

Sometimes, by heritage and accomplishment, one grows into the stature of a man that fits the term "Texican." The appellation sits well on Lieutenant Governor Coke Stevenson. His mother tells of pioneering into the Heart O' Texas country, where her father's plowshare cut the first furrow from the Colorado River to Brady, blazing a trail for others to follow. The family pushed on into Mason country near the Brown School house. Here she married into the Stevenson family, that virile tribe that has spread like Johnson grass all over Texas, sending down roots that stay. Near Camp Air, Coke was born. His youth was spent in such schools as the frontier afforded, but in his teens he got his hands on some law books, and that settled the career of the Stevensons' son, Coke. He read law while janitoring in the Bank of London—at London, Texas, while driving a freight wagon through the Hill Country and while waddying for ranchmen. The janitor job led to the cashier's window, from which he was drafted by the citizens to the office of County Judge, the prime job being to build a road through the hills of Kimball County on a specified sum. He built the road, and right there he began the labor of turning a country-bred boy, self-taught and self-propelled, into a professional politician—a profession he owns with honor and dignity, having made the study of laws, the enactment of them, as well as their execution, his life's work. The only man ever to be twice elected Speaker of the House, he has made a record of meditated, considered legislation unequalled by any living Texan.

So, a special thanks to the Jubilee Committee for bringing over to see us on our holiday the Lieutenant Governor of the State of Texas. He is an old cowhand a lot of folks are predicting will become more and more familiar with matters political in the Lone Star State.

And welcome to town, your honor. You're our kind of cattle. We like your brand and understand your breed!

August 14, 1941

"All it takes is a little faith . . . ."

Out of the Hill Country of Texas comes Coke R. Stevenson with a new word on his lips—faith. "A little faith," he says, and two millions of dollars piled up of idle surplus will be set to work; "a little faith" and 9½ millions more will not have to be taxed from the property owners in Texas counties; "a little faith" and 11½ millions more collected from gasoline tax will not be frozen from the road funds of the state.

"A little faith . . . ."

Other words that pinch-hit for "faith" are "loyalty," "belief," and "reliance." "Faith" is a word I have often connected with the Bible. So I turned to it in my concordance and found to my surprise that it is listed for the Old Testament only two times; but in the New Testament it is the key word, used over and over and over again in divine dealings with a people now mature enough to be asked to live by a principle instead of by a set of rules.

Living by principle—that is the thing that is fundamental in a democratic government. But living by principle presupposes a mature people—one which can elect one of its own members, delegate powers to him, and trust him to use those powers wisely and well. Are we mature enough to trust those we elect?

Are those we elect honest and sagacious enough to deserve the trust of a people? If democracy is to survive, it will survive because we can justifiably place "a little faith" in those we elect to chart the course for our government.

Governor Stevenson's has been a life built on faith; as a banker, he rested his faith in his fellow man; as a ranchman, he rested it in the weather, in his own ability as a herdsman, in the economic status of his country; as an office holder he rested it in the people. Today as governor, he will need the bulwark of his faith to guide him at the helm of a mighty state.

In his case, faith is a double-action affair. Just as he must build Texas on his faith in us, we must build Texas on our faith in Governor Stevenson. And right well has he deserved Texas' loyalty, belief, and reliance. Self-made, self-taught—he is a man Texas understands. Already he has shown us what a man with ability can do in business and governmental affairs. He has the brand and earmarks of a statesman, together with the sagacity of a good horse trader. He doesn't send his thinking out to be done for him; yet we have seen his ability to compromise on an issue and, at the same time, keep faith with the principle involved. The open-door policy at the Capitol whereby he makes himself available to all callers is prompted by his schooled tolerance, which has taught him the wisdom of considering the opinions of all men. He has humility. He gets along with people, but even his enemies respect his courage.

A turn in the fortunes of politics has given him to us for a governor at this time. The miracle of "a little faith"—in him by us and in us by him—can make a new day for Texas. And "Who knows whether thou art come to the kingdom for such a time as this?"

January 8, 1942

The earth of Texas Hill Country was made richer last Sunday when the dust of Fay Stevenson was laid in its bosom. "The handsome silver-haired lady of the ranch country" is the way reporters in the great dailies referred to her. The sonorous roll of it would have brought a merry twinkle to her eyes. Newspaper men loved Fay Stevenson. They loved her graciousness, her simplicity, her tact, her sense of humor, her genuineness.

No public figure ever had a better campaigner than she was—though she would have laughed at you if you had called her a campaigner. "Oh, I don't campaign," she would have said. "Why, I only go along with Coke for the trip—sort of to look after him and to see the people. I like to meet people. I like to visit with them and to listen to them." And how she listened! Whether it was your story of abuse by special privilege, of unfair tax rates, of the long arm of the federal government reaching out for the state's submarginal lands, of your proposed new venture, of Texas' needs—she listened. When your tale was told, she sagely replied with, "Coke says . . . ." and constituents felt their case had been given ear.

She was brimful of big and little stories of the doings of that long, tall, loosely-strung-together Texan who was forever getting into the public eye of Texas. When successes came his way, she accepted them as his just deserts. When reverses came, she never gave them recognition. For him, she never admitted defeat. Always she had one platform. It covered all situations. It was "Coke says . . . ." It was sufficient.

Fay Stevenson listened, too, to your personal story, to your sorrows and your joys. Or perhaps it was a new crochet pattern or the selection of a piece of old furniture or a treasured recipe. Whatever it was, she listened. Then she shared delightedly with you her little triumphs and failures, those feminine bric-a-brac we women treasure on the shelves of our lives and bring out in friendly intimacies to dust with tears and laughter.

I am glad that she who loved warmth and beauty and the richness of lived-with things saw her last Christmas in the State's White House, surrounded by children's laughter and the warm gladness of the family's love and with friends. How happy she must have been and how happy the others must have been to have her there, for she was pleased with the idea of life in the Governor's Mansion. Last August she said in a letter, "I am improving and hope it will not be long until I can open wide my doors and have you help me enjoy it here." She had no illusions about her responsibilities as the First Lady of Texas, but like all her other responsibilities, she made it her pleasure to meet it. Given the health and strength, how she would have loved transplanting the full hospitality of her ranch home to the Texas capital! And how Texas would have enjoyed the sincerity of that hospitality!

Hers was an easy way, yet eloquent with simplicity. "Stay for dinner," she urged when I dropped in last summer, dusty and road-smeared to leave her some wild flowers gathered between Louisiana and Austin. "Do stay. Magnolia's cooking turnip greens!" My corsage of wilted tuberoses she asked me to unpin and set in water so she could smell them. She substituted in its place a boutonniere of fresh pansies.

She loved flowers, loved to grow them, to have them all about her always. Once with the house full of company, I found her laughing gaily because the ice box was packed lipping full of talisman roses! She loved flowers, yet for her funeral it was urged that flowers not be sent. Rather, the request was that—instead of blankets of flowers for covering her last going away—friends should make, in her memory, gifts to the Red Cross, to the world's living needy ones. That, too, was like Fay Stevenson—kind, helpful, selfless. So it was that when earth received her into its long rest, Texas skies laid over the land a blanket of winter's cleanest cold. I think that pleased her, too, looking back from the wide open doors of All the Tomorrows.

The War

On the afternoon of December 7, my best friend asked me, "What do you think about the war?" and I said, "It looks serious."

Yeager's writing before the American entrance into World War II is full of the rumors and rumbles of wars elsewhere; after Pearl Harbor, it all came home to Claxton and Rochelle and Brady. Although she pitched in both literally and in print to support the war effort, she is quite frank in being unable to find it all uplifting. Neither a viewer-with-alarm nor a Pollyanna, her struggle to find a way to *think* about the war, a way to be both honest to herself and loyal to her country, is typical of her lifelong juggling act between individualism and connectedness.

o o o o o o o o o o o o o o o

September 7, 1939
With millions of men equipped to take the lives of other men equipped to take the lives of them, we sit at our radios or snatch ink-wet papers to see how one man thinks. This story tells all for the manly art of war: two sentries on guard outside the tent during a council of war heard the general raise his voice and demand, "You take that position tomorrow if it costs us ten thousand men!" Said one raised-sentry-eyebrow to the other raised-sentry-eyebrow, "Liberal old so-and-so, isn't he?"

I thank God that I live in a country where on September 1 a housewife could get so engrossed in the making of a pumpkin pie that she forgot to tune in for the latest newscast.

My visitors this week talk about war. Grandpa Brown makes no predictions, offers no opinions, but can tell you the last minute's war news by press and radio. Elmer Davenport thinks the Big He of Berlin is bluffing. Clara Rice thinks we should forget about it. Ida Stewart pins her faith to arbitration by Mr. Roosevelt. Mackie Ma at seventy-seven considers herself an onlooker, yet when she hears a special bulletin right into the middle of the Ma Perkins program that wheat has advanced seven cents, Mackie Ma humph-humphs sardonically through her nose: "Rich man's war; poor man's fight."

It is a crime in Germany, punishable by death, to listen to certain radio broadcasts. My countryman says that a similar situation prevails here, but we just haven't found it out.

Nazism for German women may have talking points. In rationing clothing this week, it was announced each woman is allowed to possess six pairs of stockings. Six pairs all at once! The mere contemplation of the personal ownership and operation of twelve leg sheaths at one and the same time gives me a sort of centipedish outlook on life. Among my acquaintances, multiplicity of leg coverings is rarely enjoyed by other than brides and campus cuties and the filthy rich. The rest of us pretty generally hobble along on one good pair ("good" being a relative term) and a pair that's just started or is about to start a runner.

Of course, frau Nazi's six pairs may in reality be stockings and not hose. In which case, not a democratress in all our fair land would swap her one good (relative term) and her just started or about-to-start a runner pair of hose for the whole cache of Swastika sox.

Newspaper headlines in order to be newspaper headlines this week must feature the name of Hitler, but news in our neighborhood is about hay. Ours is stacked, two mounds blocking out twin humps against the sky, if you get the right angle. Of course, they are not great bulwarks of winter rations like Walter Mooring haystacks, but I think they are quite beautiful. Himself says they are not really so hot, being sort of unduly fluffy or something. But we are both delighted with them. You see, they are ours, and it's been too long a time since we had a haystack. It makes us feel respectable again.

September 28, 1939

"Teach Us to Pray"

Once I heard a story which amused me. It was about an early cowboy who turned evangelist. Having dared to defy in fiery sermons the vice he knew existed in the community, he refused to get out of town, as he had been ordered to do, and so waited in his hotel room for a call from the tough guys who had promised him, for his failure to obey orders, a personally conducted neck-tie party. Left alone, the evangelist and his singer sought comfort in Holy Writ. They found a text: "Watch and pray," they read. Suddenly there was the sound of feet and the muffled growl of angry voices. Closing the Bible, the evangelist cowboy caught up his pistols that he had holstered on the range and had not learned to feel comfortable without and muttered to his companion, "Cumbie, you pray; I'll watch."

While this story—as I have said—amuses me, I have always felt it would have grieved the Man of Galilee. It's a lusty yarn, full of high courage and self-reliance, but no doubt about it, there's something wrong with it.

Something of the same feeling I get about praying for peace. The King of England kneels in Westminster and prays to God for peace—while the munitions works of Vickers grinds day and night in the production of arms for killing men. Likewise in an ancient cathedral of Paris, leaders pray for peace, but the voices of the supplicants are lost in the roar of munitions factories, speeded to double-quick, turning out implements of death. Nor are we more consistent nor holier in our own land. I doubt that God can hear the cries for peace above the din of the world's munitions works.

And your prayer and my prayer—how do they square with the pattern laid down by the Prince of Peace when one came to Him and said, "Teach us to pray"? How near to the Lord do we get when we say, "Our Father, who art in heaven, hallowed be Thy name"? How, exactly, have we gone about, today, honoring God's name—within the past week, then—well, within the past month?

"Thy kingdom come." How much time and study have we put in satisfying ourselves as to the meaning of those words? What is "Thy kingdom"? How empty, then, to pray for "Thy kingdom" to come when we don't even know what it is. Or, if we know what it is, what have we done today to make it come?

"Thy will be done on earth as it is in heaven." Same as above. And do we mean "Thy will be done" before or after our will is done?

"Give us this day our daily bread." Who is "us," and does bread mean nourishment for babies of all colors in all lands, and could it mean sauerkraut as well as leg of mutton?

There be those who choke on the rest of it.

"Suggestions for a More Timely Pattern"

On the whole, a more timely pattern of prayer for American today would be that of the humble one who said, "Be merciful to me, a sinner—for I am a sinner of omission. I have omitted to school my emotions, so that I am swayed by every wind that blows. I have omitted to train my intellect for thinking until I let the other fellow do my thinking for me. I have omitted to learn humility, so that I am a swaggering braggart, an easy tool for dragging out of the coals anybody's chestnuts when I am a little flattered. I have omitted to learn to love mankind and have not taught my children to love peace. I have held the priceless heritage of American freedom cheap—thoughtlessly, impulsively risking it on slim chances. Be merciful to me, a sinner."

"Putting Feet to Prayers"

I have small faith in the efficacy of the governor's plan to have all people pray that "each member of that great body (Congress) and our President and his Cabinet members have Divine guidance" when they meet in called session. That is, I have small faith that the prayers will get anywhere unless the pray-ers write, telephone, telegraph, and have their friends write, telephone, telegraph, to Washington, telling the representatives of the people that it is the wish of the voters that they keep us out of war.

A better prayer, it seems to me, would be one asking God to make America worthy of peace—a great nation where, should Old World civilization leach its strength in wasting wars, England's province for ruling, Germany's gift for organization, France's zest for living, and Russia's great vitality shall find fertile soil for growing strong again. That is, it seems to me, this would be a better prayer, provided the one who prays gets up from humble knees and sets about making this that sort of a country. For too long we've worded a prayer to God, then washed our hands of the project, leaving the labor to God.

"Intriguing Facts about Non-Intriguing People"
Infant mortality is the lowest in the world in Scandinavia. Likewise, illiteracy. There are no slums nor aged poor in Denmark. Sweden has no foreign allegiances of any kind. She has had no war since 1814. In 1930 Denmark tried to abolish her army and to make keeping peace a fine art—arguing that if she were invaded by a great power, she'd be sure to be defeated. There is no entente in Scandinavia—Sweden, Denmark, and Norway each refusing to pull the others' chestnuts out of the fire. Holland and Switzerland each stayed out of the last World War by nurturing the idea that the future of all humanity didn't rest on their shoulders.

"Impractical"
Political hot-air is full of pop-offs about the impracticality of cash-and-carry, of non-intervention, of non-participation. Have you ever heard anything less practical than the injunction, "If any man will sue thee at law and take away thy coat, let him have thy cloak also, and whoever shall compel thee to go a mile, go with him twain"? There are other things—things more important than being practical.

June 6, 1940

"Myopia"
Ogden Nash tunes "worsens" with "persons" in a delightfully barbaric rhyme, if it is a rhyme, that expresses the

reaction of me and a lot of other people I know who listen to and read the news these days when we'd rather not—but can't keep from it, somehow. Says Ogden, "All you get is news, and just when you think at least the outlook is so black that it can grow no blacker, it *worsens*, and that is why I do not like to get the news, because there never has been an era when so many things were going so right for so many of the wrong *persons*."

Yet, one thing about belonging to a great country or an old family that is encouraging is the fact that regardless of what happens—life, death, birth, disgrace, sorrow, victory, defeat—it has happened to others of yours before; and like others, you can rise Phoenix-like from the gray ashes. I find juicy quotes from the wise ones of other days of doom cheering today, since time has proved them groundless. There was, for instance, England's Prime Minister William Pitt, who, 157 years ago, said as he saw America breaking away from the empire, "There is scarcely anything around us but ruin and despair." And see how that thing worked itself out.

Then ninety-two years ago Lord Shaftesbury, that grand old fighter for England's underprivileged, seeing the map of Europe break out in a periodic rash of revolutions, wailed, "Nothing can save the British Empire from shipwreck."

The following year the energetic Disraeli got out of bed on the wrong side and viewed the situation with alarm. Said the generally shrewd little Jew, "In industry, commerce, and agriculture there is no hope." But industry, commerce, and agriculture kept right on after things settled down, and they are in a right healthy state even today.

Eighty-nine years ago the Duke of Wellington, he who with the assistance of a thundershower licked thunder out of the great Napoleon at Waterloo, saw things darkly and sighed, "I thank God I will be spared from seeing the consummation of ruin that is gathering round," and went ahead and died, but the ruin didn't come—not even yet.

It seems to be the near vision that focuses the disaster. My countryman says he has cut his news analysis down to H.V. Kaltenborn of NBC and Dub Doran of Rochelle. They both think the Allies will win and can both tell you why.

"Naked"

About our preparedness, it seems we were innocent—as the little duck who didn't realize that his pants were *down*.

We told ourselves that with the world's best or second best navy, an army ranking twentieth gave us a benign look, at the same time that it provided us with a sense of security—for weren't there two oceans between us and the Rhine? Then, too, there were some airplanes. Behind this wall of defense, we felt secure enough to keep on building up big business and fat relief rolls. All our pals said we were safe, and we believed them. The lust to fight our fellow man as a brute, the law of tooth and claw, we said were past. They belonged to the twilight times of man. We lived in a civilized world. Of course, there were calamity howlers who warned of a bumptious, unfulfilled people, but mostly the bumptious ones were far away, and the world has always had its viewers with alarm.

Then one day we saw a thing that could not be. We saw mass murder called war. We saw the world's best soldiers, the world's proudest navy suffering at the hands of a mechanized force the like of which only dreamers had envisioned—dreamers and plodding scientists. The man that has been called Europe's Emperor began dealing from the bottom, and the tricks he turned out called Orson Welles a sissy. It was real. It worked. And suddenly we knew that we were naked.

As shocking as that was, we unfortunately cannot do as the embarrassed emperor in the old story did and rush to our wardrobe to clothe ourselves. Even with the appropriation of four billions of dollars for defense, we are still naked. Nobody knows how soon airplanes can be built by machinery in sufficient quantity to protect us, or how many airplanes that will take anyhow. This is a thing that has never happened before, However, this we do know: it has been taking us four to six years to build a battleship. Also, in this land of the free, battleship workers can and do strike. We are embarrassed. We are in danger, however remote we can only guess. We know we are naked, and it is the part of wisdom to behave like naked folks. Today the familiar "Now is the time for all good men to come to the aid of their country" is more than a typewriter exercise.

April 17, 1941

On Army Day, according to reporter J.B. Krueger, six or seven thousand citizens watched twenty thousand armed men of the 36th Division, an Army unit under continuous training for the past twenty years, as it passed in review. The reporter said Army officers were proud of the "thrilling sight of armed men, tough as leather and armed to the hilt . . . on the march." But, he said, they were disappointed that there were only seven thousand onlookers. More, they were somewhat appalled with the idea that the Texan and the American heart is not with the Army. So poignantly did they regret this that they freely voiced their disappointment in an interview for the state newspapers in which Brevet Lieutenant General John A. Hulen is quoted as saying that the failure of the public to respond to the review of the 36th Division indicated that "the terrible situation we are facing has not soaked into the thoughts and emotions of ordinary Americans."

I was a part of the six or seven thousand ordinary Americans watching the parade of the 36th Division. (Another reporter estimated the crowd at fifty thousand, a considerable plus to reporter Krueger's—but I wouldn't know who is right, as I can't ever guess a crowd.)

At the review I saw long lines of khaki legs and arms moving across the drills on a former oat patch as if they were one arm and one leg. There were the horses of the mechanized cavalry, great trucks and heavy equipment of the 111th Engineers, medical, quartermasters, and field artillery units. There were pontoon boats, power drills, graders, ambulances, troop trucks, mobile repair shops, howitzers, and cannon. And bands. There were airplanes. I saw them, but I was not thrilled. Awed seems a better word for what went on inside me.

Up and down the long line of spectators I walked. I talked to mothers and fathers, soldiers in uniform, boys and girls and small children. They didn't seem thrilled either. Most mothers talked, not of the mile-long review, but of where their boys are—some in camp, some not yet called, some officers. Even the mothers of officers had not yet lost themselves in the tradition of the Army. They seemed to speak of their sons rather than of the Army's officers. Fathers mostly turned the talk to crops or to the war in Europe. Soldiers talked a little of camp life, but more of home. One showed me a picture his baby. Boys on the sidelines displayed little enough personal enthusiasm for the show. I thought they seemed puzzled a bit. Girls like the color and the uniforms, and the children loved the rhythm of the bands and the marching columns. As for me, I kept seeing the guns. Twenty thousand men trained to think in terms of guns—guns for hunting other men. It seemed pretty awful to me.

No, I'm not a pacifist. I've not the grace for turning the other cheek. Pushed to it, I'd claw and jab and bite and choke my fellow man with the worst of them. It's just that I'm not pushed yet. Today, I'd rather not be bothered. I'm not a pacifist. I'm a somnambulist. I'm afraid Brevet Lieutenant General John A. Hulen is right.

January 1, 1942

There is war in the Pacific. It is ours. There is war in Washington. It is ours. It's on our radios, in our newspapers, in every conversation. It sits at our firesides, eats at our tables, and goes to bed with us. Yet we go about our daily affairs pretty much as we ever did. Our daily affairs, as do the daily affairs of most other country people, center about providing ourselves with food, shelter, and clothing from the soil under our feet. With the surplus the world is fed, sheltered, and clothed. That is the normal procedure.

In war times we begin to feed, shelter, and clothe the world before a surplus has accumulated. That is, we who provide the world's necessities must share. Our work is important this January. It is important every January—and all the other months. Soldiers sleep warm in Iceland because the wool grows long on our sheep. Sailors and soldiers and airmen wrap our cowhides around their feet, and tomorrow or Saturday or whenever they are scraping the mud of Hawaii off them or wiping them clean of the dust of Lybia, Manila, or wherever. Bread made from the grain from our fields keeps their stomachs full and their hearts brave.

Realizing that the fate of our way of life is depending in a large measure on how well we do our job, we go about our chores with more earnestness than usual this January. Peace times or war times, ours is a good job and important. Shakespeare had a sheepherder who spoke a memorable line in explanation of his way of life. "I am a true laborer," said he. "I earn what I eat, get that I wear, owe no man hate, envy no man's happiness, glad of other man's good, content with my farm, and the greatest of my pride is to see my ewes graze and my lambs suck."

'Twould be a sweeter world by far, and even the simple can see it, if it had more sheepherders in it.

February 19, 1942

What Do You Think About the War?"

On the afternoon of December 7, my best friend asked me, "What do you think about the war?" and I said, "It looks serious."

Ever since then I've marveled at the brilliance and the sufficiency of my answer, for to this day that's about as far as I've got in analyzing anything that I think about the war. And as I see it, I've got even farther than most people I hear talking about the war. "Make a column on what you really think about the war," readers have suggested with some earnestness. Well, here 'tis.

"Getting Nowhere Fast"

"What do you think about the war?" opens a variety of types of conversations that get me and the converser about as much results as if we'd spent the time weaving ropes of sand or trying to extract sunbeams from cucumbers. Among the kinds I am becoming particularly allergic to are these:

1. Citing Nostradamus, the mathematical prognostications of the Pyramids, and Revelation: any one of these sets of prophecies is interesting; and escapists, who had rather dawdle with an idea than face it and attempt to solve it, hug the delusions of these prophecies with the devotion of a zealot. The trouble with these and other mystic forecasts is that any interpreter can and does make any one of them say anything he wishes to say, and the gullible gulp it.
2. Offering a plan of one's own to get the thing over in a hurry: you know the fellow who bears the burden of this conversation. You've heard him at every football game. He's brimful of hindsight and free advice for the coach, and criticism of whatever is. The impressive thing about him is the surprising fact that, full of brilliant ideas for running the other fellow's business, he seems to have such a dearth of ideas and energy for running his own.
3. Saying that the Japs can't and that Hitler can't and citing excellent authority to prove it: you know his line. The Japs can't take Hong Kong, feed their armies, feed their civilians, train precision pilots, get the ships or the planes or the supplies or last another week. Hitler can't take the Maginot Line, control his conquered peoples, feed his armies, supply his motorized units, get the gasoline. The only trouble with the sweet comfort of this line of talk is the disturbing fact is that the Japs do and Hitler does.
4. Getting cocky about the undertaking, as if it were a before-breakfast spell in which "we'll slap the dirty little Jap" and it will all be over without mussing us up in the melee: sure enough, we do slap him, but the little son-of-a-gun doesn't stay slapped. He deflates our ego and invites us to real carnage with great lust and little cockiness.
5. Saying, "Win, lose, or draw, this country won't be fit to live in": this fellow has generally spent a gloomy lifetime draping crepe, and you can record the history of

his service to others on your thumbnail. He loves this dark day, and is he happy in his crepery!
6. Wailing in self pity about remembering Pearl Harbor: we are beginning to learn that remembering Pearl Harbor involves Kimmel and Short and stinky things in Washington. Mending the holes in our own armor is a healthy thing to do.
7. There are others.

"The War as I See It"

The war is far too big for me to see it. Isn't it too big for your vision? So the question becomes not "What do you think about the war?" but "What do you do about the war—here, now, today?" That's something I can think about, and I do. I am a woman without sons to send to the war, so I send young relatives and neighbors and friends. While they are gone, I'll do a homemaker's part to make this country a place worth fighting to come back to. Here's some of the how:

1. I work to make my home a place where tired folks may rest, where friends may meet for companionship, where laughter comes free, and one may cry if one must, and children may feel secure.
2. I am trying to clear myself of debt and arrive at an economic independence so that society will not have to care for me when this is over and society is heels-over caring for other needy ones. I may even aspire to provide the economic security of another when need arises. I am guarding my health and the health of my family for the same reasons.
3. I accept as a privilege the sacrifices that come with this tragedy. I have the imagination and the will to make mush and milk taste like manna, and be gay on any amount of sugar or no sugar. I can move off rubber tires and back to the spring seat with neatness. I can buy bonds with folding money and stamps instead of stockings. I can accept the loss of loved ones with understanding and humility and pride.

4. I can accept the bombing of my home and my town and my country. I've never experienced the risks of war at home, but my mother has and her mother had and millions of others do it every day.
5. I can keep my hates and prejudices and unweighed criticisms under control, remembering the enemy's slogan is to divide us and conquer us.
6. And I can fight to believe in the civilization we have inherited and built onto—to believe that it has enough of the eternal in it to endure even this and more. I don't merely say it; I believe it. I will improve on the ancient poet Doer who comforted himself dolefully with the refrain, "This sorrow passed away; so will mine." My new song will be, "With God's grace, we shall pass this sorrow away, and when it is gone, there shall be again in this world freedom and opportunity and hope; there shall be courage and optimism and faith; and truth and honor shall prevail."

March 26, 1942

For a year now, I've been driving past the Civilian Basic School at Curtis Field where Air Corps pilots are being trained. From time to time, I've seen boys marching there in formation; boys at recreation; boys turning in at the mess hall, the barracks, the canteen; boys in helmets and flying gear; boys driving into camp; boys on leave from camp—boys, boys, boys, all of them engaged in some part of the routine of making themselves into Air Corps pilots. These fellows have ridden into and out of town with us in the family car. We've talked to them wherever we have found them. We've broken bread with some of them under our own roof. We've stood before the flag with them at retreat. Once we sang with them at recreation about the sound effects on Old McDonald's Farm.

But last week, under the guidance of Captain Del Bueno, I tried to see all that I could of Curtis Field in two hours. As best I can, I want to share with you the things I learned there. I was made aware as I had not been before that Curtis Field is the scene of a big job, that it is being done in a big way, that it is being done for me and for you and for you and for you, and that, like me, you want to know about it, too. I didn't learn all about Curtis Field. I just learned my two hours' worth, but the things I learned have somehow come to live with me, and I want you to know them too.

What I learned from the Commanding Officer

On the wall across from Major Gunn's desk there is framed a slogan with a picture above it. In fact, wherever Major Gunn goes, I am persuaded slogans spring up like grass on the heels of a late spring rain. I found slogans of his making all over the camp—terse, pungent, at times witty, at times as incisive as a surgeon's knife, provocative of thought, always apt. And the one that meets the Major's eyes as he raises them from work on his desk is an epitome of the spirit of aviation wherever men make themselves at home in the air. It says, "Me worry?" and the picture above is a caricature of all the gay, roguish, laughter-loving, fresh faced, altogether lovable simpletons a carefree world ever dreamed of. The philosophy of the camp, as I got it, seems to be that there are exactly two things to worry about in this world: the things you can help and the things you can't help. It becomes the every-breathing-minute business of an aviator to go ahead right now and help the things he can help. That's what he studies for. That's what he piles up flying hours for. He eats it, sleeps it, wakes up and works at it again. And the things he can't help? "Those," the Me-worry caricature seems to say for flyers everywhere, "well, those things are in the lap of the gods, and pretty generally the gods and me, well, we get along just like this!"

Major Gunn speaks of his job of training pilots for the Air Corps as a real job—now stripped of all its trimmings, with every man's shoulder to the wheel for a mighty heave that will be felt on tother side of the world. I asked how well the schools had prepared the boys for taking the training at Curtis. The officer's brow became a line. "Too many of them," he said, "are hindered by their inability to read a thought clearly from the printed page, and most of them have not been taught to think with precision in numbers." That was true, too, he added, when two years of college was required. I thought the major's trouble was a hole in the dyke today's educators might do something better about than hold their fingers in.

What I learned about parachutes

From the two young men who care for the field's parachutes, I gained the comforting information that since 1918 no parachute has failed to open for the bailer-out, provided the bailer was the required number of feet in the air. I learned to my dismay that every parachute is made with a hole in the top of it big enough to run a birthday cake through and never bobble a candle. The hole is not for running birthday cakes through, though. That's just the right way to make them.

In the building with the parachutes were pictures of every airplane wreck Curtis Field has suffered. Under each picture I found a Major Gunn summary of slogan proportions. The major does not play up the flying field's tragedies. He does not play them down. He is a realist, as majors must be, and each summary bears the mark of a realist's analysis. Under the pictured shambles of a plane there was written, "Deliberate disobedience of regulations, lack of responsibility, and a childish desire to show off, combined with over-confidence, cost the government one complete airplane and two pilots." This diagnosis, it seems to me, might keep another Curtis Field flier and his plane flying.

Nobody is prouder than Major Gunn of the field's record of the ratio of two million miles plus in the air to one crack-up; but nobody is more concerned than he to make that two million more miles and the crack-ups fewer.

Continued in the next issue

Two hours of Curtis Field show a lot of things cooking, and a Yeagitorial is hardly any space at all for telling you, so next week's stint will be more about the Civilian Basic School at Curtis Field. You will want to know about the classrooms and the boys in the classrooms. There were trainer planes, hangars, radios, and the supply division. There were airplanes. And there was Captain Del Bueno. They weren't the way I thought they'd be. They were different from the way I see them in movies. There is, for instance, the matter of the salute and who speaks to whom and how and when. I had picked up the idea somewhere that military howdying is somewhat exclusive—you know, like the Bostonian aristocracy, where "the Lowells speak only to the Cabots, and the Cabots speak only to God." Well, folks, it isn't that way in our Air Corps. Curtis Field folks are the howdyingest people I've met since last election—and they are not running for anything!

April 2, 1942

More about Curtis Field

April 6 is Army Day. On next Monday fitting recognition throughout the nation will be given to our army. Such will be the demonstration that, when it is over, the American citizen will have a better appreciation and evaluation of the men in our army; and by the interest we show in Army Day, the men of the armed forces can judge somewhat the American citizen's appreciation of the job the army is putting up. Army Day will not pass unnoted at Curtis Field; for, though the Air Corps does not look like the army, nor does it look like the navy, yet wherever the army is in action, you'll find the Air Corps, and wherever the navy is in action, you'll find the Air Corps. Too, the Air Corps is frequently in action nowadays where they have neither soldiers nor sailors to augment them, at which time it is their fervent, sincere prayer that nobody finds them till their stint is done.

In the hangar

At Curtis Field, where I was recently a visitor for the *Heart O' Texas News*, I saw an airplane undergoing a field repair job. I wondered whether the plane had "developed a knock" or needed new rings or had been into trouble, the way our own transportation facility behaves. "Oh, no," explained the adjutant, "there's no trouble with the plane. We can't afford to allow trouble to show up in this business. That is just the way we go over a plane when it has been in the air fifty hours. Not only that, but when a plane has flown its specified hours, its motor is crated and sent to the repair depot for complete reconstruction." I got the idea that the goins-over of airplanes were somewhat in the class with our Saturday night baths—they get the goins-over periodically, whether they need them or not.

You would be interested to see how the field goings-over work. One doesn't simply turn a plane over to a mechanic and say, "Here she is; tune 'er up." An airplane repair job is the work of specialists, bunches of them. The plane I saw being repaired was lousy with men—each man or group of men working on and testing the part of the machine he or they knew about. As I watched them at work, complicated instruments all about, so intent on their various jobs that they scarcely noticed visitors, I experienced an appreciation of that army behind the Army, that army eighteen times as many in number as the army of men who do the shooting, that army of mechanics and helpers—producers everywhere—which must function before the enemy feels the force of our steel. I got a new evaluation of the faith the flying fighter rests in the ability and responsibility of the mechanics that keep 'em flying!

Instrument trainers

I saw training of pilots by use of instrument trainers. With a student shut from sight of all except the instrument board of his dummy plane supported on a pedestal, an instructor, connected with the student by radiophone, worked out hypothetical flights, while an instrument on the instructor's desk plotted on paper the movements of the imaginary flight. In short, the student pilot, shut into the dummy plane, did a complete job of instrument flying such as he will do in the air—except he didn't go anywhere and he didn't take any chances. How they did it was completely over my head, but the instructors weren't worried about that. I stood agape before the array of instruments at the command of the instructor, and did a mental hat-raising to the ingenuity of man, that he has wrought devices of such astounding mechanical wonder. I thought a little, too, about Orville and Wilbur, the Wright boys, who brought it to the attention of the world that man might successfully overcome the law of gravity. I wondered what their reactions would be to a trip through Curtis Field. I still do.

In the supply room

You don't know how many pilots are trained at Curtis. That is a military secret, though from the business-like looks of things I saw there, I doubt that the information, especially when multiplied by the number of similar fields over the nation, would be calculated to give aid and comfort to the enemy. In the supply room, I took a housewife's-eye view of what it takes to keep 'em flying—especially in clothes and planes. This is to tell you that the next time you see a plane high in the blue, playing hide-and-seek among the cumulonimbus, you may know the pilot in the plane is dressed up in clothes. I thought I had seen sheep-lined coats before, but the rich, deep pile of the pilot's coat has a softness and warmth that beggars the finest sables in milady's wardrobe. And he has pants and high shoes and gloves lined with the same. Running my hand over the wool of the pilots' garments, I thought of the farms and ranches where the wool comes from. Our job, too, I told myself, is a part of the Air Force.

There was a stack of scarves. When flying, the boys wear them tucked in about their necks. Most of the scarves are around two yards long and three-fourths of a yard wide. They are made from the silk of old parachutes.

Stacked on the floor were the garments of last week's graduating class like mantles of departing prophets fallen to the new recruits.

I didn't see the supply of undies. I am sure they are there, though, for at Mrs. Hobbs' Helpy-Selfy Laundry, where I do my weekly wash, I learned that Curtis Field washes are weighty with heavy longhandles. No short-panty, Clark Gable sissies these! They are he-some fellows and require real he-man body swathings!

Was it your kettle that went into the making of the propeller Captain Del Bueno showed us? I judged it was about a dozen feet long, possibly less. "This piece of aluminium," he said, "cost the army $700."

April 9, 1942

What I learned about Curtis Field

The aviation students at Curtis Field will be non-commissioned pilots of the Army Air Corps when they have finished another period of training in another school after completing their term at Curtis. They had three months aeronautics before coming to the basic school here. They are between eighteen and twenty-two years of age, high school graduates with one and one-half years in mathematics. They receive the same ground and air instruction as that given cadets and are paid according to their rank plus fifty percent while engaged on flight duty. They are enlisted men of the Army, and when their training is finished, these non-commissioned officers will be that part of the army known as staff sergeant pilots, for it is the army's intention to build up its non-commissioned pilot personnel to twenty percent of the Army's total pilot strength.

In the classroom

A trip through the empty classrooms gave me some evaluation of the kind of young fellows who train at Curtis. The classrooms are, in equipment and design, little different from those you would find in any modern high school. There are lecture chairs, teachers' desks, blackboards, maps, and charts. Yes, and there are Major Gunn's silent teachers, his mottoes. One that struck me amidships said, "Aviation, to an even greater extent that the sea, is terribly unforgiving of any carelessness or neglect."

This idea of the carelessness and neglect carrying their own penalty seemed to have sunk in on Curtis Field students to the extent that even the appearance of the classrooms is different from any other classrooms for young gentlemen I have ever seen. Last month the field observed its first birthday. Some of its classrooms have been in use for twelve months. Many boys have graduated from them, and it is hardly a debatable question among teachers that boys, as such, are a bit rough on classrooms and classroom equipment. This isn't true at Curtis. Property is given use with care at the training school. The chairs, the walls, and all equipment show the use of careful craftsmen. True, the hard, brash newness is gone, the empty rooms hold a sense of having been lived in, but there are no jackknife carvings, no charcoal frescoes, no careless abuse of the schoolrooms.

Though the instruction begins on the high school level, considerable of the work I saw indicated that the course is addressed to such of the high school boys as those who were more than average diligent during their high school experiences about the materials inside textbooks and who have learned a degree of responsibility and industry. I liked this motto about the industry: "When God made us he gave us two ends: one to think with and one to sit on. A man's success depends upon which end he uses most." In one classroom I was amazed to find a board full of dah-dah-dit and dit-dah-dah. I was chagrinned, too, at my own ineptitude in familiarizing myself with the code. Until I saw the chart full of the, to me, senseless spellings, I had thought that dah-dah-dit belonged exclusively to the flying funnies of Smiling Jack.

About boning

In the schools where I have been, I have seen the fine art of boning developed to an astonishing degree, or was cramming, grinding, or some other happy term your word for it? The perfidy, as I have observed and practiced it, consists of attending class in a sort of haze, picking up a smattering here and a smidgen there throughout the course, then humping like the devil to get together enough information to pass the examinations. Midnight oil, grind sessions, tutoring, something up the sleeve, and all that sort of thing. I got the idea out at Curtis Field that that sort of thing doesn't go on with aviators.

On the trip through the school, Captain Del Bueno opened a door upon a class in session. The instructor was lecturing, and the opened door faced the roomful of boys. As we stood there before them, hardly an eye turned our way. They listened to the instructor. There was an alertness in their faces—young faces with something of the choir-boy look still with them. Keen faces, nonetheless, with purpose firming their eyes and squaring the set of their shoulders. I was impressed with the appearance of this cross-section of young students from all over the country.

In the training course following Curtis, there will be a few more pilots to fail the course. Young fliers don't like "wash outs," but therein does not lie their chief concern. These youngsters aim to master ground school instruction because they realize that only mastery of ground schooling will be sufficient on that occasion when they themselves go to put into practice the theory of their art. Here "good enough" just won't do. Records show that the greatest number of tragedies in aviation are marked up by the students who fumbled their ground schooling. On a classroom wall I saw Pope's well-turned lines rhyming their ancient warning with a new accent. Says Alexander Pope to the young pilots at Curtis Field, "A little learning is a dangerous thing. Drink deep, or taste not the Pierian spring; there shallow drafts intoxicate the brain, and drinking largely sobers us again."

April 16, 1942

Conclusion of remarks on Curtis Field

I didn't believe it a little while ago when people said that Mayor Curtis and the United States Government were going to build a Basic Training School in Kirby Huffman's cow pasture. Not, I told myself, a school for fliers, and certainly not in Kirby's pasture. You see, I was accustomed to seeing his cows graze there. Besides, I had no vision.

But Mayor Curtis had vision and the United States Government had vision, and now the Huffman cows graze in quieter spots—and we have Curtis Field.

Even a groundling like me gets a lift out of Curtis Field. Boys and girls I have taught work there, doing their share to give the nation pilots. My neighbors and my friends are employees of the field, each realizing that he has more than just a job to perform. In the radio department of the Maintenance Division, three Brady men under the direction of Dan Linville are a part of the staff that twist knobs, pull switches, and otherwise do the chores that keep the aerial broadcasting system and radio communications clicking over the field and in the planes.

On Army Day

When the field was host to the public on Army Day, I loved seeing all of us seeing Curtis Field. Students at the school steered us in big and little bunches out to see the airplanes, through the instrument training department, the ground school building, the barracks, the mess hall, and the recreation hall, where I was impressed again with a Major Gunn motto over the door which says to Curtis Field and the world in general: "What you earn in the daytime goes into your pocketbook. What you spend at night, into your character."

Back at the canteen, I talked with my young host. "Now," I said, "I know everything about airplanes and about Curtis Field, except one thing."

"And that?" he asked.

"I don't know why you do it—why you want to fly. Why do you?"

I suppose the question was a little blunt, and so for a few minutes we sat out an awkward silence, till the boy, looking me straight in the eye, said simply, "I like flying, see? It's a job, and somebody has to do it."

"Afterwards?" I asked.

"Oh, afterwards," he laughed, sure of himself, I thought. "I shall have a plane of my own. My brother at home—he wanted to fly, but he didn't get to. There were other things. Now I am to go ahead; when it's over, I am to go back home and teach him to fly. We like flying—see?"

The Adjutant's point of view

I am an earthbound creature and content to be earthbound. So I followed Captain Del Bueno about over the Field, trying to learn about it. I kept trying to find a place to ask the Adjutant why the fellows chose the Air Corps with such eagerness, realizing as they must the strenuous life a flyer leads and the dangers that attend it. I nailed him with the question when we reached the hangar. He gave me a lifted masculine eyebrow, something that might pass for a smile and—if he were not the Adjutant—I would say an impudent look. "Perhaps that's why," he said. "Perhaps they like the strenuous life, spiced with danger. Or perhaps it appeals because the air is not man's element. Then there are fellows who like to do things with machines."

And he climbed into the cockpit of an idle airplane and dived into its innards, pushing this and twisting that. We stood on the wings and gaped as he carried on an animated conversation with himself about how it climbs and banks and turns, how the pilot gets into communication with the other fellow in the plane with him and with the air field, how he tells how he's sitting in relation to the earth, how he checks on fuel, what he does when he goes to land and this and that and a hundred other things that left me with the impression that the flyer could do with a bunch more hands and feet, and heads, too, provided the heads were cool, deliberate and in good working order—but it left me a fuzzy idea about why young men choose to become pilots.

So I am still in the air. Captain Del Bueno's philosophy nor his beautiful airplane with all the surprising gadgets nor his very fine shrug at my helplessness when he says, "That's all there is to it," nor the student's "I like flying, see?" have really told a prosaic, plodding woman what allures in modern aviation.

John Gillespie Magee, Jr., explains

Back in the headquarters office, however, I was given a copy of a poem that hangs on the wall. Written by a young pilot, the poem says some things I do understand and appreciate. I'll let John tell you.

High Flight

Oh, I have slipped the surly bonds of earth,
And danced the skies on laughter-silvered wings;
Sunward I've climbed and joined the tumbling mirth
Of sun-split clouds—and done a hundred things
You have not dreamed of—wheeled and soared and swung

High in the sunlit silence. Hov'ring there,
I've chased the shouting winds along and flung
My eager craft through footless halls of air.
Up, up the long delirious burning blue,
I've topped the windswept heights with easy grace,
Where never lark, nor even eagle flew;
And, while with silent, lifting mind I've trod
The high untrespassed sanctity of space,
Put out my hand, and touched the face of God.

John Jr., likes flying, see? And so I've made a crude sonnet to tell him that I like his liking flying. This goes for him and all the other earnest young fellows who like flying because they like flying.

From Ma Yeager to John Gillespie Magee, Jr., *et al.*

Yes, boy, I caught the glint of your bright wings;
Your motor crooned a cloud-tossed lullaby.
I hailed you through the wash of baby things,
Like wind-socks hung out on the line to dry.
Again, I saw your high-flung craft swoop low
As in the soil I stooped and mucked in lime
To grow my beans. I like to garden so—
For God walks with me in the cool, sometimes.
Go to it, Johnny, Jr.; this adds up.
When Adolph Shicklegruber and other heels
Let slip their dogs, God's known will drink the cup—
You dreaming sunward, I earthward, each seals
Himself to break the hell-fiends' rod
So man is free again to search for God.

May 14, 1942

During World War I, I bought sugar over the counter at thirty cents a pound. There weren't any ration cards, and one could have the sugar if one could produce the thirty cents. Skimping on recipes, substituting molasses and honey for sugar, pretending that sweetless meals were a lot of fun, I learned a good, solid, housewifely object lesson in the proper appreciation of sugar. So when the commodity tapered off to two-bits, I had a sugar bin built for my kitchen, pitched it with precaution inside and out, somewhat after the manner of Noah's ark, took a quarter of a hundred dollars from deep in the family sock, went to town and bought a hundredweight of sugar.

From that time to this, I have rarely seen the bottom of my sugar bin. Its fullness has been a comfort to me. It has been a challenge to my frugality. From time to time, I've made it a habit to buy a ten or twenty-five pound sack of sugar when the family budget could budge it. If I took in eggs and butter and the shopping list totaled in my favor, I generally added a measure of sugar. During canning season and when and if I found the exchequer flush, I bought a hundred pounds. Somehow, it seemed to sort of give me a sense of well-being to know it was a comfortable distance to the bottom of the bin. Besides, it is a quaint old American custom to enjoy a plethora of the roundabouts of living, whether it be bear grease, a full root cellar, a box of quick freeze, or plenty of sugar.

So with the coming of May and ration cards, I examined the status of my sugar bin. I unloaded. I called my chagrined countryman and loaded him up with seventy pounds of sugar, none of it bought before the seventh of December, and sent him into town by the back roads to sell it back to the grocery man like a common sugar hoarder!

I've taken the sugar bin out of the kitchen for the duration. Again I am skimping on recipes, substituting molasses and honey for sugar, pretending sweetless meals are a lot of fun. But just as soon as Hitler and Hirohito are in the bag, I intend to move my sugar bin back again and fill it lipping full. I like sugar. Besides, I like living in a country where I can turn my earnings into that which satisfies my wants and nobody raises a ruckus. I am a natural born hoarder. Sugar just happens to be one of my specialties.

My countryman says that this is not hoarding. He says it is simply employing the principles of the system of free enterprise. He says that my sugar bin is a product of the capitalist system. I don't know. I only know I like my sugar bin full when I can afford it.

September 17, 1942

I'm writing this in the shank of a long, warm Sunday afternoon in the middle of September. My winter greens, two leaves above the ground and so crisp and perky in the morning cool, are now flattened dispiritedly against the ground in the baking sun. We went to Sunday School this morning and had a lesson about Israel's being partial to Joseph. Mine is largely a class of fathers, who for the most part have well raised or reared their families, whichever they are going to do about it; and what we had to say about paternal partiality likely fell on winter soil, but it was all very pleasant and agreeable talking—though as I read about the behavior of Father Israel's somewhat haphazardly thrown together family, I didn't blame him too entirely for favoring his obedient, cooperative son.

Our church isn't really pastored. We are what is, more or less aptly, called a half-time church. Though one might get the suggestion, the term is not intended to imply that half the time we are in church and half the time we aren't. We are a half-time church because half the Sundays we have a pastor and the other half our pastor pastors some other church. On Sundays when we are un-pastored or absentee pastored, we meet for Sunday School. If there is church business which demands immediate action, we make motions, mumble seconds at them, and vote a so-be-it. Then the next Sunday the pastor is back and more of us come, and it is really a Sunday.

Hitler moved our half-time pastor this week from half-time Jordan Springs to half-time Camp San Saba church. For some time he has been serving alternate Sundays between us and Jordan Springs, a community church on the outskirts of Camp Bowie. (I mean our pastor has been serving, though it looks as if Hitler had got in some time for himself.) Now Camp Bowie is extending itself in the direction of the Jordan Springs community; so Sunday was the last day for worship in that church before the congregation disbanded in order for the Army camp to move in. Mark up another Axis victory: another community uprooted and another church sacrificed.

As we were coming home from Brownwood last week, a couple of uniforms hailed us. "Brady!" they yelled; and we stopped, shifted our heterogeneous ("messy" to you and me) cargo, and took them aboard. One uniform had Jimmy Harrison inside it—Brady's Jimmy Harrison, shortly transferred from an army camp in Wyoming back to Camp Bowie. He was on his second trip to Brady within the week. Jimmy was full of eager questions about how is everybody? and where? and about the range and recent rains and price of wool and lambs. Jimmy is still rooted in a business venture at home and means to wipe up this mess for Uncle Sam and come back as soon as he can get around to it. "Half of Wyoming heard me whoop when they said I was transferred to Camp Bowie," he said. Jimmy is in quartermasters and has just finished a course in a school of baking—field baking. He told us about hardtack, also what a boy in the army wants. "It's news from home. Letters are top crust, but the hometown newspaper is more dependable. It comes through on schedule." Jimmy said that in camp he read his Brady paper from kiver to kiver, including the ads.

The last party of Curtis Field boys we picked up going into town had in it a lad from Utah, one from Idaho, and one from Pennsylvania. "What do you do when you get to Brady?" I asked. "Where do you go?"

"Picture show, poolhall, and preaching," they said.

August 13, 1943

Mussolini is a prisoner. Mussolini is living unmolested and comfortably in his own home in the heart of his family. Mussolini has escaped to Germany. He has lost all his hair. He has cancer. Hitler is down. He's out. He's dead, and a puppet who looks like Hitler appears in his place. Roosevelt is in Sicily, Russia, China, Fort Worth. Eleanor is in Reno. The cook is in love with the gentleman of the house. The pastor is casting eyes at a prominent member of the choir. There are polio germs in chewing gum. Horned toads spit blood.

In these times of startling developments, when Hess drops down in England, when the Japs sneak up on Pearl Harbor in the midst of peace negotiations, when Mussolini is suddenly "out" in Italy, anything can and often does happen. If one disbelieves all the dramatic stories, he finds himself in the wrong too many times. If he believes them all, he is in the same category. And any story of possibilities has a way of getting repeated enough times to take on the color of truth. How is one going to keep himself from being taken in too many times? Especially so, when organized propaganda sets about artfully to make one believe what it wants believed?

By the way, one does well nowadays to withhold judgment when a colorful tale unfolds, even if our friends tell us the story and/or we hear it on our radios. If we wait a little, we can generally learn who originated the story, to whom it was told, what will be the effect of its telling, who will be sorry and who will be glad. If we can make ourselves wait and answer even some of these questions before we accept or reject highly colored stories, we ordinary folks can sometimes discern the why of a half-true, half-false story. Such sagacity, if it becomes sagacity, will make us more reliable, less panicky citizens, friends, and neighbors.

August 27, 1943

One ticket—three gallons, and the Southwest doesn't like it one bit, especially the oil-producing Southwest. Nor does it make the Southwesterner like the deal he is getting because somebody invoked patriotism. The Southwesterner loves his country. He gives his sons and daughters to it. He buys bonds, pays taxes, and shoulders his share of the burdens of government in peace and in war. But he does not like the gasoline situation. The reason is that history and life in the Southwest have conspired to make an adult of him. The Southwesterner is, by and large, a countryman. He comes from generations of countrymen. He lives nearer to nature than any other man left in the United States. The seasons, drought and flood, hot weather and cold, lush crops and scanty—these things have made the Southwesterner a man who reasons from cause to effect, and they have made of him a man who regulates his comings and goings, his daily living, in accordance with cause and effect. Bullnecked where he cannot see the workings of reason, he becomes the most cooperative fellow on earth when the whys and wherefores are shown to him.

Is the gasoline curtailment a means to save rubber? Then why not actually reduce speed on the highways? Is the curtailment due to a shortage? Then why fetter the oil industry all these months with a price ceiling which makes exploratory drilling an impossibility? Why shutdowns? Why the low price of crude? Why starve to death the land of plenty?

None deny that the Southwest is eager that war needs be met with full Southwestern measure. They would withhold no thing from the men at the front, for that is where Southwestern youth is today. But the Southwesterner doesn't like what has happened to his gasoline, and he will continue not to like it until some power is frank enough to tell him the honest-to-goodness grown-up reason why, without baby-talk of a "teensy-weensy bit of a little bitsy gasoline shortage," and a "dreat big old ugly political setup that'll get you if you don't watch out!"

Southwestern circumstances and Southwestern history have made of the Southwesterner an adult. He is old enough to be told the facts of life, and he is tough enough to take it straight from the hip. He simply feels silly when he's chucked under the chin.

February 4, 1944

Last week our government told us the hell that was the surrender of Corregidor and Bataan. The story burns in blue flame in our land. In the nation, it leaves few lives untouched. One has a boy there, or had a boy there. One has a husband. One a friend. One a friend's friend.

This day the ghastly thing moves us to action. We are an angry nation. What will the pattern of our angry behavior be? Such anger must find relief in action. Of this you may be sure: our angry behavior over this tragedy will weave a pattern into the warp and woof of our national life that will be there forever for the world to see. It will become history. By that pattern, the worth of our civilization and our culture will be judged—and justly judged—by the ages.

What will you do about it? Well, what can you do? You can rant and rave. You can criticize and upbraid. You can cuss. You can demand whyinthehell! You can armchair-general us out of Germany and into Tokyo. Or this thing can bring from you sweat-earned sacrifice and that unity of purpose that makes a nation strong. It can consecrate you to a cause bigger than you are.

Vengeance? That's the first, the elemental urge. Many will yearn for it and nurse the desire like a cancer. Some will demand it. Others will go out and get it.

Justice? That is what the mind, with emotions under control, sets grimly and awfully to attain.

Vengeance and justice—they are the sweet morsels the strong sometimes are privileged to taste. But sweet as they are, they always turn out to be morsels. They give us only a taste.

Men died at the brutal hands of the Japs, died without the dignity of a soldier's death, as the conquered of an "honorable" enemy, and they are dying every day that you and I may have—not tastes—but the full meat of living.

Whatever the pattern of action your anger evokes because of the indignity brave men suffered from the beasts in human form, God grant that the pattern be one the dead of Corregidor and Bataan can honor.

ABOUT THE AUTHOR

Ethel Neal Yeager was born in 1896 in a ranch house seven miles deep in the countryside from the village of Rochelle in McCulloch County near the geographical center of Texas. Raised with nine siblings, she was a happy child in a large, rowdy ranching family, known and respected throughout the area. She was married in 1917 to a "city slicker" from Brownwood, Aaron Yeager, a railroad man, and lived with him in Brownwood and subsequently in a tiny frame house on a small farm in the Claxton community, five miles north of Rochelle. There they raised a daughter, Jane, and struggled to keep body and soul together in the face of considerable odds.

In 1926, Aaron lost a finger in a railroad accident and was dismissed. They moved to the farm. Aaron farmed and Ethel taught school nearby. In 1936, however, Ethel lost her school teaching job because she was diagnosed with tuberculosis—which turned out not to be tuberculosis at all, but it sent her nevertheless to a sanatorium for six months. The upshot was, neither of them had work other than the farm. In the very depth of the Depression, they were quite literally "backed up on the land." And with remarkable energy and very little complaining, they made the most of it.

To earn a little money and to regain her psychological equilibrium after half a year's battle for her health, Ethel started writing weekly columns for the newspaper in Brady, the county seat. At once, her columns attracted attention from journalists in the larger papers around the state. She won various prizes and contests. Once she found her voice, she produced over a period of eight years a great treasury of observation and commentary, reaching into virtually all aspects of life on a hardship farm in Central Texas during the most trying years of the twentieth century. She retired from writing in 1944, when her mother came to live with her and occupied much of the time she had previously spent writing.

In her later years, Ethel Yeager returned to university studies—a Master's Degree in Education in 1954—and returned to school teaching until she retired.

Bruce W. Coggin is the son of Ethel Yeager's daughter, **Jane Yeager Coggin**, who provided the foreword for this collection and made the original selection of items to include. She lives in retirement in Brady. Dr. Coggin, the editor of this collection, is presently Director of the Foreign Language Center at the University of Monterrey in Mexico.

9 781588 202376